*third edition*

# ESSENTIALS
# OF
# MARKETING

**RICHARD R. STILL**
*Florida International University*

**EDWARD W. CUNDIFF**
*Emory University*

PRENTICE-HALL, Englewood Cliffs, New Jersey 07632

*Library of Congress Cataloging-in-Publication Data*

STILL, RICHARD R.
   Essentials of marketing.

   Includes index.
   1. Marketing.   I. Cundiff, Edward W.   II. Title.
HF5415.S84   1986        658.8        85-19297
ISBN 0-13-286444-4

Editorial/production supervision and
   interior design: Sonia Meyer
Cover design: Wanda Lubelska Design
Manufacturing buyer: Ed O'Dougherty

Printed in the United States of America
10  9  8  7  6  5  4  3  2  1

ISBN    0-13-286444-4    01

Prentice-Hall International (UK) Limited, *London*
Prentice-Hall of Australia Pty. Limited, *Sydney*
Prentice-Hall Canada Inc., *Toronto*
Prentice-Hall Hispanoamericana, S.A., *Mexico*
Prentice-Hall of India Private Limited, *New Delhi*
Prentice-Hall of Japan, Inc., *Tokyo*
Prentice-Hall of Southeast Asia Pte. Ltd., *Singapore*
Editora Prentice-Hall do Brasil, Ltda., *Rio de Janeiro*
Whitehall Books Limited, *Wellington, New Zealand*

# CONTENTS

## 3 THE MARKETING PROCESS 18

## 4 ORGANIZING FOR MARKETING 31

## 5 MARKETING INFORMATION 41

## 6 BUYER BEHAVIOR 58

*part two* / *MARKETING INSTITUTIONS*

## 7 PRODUCERS, MIDDLEMEN, AND FACILITATING AGENCIES 77

## *12* MARKETING CHANNELS     **150**

## *13* PHYSICAL DISTRIBUTION     **160**

## *14* PROMOTION     **170**

## *15* PRICING     **188**

# *16* INTERNATIONAL MARKETING 200

# INDEX 211

# PREFACE

*Essentials of Marketing* is a concise introduction to marketing. It provides the foundation for later and more intensive study of key policy areas. It is designed for courses providing a general survey of the field.

The plan of presentation is simple, and, we hope, logical. Part One focuses on the nature of marketing, markets, consumer motivation and behavior, and on planning and organizing. Part Two describes and analyzes the various institutions that are involved in marketing operations and that make up marketing channels. Part Three provides short introductions to the key marketing policy areas and concludes with a summary of how marketing strategy is developed in the work setting.

We owe special thanks to Elizabeth Classon, former Marketing Editor at Prentice-Hall, for her help and encouragement in revising this third edition. We also owe thanks to fellow faculty members at Emory University and Florida International and former colleagues at the University of Georgia and the University of Texas for their helpful criticism and suggestions.

*Richard R. Still*

*Edward W. Cundiff*

# 1

# MARKETING AND MARKETS

Marketing is concerned with product-market interrelationships and transfers of ownership. Marketing management seeks to match up products with markets and to effect transfers in the ownership of products. In this chapter we define marketing, consider the different approaches to marketing study, and introduce the market and market-segmentation concepts.

## DEFINITION OF MARKETING

Marketing activities are those most directly concerned with the demand-stimulating and demand-fulfilling efforts of the enterprise. These activities interlock and interact with one another as components of the total system—by which a company develops and makes its products available, distributes them through marketing channels, promotes them, and prices them. Specifically, then, we define *marketing as the business process by which products are matched with markets and through which transfers of ownership are effected.*

### Product-Market Interrelationship

Our definition states, in part, that "marketing is the business process by which products are matched with markets." Marketing and production activities are interlocked—we can only market products that can be produced, and we should only produce those that can be marketed. Thus, it is logical to think of marketing as the business process by which specific products are matched up with specific markets and to think of production as the business process concerned with manufacturing these products.

Matching products with markets is both a marketing and a production problem. It involves selecting, manufacturing, and marketing products that possess as many as possible of the characteristics desired by those who make up the "markets" while, at the same time, achieving the company's overall goals. Although top management bears the ultimate responsibility for satisfactorily solving these problems, marketing management plays a highly important role.

Consider how products are matched with markets. In some cases, marketing research first uncovers the product characteristics wanted by final buyers, then top management (working with both production and marketing personnel) translates these wants into product specifications. In other cases, the products are the result of technical research carried on within the company, and marketing research focuses on finding and measuring potential markets. In all cases, if management decides to "go ahead and market the product," marketing management is responsible for applying the marketing controllables (personal selling, advertising, other promotion, distribution policy, and price) to gain and hold market favor. In addition, marketing management is responsible for the continual adjustment of marketing controllables for products already on the market, while production management, of course, is responsible for making them. Management regards marketing and production as interdependent subsystems—marketing as the subsystem by which specific products are matched up with specific markets and production as the subsystem charged with manufacturing these products.

### Ownership Transfers

Ownership transfers occur repeatedly as products flow from producers to final buyers. A manufacturer may sell its output to wholesalers who, in turn, resell to retailers who, again in turn, resell to consumers. In this instance, every unit of the manufacturer's product that is finally purchased by a consumer has had its ownership transferred three times (from manufacturer to wholesaler, from wholesaler to retailer, and from retailer to consumer). Of course, for an ownership transfer to take place, buying as well as selling is necessary, and in moving a product to market, the producer only sells. The resellers (wholesalers and retailers) both buy and sell, and the consumer only buys. Consumers are the "targets" of marketing activities—the whole movement of products from producers to consumers anticipates this final buying action by consumers. There can be no marketing, then, unless ownership transfers are effected.

## APPROACHES TO STUDY OF MARKETING

Marketing can be studied through analysis of (1) the marketing of individual products, (2) the problems and operations of different marketing institutions, (3) the activities performed in marketing, and (4) the decisions required in the marketing process.

### Product Approach

In applying the product approach to marketing, description and analysis center on the problems encountered in marketing a particular product—for example, wheat, paper, furniture, or building materials. The marketing of each product is examined from such standpoints as: sources and conditions of supply, producers' marketing organizations and policies, the different middlemen who help in distributing the product, and characteristics and extent of the market. The product approach, then, gives detailed analysis to the specific problems met in marketing particular products, and that is its great advantage. If, for example, you want to learn a lot about marketing lumber, cotton textiles, or some other product, the product approach is an appropriate way to study marketing. However, this approach is repetitious and time-consuming. Numerous products are traced through from producer to consumer to determine marketing differences among products. Since there are many more similarities than differences in marketing most products, continual reference to similarities makes for repetition.

### Institutional Approach

The institutional approach concentrates on description and analysis of the different institutions engaged in marketing: producers of all kinds, wholesalers, agents, retailers, and so on. It pays special attention to the problems and operations of each institution. In applying this approach, for example, we might start with retailing. Consider the nature and significance of retailing in general and then the operations and problems of such institutions as department stores, supermarkets, mail-order houses, and shopping centers—then, perhaps even more specifically, the operations and problems of hardware stores, automobile dealers, and bookstores. For each institution, we would seek to explain the marketing role it performs and how it fits into the overall marketing system with regard to both the products it handles and the markets it serves. Next, we would examine wholesalers and institutions on other distribution levels. The institutional approach involves going through a great deal of detailed information about each of many types of institutions, and it is usually tedious and repetitious. But this is an appropriate approach for those who are primarily interested in studying how a particular class of institution—for example, supermarkets—fits into the overall marketing structure.

### Activities Approach

The activities approach breaks marketing down into the activities involved in the performance of marketing: buying, selling, storage, and transportation, among others. Each activity is analyzed relative to the importance of its performance in the marketing of different products and according to its performance by different marketing institutions. Thus, for example, we might study the selling activity in relation to its importance in marketing grocery products and its performance by the different institutions (manufacturers, wholesalers, and retailers) engaged in grocery marketing. Because marketing involves a smaller number of activities than it does either products or institutions, the activities approach has two great merits: conservation of time and avoidance of repetition.

### The Decision-Making Approach

The decision-making, or management, approach combines certain features of the other three approaches and relates them from the decision-maker's viewpoint. In this book, a modified version of the product approach is used in Chapter 14. An analysis of the activities performed during the marketing process forms the basis for Chapter 4. The institutional approach predominates in Chapters 7 through 13. The areas of marketing decision, including the marketing organization, the product, promotion, distribution, and pricing are analyzed in Chapter 5 and throughout Part III.

## MARKETS AND MARKET SEGMENTATION

Two key concepts in marketing are those of a "market" and "market segmentation." A *market* is defined as the aggregate demand of the potential buyers for a product. An aggregate demand is a composite of the individual demands of all potential buyers of a product. But an aggregate demand, or total market, also is the sum of the demands of different *market segments,* each made up of a group of buyers or buying units, who share qualities that render the segment distinct and make it of significance to marketing. A market is not only an aggregate demand for a product but the sum of the demands of different market segments.

Existence of a group of individuals with common characteristics does not in itself constitute a market segment. Only when they have common characteristics as *buyers* do they form a market segment. For example, to the extent that teenagers as consumer-buyers behave differently than do other age groups, there is a teenage market segment. The distinctive marketing characteristics of each such market segment make it profitable for the marketer to adapt his product and marketing program to meet the needs of each.

### The Consumer Market and the Industrial Market

The broadest market division is that separating the consumer from the industrial market. This division, so broad that each part is too extensive to be a market segment, separates potential buyers into two categories: ultimate consumers and industrial users. *Ultimate consumers* buy either for their own or for their family's personal consumption. Industrial users buy to further the production of other goods and services.

There are striking differences between ultimate consumers and industrial users, because their ways and means of purchasing differ considerably. Ultimate consumers buy in smaller quantities and for consumption over much shorter time periods than do industrial buyers. More important, ultimate consumers are not so systematic in their buying as are industrial users. Some industrial users are business enterprises that exist to make profits, which encourages them to adopt systematic purchasing procedures. Other industrial users are nonprofit institutions (such as governmental agencies, schools, and hospitals) whose operations are audited and reviewed by outside authorities, which also encourages systematic purchasing procedures.

Ultimate consumers spend only part of their time buying, whereas industrial users employ professionals who devote all of their time and effort to purchasing. Furthermore, the ultimate consumer spreads all his buying skill over a wide range of goods and services, whereas the professional tends to specialize and, therefore, has more opportunity to perfect his purchasing skills. These are only a few of the differences between ultimate consumers and industrial users, but they indicate that marketers must use significantly different approaches to the two broad types of markets.

### Market Segmentation

The concept of *market segmentation* is based on the fact that markets, rather than being homogeneous, are heterogeneous. No two buyers or potential buyers of a product, in other words, are ever identical in all respects. However, large groups of potential buyers share certain characteristics of distinctive significance to marketing, and each such group constitutes a market segment. When we consider the market for automobiles, for example, we think of a most heterogeneous group of buyers—buyers representing every income group, every age group, every section of the country and world. If we segment the automobile market by income groups—for example, into lower-, middle-, and high-income groups—we achieve some homogeneity. If, next, we segment each of these income groups into further subsegments—for example, into such subsegments as the Eastern urban, age 30–39, middle-income group—we gain still more homogeneity among buyers within each subsegment. Through market segmentation management sets the stage which will enable it to plan marketing uniquely fitted for each segment.

TABLE 1-1 Summary of bases for segmentation and typical products that would benefit from each segmentation basis

| BASIS FOR SEGMENTATION | TYPICAL PRODUCTS |
|---|---|
| *Geographic* | |
| Region | Cowboy boots |
| Urban, suburban, rural | Tennis equipment |
| Climate | Ski clothes |
| City size | Rolls-Royce |
| Density | Riding lawn-mowers |
| *Demographic* | |
| Income | Dishwashers |
| Age | Baby food |
| Education | Books |
| Stage in life cycle | Home furnishings |
| Social class | Wrestling matches |
| Sex | Clothing |
| Occupation | Job-oriented equipment |
| Religion | Food and drink |
| Race | Cosmetics |
| *Psychographic* | |
| Personality | Home furnishings |
| Life-style | Leisure clothing |
| Use of product | Coffee |
| Frequency of use | Beer |
| Readiness to purchase | Computers |
| Benefits desired | Automobiles |

*Source:* Cundiff, E.W., Still, R.R., Govoni, N.A.P., *Fundamentals of Modern Marketing.* (Englewood Cliffs, N.J.: Prentice-Hall, Inc., 1985), p. 84.

Most major consumer market segments used in analysis of consumer markets result from groupings based on income, age, degree of urbanization, and geographic location, but there are many other bases. (See Table 1-1.) Because income is the main source of consumer purchasing power, market segmentation based on income is widely used; an individual's income, in most cases, limits not only how much can be bought but also what is bought. Market segmentation on the basis of the prospective buyer's age is important for many products, especially those designed specifically for certain market segments, for example, breakfast cereals. Segmentation—based on whether buyers live in urban, suburban, or rural areas—isolates buying behavior for products such as gasoline and oil, lawn furniture, gardening supplies, and automobiles. Geographical market segmentation is based on variations in buying patterns resulting from differing cultural heritages, topography, and climates; for example, furniture manufacturers find that consumer-style preferences vary considerably among different regions, with southerners having a much stronger preference for traditionally styled items than midwesterners, and far westerners having a noticeably strong preference for furniture styles with certain Oriental influences.

Market segmentation of the industrial market is accomplished along similar lines. For instance, market segmentation by kind of business is usually approached through use of the Standard Industrial Classification System (known as the S.I.C. system), under which all places of business are classified into one of ten divisions covering the entire field of economic activity. Each division is, in turn, broken down into several "major groups" representing specific kinds of business, and, again, into still further breakdowns of even more specific kinds of business. Thus, with the use of the S.I.C. system, the industrial market can be divided into relatively small, medium, or large market segments—depending upon the degree of homogeneity desired in the analysis. For instance, manufacturers of furniture and fixtures are classified under S.I.C. No. 25. Further classification is effected through three- and four-digit numbers, with manufacturers of household furniture coming under S.I.C. No. 251 and manufacturers of metal household furniture coming under S.I.C. No. 2514. Other bases for segmenting the industrial market include segmentation according to geographical location of the user, usual purchasing procedures, and size of user.

## CONCLUSION

Marketing is the process by which products are matched with markets and through which ownership transfers are effected. There are four main approaches to the study of marketing: (1) through considering problems in marketing particular products; (2) through analysis of marketing institutions; (3) by breaking down the field into marketing activities; and (4) by combining the first three approaches and relating them from the decision-making, or management viewpoint.

Among the most basic concepts in marketing are those of "market" and "market segmentation." A "market" is the aggregate demand of all the potential buyers of a product. "Market segmentation" refers to the analysis of a total market in terms of its component segments, each made up of a group of buyers who share common characteristics as buyers.

# 2

# THE MARKETING CONCEPT

A company operating under the marketing concept takes its principal guidance from the marketplace; i.e., from its knowledge and understanding of its customers' needs, wants, and desires. This understanding becomes the main basis for organizing operations. Not only marketing, but production, financial, and other organizational units are geared toward satisfying customers' needs, wants, and desires. But the organization of operations is also influenced by the company's overall goals; department heads must recognize what results top management is looking for if they are to manage their departments in ways that not only satisfy customers' needs, wants, and desires but also facilitate achievement of company goals. Thus, the marketing concept has three main features: (1) a market or customer orientation, (2) a subordination of departmental aspirations to company-wide goals, and (3) a unification of company operations. (See Figure 2-1.)

## ENVIRONMENTAL FACTORS INFLUENCING ADOPTION OF THE MARKETING CONCEPT

Certain key environmental factors provide the setting within which companies adopting the marketing concept can reasonably expect profitable results. Consider the consumer market: population and income trends cause large potential markets to exist for the continual stream of product improvements and new products made possible through advances in technology. These "market" and "product" factors produce a rising crescendo of com-

**Figure 2-1** The marketing concept

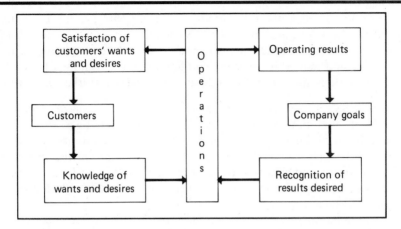

petitive activity, as more and more marketers seek shares of consumers' buying power. Competitive activity is further heightened by evolution and change in marketing channels and by development and growth of successive new waves of mass communications media, which make it possible to adjust marketing controllables in more ways.

These environmental changes are causing marketers of consumer products to alter both their marketing philosophy and organization. They are becoming less "product-oriented" and more "market-oriented," gearing their operations primarily to customers' needs, wants, and desires and only secondarily to particular products. Promotional emphasis, at the same time, is shifting away from selling the product *per se* to selling the *function* that the product can perform; e.g., rather than promoting the technical features of a self-cleaning oven, one marketer advertises "this oven will clean itself, permitting the user to avoid a dirty and time-consuming job."

Marketers of industrial products have been slower in adopting the marketing concept. Nevertheless, developments in the consumer market have "spilled over," and industrial marketers also are adjusting their operations according to the marketing concept.

### Changes in Markets

*Population Growth.* Consumer markets are made up of people with money, and the American market has been growing both in population and income. Total U.S. population has grown from fewer than 100 million people in 1910 to around 226 million in 1980, and the projection for the year 2010 is that population will then exceed 300 million. The American population is growing at a net rate of between 2 and 3 million persons a year. Thus, large and growing potential markets exist for the widening stream of new consumer products being introduced to the market.

*Growing Number of Households.*   For some products (e.g., household appliances, automobiles, and other consumer durables) market growth is more closely related to the total number of households than it is to the total population. In 1980 the number of U.S. households approximated 80 million. The number of households is increasing at a faster rate than the total population, and marketers of many consumer durables can look forward to potential markets that grow faster than the consumer market as a whole.

*Increases in Discretionary Income.*   Households have increasing amounts of discretionary income, which is money left over after buying essential food, clothing, shelter, transportation, and other items it regards as "necessities." Such income may be spent, saved, used for buying "nonnecessities," or for a combination of these. Experience indicates, however, that a rise in discretionary income usually results in more spending for nonnecessities (*discretionary spending*).

Continuing increases in discretionary purchasing power in consumers' hands have resulted in dramatic expansions in the market potentials for such items as automatic dishwashers, color television sets, and home swimming pools. Moreover, with consumers becoming more affluent, they also are becoming more particular about what they buy and more choosy in what they accept. Increasing consumer sophistication has led more manufacturers to research consumers' wants and desires more thoroughly and to develop and market products more in line with these findings. Simultaneously, growth in market potentials for nonnecessities has encouraged other firms to enter such markets, thus adding to the incentive all competitors have for adjusting their products more closely to what consumers demand.

*Leveling Off of Income Distribution Pattern.*   There is also a trend toward a leveling off of income among consumers, a trend which is contributing importantly to growth of mass markets for such "luxury" items as motorboats, which, until recently, only a few could afford. A few generations back, income distribution resembled a pyramid with the vast bulk of the incomes (i.e., the low incomes) at the pyramid base. Today, this distribution more closely approximates a diamond shape, with a large middle-income group positioned between a "rich" minority above and a "poor" minority below.

More people tend to have more income, and this is causing new mass markets to develop. More and more products once regarded as "luxuries" become "necessities." Washing machines, radios, television sets, telephones, and automobiles all have—for ever-increasing segments of the population—moved from the luxury class to the necessity class.

*"New" Attitude Toward Debt.*   Less and less stigma is attached to credit buying, and fewer people save in order to pay cash for such products as automobiles, television sets, furniture, and major household appliances.

Each year, for instance, more than six of ten new car buyers and five of ten used car buyers buy on credit. Many "cash" buyers borrow from banks, finance companies, and other lenders, so, in effect, they also buy on credit but make their payments to lenders rather than to sellers. Credit buying is a way of life for millions, including many who could pay cash but prefer not to.

The amount of credit consumers can obtain is related to the size of their present incomes and, since the long-range trend is for incomes to rise, we can expect still further expansions in credit buying. Marketers of such products as mobile homes, boats, and camping trailers have adopted credit plans to accelerate expansion of their markets; and "go now—pay later" plans make international air travel possible for the average person. In addition, the spread of bank-sponsored credit card plans makes it progressively easier to buy on credit even from those retailers who formerly sold for cash only. The changing attitude toward debt and the increasing ability of consumers to obtain credit add to the intensity of competition for the consumer's dollar.

### Technological Change

No company has a guarantee that its product will not be made obsolete by some technological advance. Time and again, and with increasing frequency in recent years, technological change brings overnight obsolescence to products, whole product lines, and even entire industries. At the same time, technology just as suddenly creates vast new markets for other products and industries.

One important result of increased spending for research and development is that product life cycles—time spans from market introductions to market discontinuances—shorten as new products account for an increasing proportion of sales. Another result is that technological developments in one industry often end in products being sold to markets traditionally supplied by companies in a different industry.

Technological change, then, is a key element in the competitive struggle among companies. An ever-growing number of new products is introduced to the market each year. The list of products from which consumers may choose also grows longer.

### Changes in Marketing Channels and Physical Distribution

Changes in marketing channels occur at a more rapid rate, generally speaking, than changes in either markets or technology. At one time, a manufacturer could expect its marketing channels to remain stable and appropriate over a long period. But appearance of new types of distributive institutions, shifts in operating methods of older institutions, and development and change in physical distribution systems are creating new distribution "problems" as well as "opportunities."

Many new types of distributive institutions have appeared since the 1930s; the consumer markets for some products also have been invaded by marketers who previously operated elsewhere. Grocery outlets, for example, now stock traditional drugstore items such as aspirin and mouthwashes, while drugstores have added certain food items. Petroleum marketers now sell such items as coffee pots, cameras, and short-wave radios to their credit-card holders by mail. The chains of redemption centers operated by trading stamp companies are important distributors of many products once sold only through conventional retailers, such as department stores and appliance dealers. Numerous similar examples exist. Thus, the range of distribution options open to the manufacturer has significantly broadened.

Noteworthy improvements in transportation also are occurring, making it possible to distribute products faster, more economically, and more widely than ever before. Among these are jet air freight, containerized shipping, piggyback, fishy-back, and the unitized train. Technological gains in the design, manufacture, and utilization of transport equipment yet to come will make possible still further gains in the ease with which manufacturers distribute their products nationally and throughout the world. Manufacturers who restrict their distribution to certain areas will find themselves confronted by an increasing number of new competitors from elsewhere.

### Growth of Mass Communications Media

With the appearance and growth of successive new waves of mass communications media—newspapers, pay and cable TV, magazines, AM and FM radio, black-and-white and color television—it has become possible to "spread the word" about new product developments faster, more widely and more effectively than before. It has also made it possible for advertising to play a larger role in marketing. Furthermore, the growth of mass communications media has been further stimulated by the increasing pressures for rapid development of mass markets brought on by ever-accelerating technological change and by businessmen's efforts to secure the economic advantages of large-scale production. At the same time, communications effectiveness has increased.

Development and growth of different mass media has made it possible for marketers to deliver advertising messages in more ways, each medium reinforcing messages delivered by other media and each boosting the combined impact on potential buyers. These and other environmental factors affecting the marketing concept are illustrated in Figure 2-2.

## ORGANIZATIONAL CONDITIONS PRECEDING ADOPTION OF MARKETING CONCEPT

Three organizational conditions, all representing maladjustments to the environmental factors just discussed, generally precede management's recognition of the necessity for adopting the marketing concept.

**Figure 2-2** Marketing and its environment

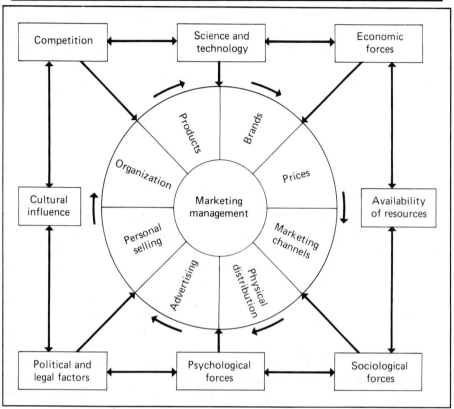

*Source:* Cundiff, E.W., Still, R.R., and Govoni, N.A.P., *Fundamentals of Modern Marketing* (Englewood Cliffs, N.J.: Prentice-Hall, Inc. 1985), p. 7.

### Product Orientation

The traditional orientation of top management in many companies, particularly those emphasizing mass production, focuses on the product. Product orientation involves falling in love with the company's products: concentrating on making them better (technically, mechanically, and aesthetically), improving the production process, bringing down product costs, and the like, while simultaneously neglecting to take into account changes in the market and competitive situation. A product-oriented company expects marketing operations to serve the seller's interests alone and not those of buyers. Focusing on achieving ever more efficient manufacturing, top management assigns marketing the task of selling increased outputs—literally, if necessary, of "forcing it down customers' throats." If the fact that the company has a "better mousetrap" doesn't cause the "world to beat a path to the company's door," the marketing department is expected to go out and sell the output any way it can.

The great danger in the product-oriented company is that top management will not know what business the company is really in; that it will fail to recognize that it is in business to serve a market and not simply to dispose of a product. The risk is that the market now buying the product will find some more satisfactory way of meeting its needs. Eventually the owners of horse-drawn buggies nearly all bought automobiles! Where did that leave the makers of buggies? As a pure matter of survival, companies with product orientations must change them in order to stay in business at all.

### Communications Problems and Uncoordinated Proliferation of Specialists

As a company grows, important functions (such as marketing, finance, and production) are split down into smaller and smaller parts, each in charge of a specialist. Complexities of administering the growing number of people in the organization also bring into existence a wide range of bureaucratic positions. With organizational growth, departmental walls tend to rise ever higher, causing some tasks to be duplicated, as department heads and other bureaucrats seek to build their "own little empires."

As the number of specialists grows, they tend to lose effectiveness in communicating with others not sharing their specialties. As various technical languages for communicating with others sharing the same specialties develop, overall communications difficulties arise because the same things and events have "special meanings" for different specialists. Additionally, specialists feel the need for justifying their own positions, and one way specialists legitimatize their positions is to transform everyday speech into technical jargon and, in some cases, even into mathematical formulae. Worse yet, in a company where this is going on, there also is a tendency for management not to coordinate the proliferation of specialists so they work at cross purposes, and frictions and inefficiencies, as well as communications problems permeate the entire organization.

These difficulties often cause top management to become preoccupied with internal operations. Painfully aware that hoped-for economies of large-scale operations are not being realized, management tends to devote its main efforts toward improving the technical aspects of operations and, likely as not, moves toward greater product orientation. Management exhibits a growing inability and unwillingness to see opportunities on the outside caused by market shifts, technological changes, and the like.

### Conflicts Among Departmental Goals

Also stemming from the strong drives of different specialists to justify their own positions is the conflict among departmental goals. In the production department, costs are uppermost in importance. Thus, emphasis is placed on reducing costs by minimizing the number of products, standardizing product variety, lengthening the interval between model changes, and maximizing production runs. In the marketing department, everything revolves around sales volume. Hence, sales are pushed by any means available, and pressures are exerted to offer the widest variety of products, to change models at short intervals, to get the products into every conceivable outlet, to promote them continuously and heavily, and to price them at or below competitive levels. Finance specialists also are caught up in the effort to justify their own positions—often seeking to maximize short-run returns to stockholders, neglecting not only to consider customers' wants and desires but also opposing research and development projects needed to keep the firm competitive, frustrating the efforts of both production and marketing to install innovations that cost money in the short run but pay off in the long run, and generally trying to minimize costs and maximize revenues at the same time. As each department emphasizes attainment of its own "natural" goals, the total enterprise's potential for serving its markets profitably over the long run shrinks. With each department trying to optimize its own performance, the company's overall performance is sub-optimized.

## *CONCLUSION—THE MARKETING CONCEPT*

Three main features distinguish the company managed according to the marketing concept: (1) adoption of a market, or customer orientation, (2) subordination of departmental goals to a set of company goals, and (3) unification of company operations, both to serve markets and to meet company goals.

### Market Orientation

In adopting a market orientation, management focuses on the customers and their wants and desires primarily and on the product secondarily. Emphasis is placed on using marketing research to keep abreast of market trends and developments and on doing research and development work (even if it makes present products obsolete). Management exerts every effort to keep up-to-date on the changing answers to five important questions:

1. What business are we in?
2. Who are our customers?
3. What do they want and desire?
4. How can we best distribute our products to them?
5. How can we communicate most effectively with them?

**Figure 2-3** Planning and operating under the marketing concept

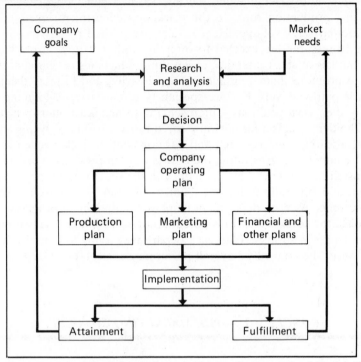

*Source:* Cundiff, E.W., Still, R.R., & Govoni, N.A.P., *Fundamentals of Modern Marketing* (Englewood Cliffs, N.J.: Prentice-Hall, Inc. 1985), p. 18.

### Formulation of Company Goals

Top management formulates a set of company goals to which individual departmental goals are subordinated, thus recognizing that the company exists to achieve something as a company rather than as a collection of departments. Such "total company goals" as achieving a given profit level or a certain return on investment become of prime importance. Therefore, in working toward achievement of a given profit level, for instance, the production department is made aware that obtaining low manufacturing costs is not enough. The marketing department is guided toward placing less emphasis on high sales volume and more on making profitable sales. The financial department is alerted to top-management's desire not only to provide a satisfactory short-run return for the stockholders but to serve the company's markets profitably over the long run. In other words, a coordinated effort is made to optimize the company's performance over the long-run, recognizing that this means sub-optimizing the short-run performance of individual departments.

### Unification of Company Operations

In seeking to achieve company goals through effectively serving chosen markets, management works continuously to weld the different parts of the organization into an efficient operating system. An orchestration of effort is required to correct such organizational deficiencies as the communications problems among the specialists and the parallel tendency for their proliferation to go uncoordinated. Management strives to secure a "synergistic" effect—to achieve greater total results than could be obtained by the individual departments working separately.

A company managed under the marketing concept plans, organizes, coordinates, and controls its entire operation as *one system directed toward achieving a single set of goals applicable to the total organization.* This is illustrated in Figure 2-3.

# 3

# THE MARKETING PROCESS

Marketing is the business process by which products are matched with markets and through which transfers of ownership are effected. It consists of combining and performing various activities (inputs) in an effort to obtain given goals (outputs). Some contend that there are only two purposes (goals) of marketing: obtaining and servicing demand. Although obtaining and servicing demand are general marketing goals, individual companies have additional, more specific marketing goals which vary with the company and its goals. Thus, for example, a company that has a reputation for leadership in product innovation not only will attempt to obtain and service demand but will continue to further its reputation as a leader. Both the inputs (marketing activities) and the outputs (marketing goals), then, vary with the company and its overall goals. Individual companies perform and combine different marketing activities in various ways, not only to obtain and service demand but to reach other and more specific marketing goals.

Identifying marketing activities might seem simple, because it would appear necessary only to itemize those steps required to move products and services from producers to final buyers. But the task is complicated by difficulties met in determining just where marketing begins and ends. It is oversimplifying to assume that marketing activities are concerned only with the flow of products and services; to achieve marketing efficiency, there must also be a reverse flow of information, from the market to the producer. This information-gathering activity is performed both before the product is planned or produced and after the product is on the market. The marketing process both begins and ends with the final buyer, with information flowing back to the producer and products flowing forward to the final buyer.

The marketing activities most easily identified are those concerned with bringing products into contact with markets. Selling is one of these. Buying, the other side of selling, is not so easy to identify as a marketing activity, the ease of identification varying with who is buying. For instance, buying merchandise for resale is one of the retailer's most important tasks, for to achieve the goal of selling goods to consumers, the retailer must buy those things consumers need and want. But, is buying as clearly a marketing activity for the manufacturer? In some cases, the manufacturer's buying decision is influenced by the effect the purchase has on its product's marketability; in other cases, it is influenced by the effect on product costs. The selection and purchase of materials for television cabinets mainly affects the finished product's marketability, but the selection and purchase of parts and materials for the receiving equipment itself is largely a production and cost problem. In most instances, both marketing and production needs influence buying decisions. So manufacturers properly look upon buying as a marketing activity whose performance is frequently conditioned by production and cost considerations.

Activities not directly concerned with bringing products into contact with markets are more difficult to identify. For instance, although planning and designing the product may not seem like marketing activities, products should possess those characteristics that final buyers want. These wants must be discovered in an early stage of product development; otherwise the product is destined for marketing failure.

Final buyers, themselves, often perform some marketing activities. Marketers strive to move products and services into the hands of final buyers, but it does not follow that all marketing then ceases. For example, storage is normally thought of as a marketing activity. Potatoes, produced seasonally, are held and sold throughout the year by marketing institutions, but sometimes individual consumers take over part of the storage activity— they may buy bushels of potatoes to store in their homes. The storage activity continues to be performed, but by consumers rather than marketing organizations.

## A CLASSIFICATION OF MARKETING ACTIVITIES

Classification of marketing activities facilitates analysis of specific situations. However, no general classification does or can apply to every marketing situation. Any classification system needs some modification to fit the particular analytical requirements imposed by an individual company's marketing circumstances. Keeping this restriction in mind, we classify marketing activities into three general categories containing nine activities in all:

*Merchandising Activities*
1. Product planning and development
2. Standardizing and grading
3. Buying and assembling
4. Selling

*Physical Distribution Activities*
5. Storage
6. Transportation

*Supporting Activities*
7. Marketing financing
8. Marketing risk bearing
9. Obtaining and analyzing marketing information

These activities are arranged in a logical sequence for discussion. Merchandising begins with an analysis of market needs and the development or procurement of products to meet these needs, and it ends with the activities involved in stimulating market demand most directly. Physical distribution makes the products available at the times and places final buyers want them. The supporting activities, generally speaking, improve the effectiveness with which merchandising and physical distribution activities are performed.

**Merchandising**

Merchandising consists of activities necessary to determine and meet market needs in terms of products and to stimulate market demand. Some marketing writers classify standardizing and grading as "auxiliary" or "supportive" activities. We include them as merchandising activities chiefly because they involve problems in managing product uniformity and consistency.

***Product Planning and Development.*** Most products, to be marketed successfully, must possess characteristics that conform rather closely to buyers' needs, wants, and desires, and this requires frequent product adaptation. In most industries, this process is endless—with product improvements flowing from changing technology while shifts in buyer expectations simultaneously create continuing product obsolescence. In rapidly changing industries, such as pharmaceuticals, products developed within the last 20 years normally account for over half the sales and profits of the leading companies. In such industries, the noninnovating company almost certainly faces gradual elimination from the market. In other industries where rates of product obsolescence are slower, the process takes place over longer time spans.

Growing recognition of the importance of satisfying buyers' changing product preferences is evidenced by the trend toward making the marketing department primarily responsible for product planning and development. Middlemen, too, increasingly regard product planning and development, which for them usually takes the form of changes in products handled or services offered, as crucial to their success.

A grocery wholesaler who begins a cash-and-carry service is engaging in product planning. A men's clothing store that adds a selection of women's clothing or abandons delivery service is also doing product planning. Both retailers and wholesalers call such changes "merchandising," but what they are actually doing is comparable to what manufacturers do under the name of "product planning and development."

*Standardizing and Grading.* These activities involve establishment of basic measures or limits to which articles must conform. A "standard" specifies what basic qualities or characteristics a product must have to be designated by certain grades. Standards should be based on the qualities desired by buyers or on the use to which the article is to be put. For example, in clothing manufacturing, it is useful to establish standards of size so that all size 12 dresses will fit the same people. "Grading" is the act of separating or inspecting the goods according to the established specifications. The specifications are set by the standards established and may include size, weight, or quality.

Standardizing and grading are important to efficient marketing. Both make it possible for customers to purchase by description instead of by inspection; for example, to order a ton of steel or coal of a specified grade by mail or by telephone. Both make it possible to "merchandise" products closer to what customers want. A mixed lot of ungraded fruits is less attractive to prospective customers and commands a lower total price than the same lot after it has been graded and priced by grade.

Grading also helps in streamlining the physical handling of many farm crops because it makes possible the mixing of lots belonging to different owners for purposes of storage and transportation. This permits the grain-elevator operator to store the crops of different farmers in a single elevator. It also allows the transportation company to mix the same crops in shipment.

"Standardization," the application of standards, relates mainly to manufactured products. Its first step involves establishing *physical standards* to which the product should conform. But prior to selecting the standards, the manufacturer should have assessed the market. Thus, a men's suit manufacturer can measure the potential market for each suit size and either produce each size in proportion to the probable demand or produce only certain sizes.

"Grading" refers to the application of basic *descriptive standards,* such as size, color, or weight, to the products of nature where growers or producers have limited control over their products' physical specifications. Since the United States Department of Agriculture has set standards for the sizes and grades of oranges, for example, growers sort their crops according to these sizes and end up with oranges in each of several sizes or grades, each of which commands a higher price than ungraded fruit. For grading to be used, all properties to be graded must be measurable. Thus, canned peaches can be graded in terms of properties such as sugar content, color, and size, but they cannot be graded in terms of taste, since there is no objective way to measure differences in individual tastes.

Standardizing is most effective when adopted on an industry-wide basis. Otherwise, a consumer may not confidently expect a size 9 to be the same regardless of the maker. Standardization in each industry is normally voluntary.

***Buying and Assembling.*** Buying, as a marketing activity, is the procurement of items for eventual resale to ultimate consumers or industrial users. Most of the items purchased by producers are used in the manufacturing process and generally reach final buyers in a different form as part of finished products. By contrast, the products middlemen buy are resold by them in essentially the same form to other middlemen or to final buyers.

Assembling is closely related to buying. It is bringing together either (1) *different quantities of a wide variety of items* for resale by a single establishment or (2) a *large quantity of similar items* for resale in a particular region. The first type of assembling is performed by retailers, such as department stores and supermarkets, who bring together products from many diverse sources making it possible for consumers to satisfy a variety of wants on a single shopping trip. The second type is illustrated by the activities of centrally located wholesalers of agricultural produce who buy from numerous growers throughout the country and distribute the assembled produce to local wholesalers for eventual resale by retailers. Although the manufacturer performs assembling when procuring parts, materials, and the like, most assembling is performed by middlemen.

Successful buying requires an ability to estimate requirements weeks and even months in advance. When ordering merchandise that will be delivered and placed on sale two or three months later, retailers, for example, are in effect trying to anticipate what consumers will do in the future, even though consumers are not sure themselves. It is important to know customers' needs and buying habits to predict their buying actions. A retailer must know the consumers who comprise the market, their income levels, their product preferences, their shopping habits, and so forth. A wholesaler must have just as complete an understanding of its customers—the retailers—and at least a general knowledge about their customers. Similarly, the manufacturer must be familiar with the buying habits, financial capabilities, promotional policies, and other characteristics of its immediate customers, and it must also be acquainted with the needs and buying patterns of other marketing intermediaries and of final buyers.

*Selling.* Selling, in its broad sense, has the purpose not only of making sales (i.e., effecting ownership transfers) but of identifying prospective customers, stimulating demand, and providing information and service to buyers. In working toward these goals, the marketer must combine such activities as personal selling, advertising, sales promotion, packaging, and customer service. Management usually does not rely on any one selling activity, but tries, through continuous experimentation, to find an effective combination. (A blend of selling activities coordinated into a sales program is called a promotional mix.) Skill is needed not only in planning an optimum promotional mix, but in coordinating the different selling activities.

**1.** *Personal Selling.* Personal selling is the chief means through which marketing programs are implemented. The unique strength of personal selling lies in its ability to personalize sales messages to individual customers. Capitalizing on this strength, however, requires trained and competent sales personnel. Substantial investments must be made in recruiting, training, paying, and supervising sales personnel—thus, personal selling is a relatively high cost selling method. The cost of each advertising message per prospect reached is much lower than the cost of each personal sales contact. But it often takes many advertising messages to move a prospect to buying action, while a single sales presentation may do the job. Management generally seeks to minimize selling costs through using some combination of personal selling and other sales activities. In theory, all selling activities—personal selling, advertising, and so on—should be used up to the point where their marginal efficiencies are all equated.

**2.** *Advertising.* Because advertising generally is a relatively low-cost way to convey selling messages to numerous prospects, it is important in most marketing programs. It is used not only to stimulate demand but for other purposes. It can secure leads for sales personnel and middlemen by convincing readers to request more information and by identifying outlets handling the product. It can force middlemen to stock the product by building consumer interest. It can help train dealers' sales staffs in product uses and applications. And it can build dealer and consumer confidence in the company and its products by building familiarity.

Marketing management's most frequent assignment to advertising is to stimulate market demand. By using advertising to "presell" customers, that is to arouse and intensify their buying interest in advance, management hopes to facilitate the personal selling task. While sometimes advertising alone may succeed in achieving buyer acceptance, preference, or even demand for the product, seldom can it be solely relied upon. Advertising usually is most efficiently used with at least one other sales method, such as personal selling or point-of-purchase display, which generally are more effective in directly moving customers to buying action. Effective advertising by a manufacturer, for instance, often arouses consumers' interest, but it will rarely send them to retail stores actively seeking the product. However, when they are in a store, and an alert clerk or an attractive display calls their attention to the manufacturer's product, the impact of previous advertising often helps in persuading them to buy.

**3.** *Point-of-Purchase Display.* Point-of-purchase display supplements and coordinates personal selling and advertising, helping to make them more effective. Thus, its main purpose is to impel on-the-spot buying action. It is used more extensively in marketing consumer products than in industrial marketing because ultimate consumers are more susceptible to making impulse purchases. Furthermore, with the spread of self-service retailing, consumers seeking product information have come to depend less on sales clerks and more on displays.

**4.** *Packaging.* Marketing management expects the package to: attract consumers' attention at the point of purchase, furnish them with needed information about the product, and provide the extra push so often required to propel them into buying. With the spread of self-service retailing, packaging—like point-of-purchase display—has risen in importance as a marketing activity. Traditionally, the package was regarded solely as a container for the product, and production departments had exclusive responsibility for packaging.

The package's basic role is still that of container but it is also expected to play important marketing roles. In most consumer product marketing programs, the package is designed to relate the product to the manufacturer's advertising, thus improving the chances that consumers will recognize the product in retail outlets. In selling through self-service retail outlets, the manufacturer's sales personnel are responsible for persuading retailers to stock the product: advertising is responsible for making consumers aware of the product, its uses, and its advantages; and packaging operations are responsible for tying-in personal selling efforts and advertising's impact.

**5.** *Customer Service.* As a seller activity, customer service provides assistance and advice on such things as product installation, operation, maintenance, and repair. For prospective buyers of many products, availability and adequacy of customer service are major factors in the choice among competing sellers. Through providing superior customer service, a seller may obtain the patronage of certain buyers even in the face of strong price competition. As more and more technical features are added to a product and it becomes more complicated to install, operate, and maintain, customer service gains in importance as an instrument of competition.

### Physical Distribution

Storage and transporation are the activities necessary to move products from their times and places of production to their times and places of consumption. In a highly developed and complex economy, such as in the

United States, most of each producer's customers are located hundreds and even thousands of miles away, and products must be transported to and stored at points more accessible to them. Furthermore, in developed countries, such as those in Western Europe and North America, most manufacturers produce in anticipation of market demand and hold inventories until orders are received and filled. In developing countries, on the other hand, many manufacturers wait for orders before they begin manufacturing and have minimum stocks of finished products, although they do maintain stocks of raw materials. As countries develop and as multi-national trade increases, both storage and transporation, as well as inventory management and the processing and handling of customers' orders, increase in importance.

*Storage.* Because in our complex economic system products are generally produced in anticipation of market demand, storage is important. Manufacturers, wholesalers, and retailers all hold and manage inventories. When consumers make purchases from retail outlets, retailers' inventories are reduced and are replenished from wholesalers' inventories which, in turn, are replenished from the manufacturer's inventory. Similarly, the consumer's own supply of products is reduced by consumption and replenished by purchases. When there is a demand for a product, stock levels fluctuate all along the line of distribution.

Marketers have three other important reasons for holding products in storage. One is to even out the seasonal factor in production or in sales. A manufacturer of Christmas ornaments, for example, has a market for its products only during the immediate pre-Christmas period, but its costs are lower if production is carried on throughout the year; so it stores its output from one selling season to the next. Similarly, many farm products are harvested in only one season but are bought and consumed throughout the year—so growers and middlemen store them from one harvesting season to the next. A second reason for storage is to obtain economies in other business operations: for instance, manufacturers who make products in a large number of sizes, such as nuts and bolts, use the same machines to produce different sizes. It often is more economical to schedule long production runs involving turning out several weeks' supply of particular sizes at a time, rather than making the total needs of each size weekly. A third reason for storing products is to improve their quality and value—products such as cheese, whisky, and tobacco must be aged or conditioned to improve their flavor and, hence, to increase their value.

*Transportation.* Because most markets are geographically separated from production areas, transportation is an important marketing activity. Many factories are located away from urban areas to avoid population and traffic congestion and high land costs, with the expectation that the lower costs incurred in a nonurban location will more than offset the costs of moving finished products to urban markets. Other factories are separated from their largest markets through historical accident. For instance, many businesses start up in the founder's home town and as they prosper and grow, the founder seeks ever farther markets for the expanding production. Eventually, strong reasons develop for building additional plants nearer the larger and more distant markets, but many manufacturers conclude that lower production costs in a single large plant more than offset transportation costs to distant markets. In some industries, such as lumber and steel, where transportation costs for raw material are higher than for the finished products, manufacturing facilities are located near raw material sources with little regard to market location. Regardless of the location of production facilities, transporting products to markets is an important distributive activity.

### Supporting Activities

The supporting activities do not relate directly to the effecting of ownership transfers but support or contribute to the carrying out of other marketing activities. Supporting activities include marketing financing, marketing risk bearing, and obtaining and analyzing marketing information. Because of the relationships these activities bear to the formulation of marketing and other basic business policies, top management often seems to pay closer attention to these activities than it does to others.

*Marketing Financing.* Marketers, both as receivers and sources of credit, are concerned with financing. As receivers, they sometimes use short-term financing to tide their operations over seasonal peaks that require additional inventory investments and higher promotional expenses. Many retailers, for instance, increase their inventories 50 percent or more during the months just before Christmas and increase their sales force and advertising outlays accordingly; if permanent capital investments were kept at a level high enough to meet these seasonal needs, much money would lie unproductive the rest of the year. Consequently, most middlemen—and many manufacturers—finance seasonal variations in expenses through credit.

Marketing organizations have two main sources of credit: trade credit and banks. Trade credit, important in short-term financing, is extended by suppliers. Manufacturers and middlemen offer their customers credit terms allowing them from as few as 10 to as many as 120 or more days in which to pay. Trade sources are willing to assume greater credit risks than are banks, but trade credit also is more expensive, especially when interest is charged on overdue balances.

Providing credit to customers is essential to the success of most marketers. Most "big ticket" consumer durables, such as automobiles and furniture, are sold on the installment plan; surprisingly few consumers are both able and willing to pay cash for such items, and there is no doubt that installment credit has contributed to the development of mass markets for many consumer durables. Department stores and other retailers use credit (in the form of charge accounts or through honoring various credit cards) as one means of attracting patronage. At the wholesale distribution level, most transactions are on a credit basis. Mercantile credit, which is credit granted by manufacturers and wholesalers, not only assists in but simplifies ownership transfers. By extending credit to buyers, the seller avoids having transportation companies make collections on delivery or asking customers to pay at the time of order placement.

*Marketing Risk Bearing.* Marketing risks arise from both supply and demand changes and natural hazards. Any institution that carries an inventory takes the risk that supply and demand conditions may change. Thus, marketers who perform the storage activity also perform not only financing (by taking ownership) but risk bearing. Most marketing institutions have the problem of deciding on the proper size of inventories. Risk always exists that an inventory will not be sold if it proves too large relative to market demand. But there is also risk that if it proves too small, orders will be lost because they cannot be filled.

A marketer may transfer part of the risk burden, eliminating some risks entirely and converting others from unpredictable amounts of potential loss to known items of expense. For example, when a seller agrees to reimburse a buyer for any drop in a product's price that may occur within a given period, the buyer succeeds in transferring the entire risk of a price decline during the period to the seller. Hedging provides another way to transfer the risks of price changes in a limited number of items traded on organized commodity exchanges.[1]

Risks attached to such natural hazards as fire and floods, deterioration of products in storage, and damage in transit can often be transferred to institutions that specialize in assuming such risks. Insurance companies cover all these risks in return for premium payments. When risks are transferred in this way, unpredictable amounts of potential loss become known amounts of expense.

Because many marketing risks cannot be transferred, marketers concentrate on trying to reduce them. Risks of changes in market demand are reduced through accurate sales forecasting and marketing research; for example, while available techniques for market measurement are by no means foolproof, a well-considered sales forecast can help reduce the margin of error in deciding on inventory size. Also, risk of a change in market demand is reducible through aggressive programs of advertising, personal selling,

[1] Hedging is a procedure involving simultaneous sales in the futures market when purchases are made in the current (spot) market, and simultaneous purchases in the futures market when sales are made in the current market so that gains or losses on current transactions are approximately balanced off against the opposite experience in the futures market.

and the like. Reasonably accurate sales forecasting should also help in reducing the "supply" risk of being out-of-stock and unable to fill customers' orders.

Other risks involved in changing supply conditions, such as the risk that an oversupply will cause competitors to cut prices, may be partially offset by differentiating products in ways that will cause customers to be reluctant to accept substitutes. To the extent that product differentiation succeeds in building customer loyalty, a marketer gains a degree of control over the supply; its customers will not switch to substitutes simply because of small price differentials. In a limited sense, it gains a degree of monopoly control over the product's supply. However, product differentiation only reduces the risk of price competition; it does not eliminate it. Few marketers ever succeed in completely differentiating their products.

***Obtaining and Analyzing Marketing Information.*** Both for the sound formulation of marketing programs and for the intelligent direction of marketing activities, management needs to obtain and analyze a great deal of marketing information. The success of a company's marketing operations largely depends upon management's knowledge and appraisals of such important information as the size, location, and characteristics of different markets for the several products; the nature of present and prospective customers making up various market segments, their needs and wants, and their buying habits and preferences; competitors' strengths, weaknesses, activities, and plans; and trends in market supply and demand. Management secures these types of marketing information, appraises the significance, and adjusts company operations accordingly.

Besides the general types of information mentioned above, particular items of market information are often important. For example, the fact that a "market glut" for lettuce exists in Chicago is important to a Texas lettuce grower planning shipments to that area. Similarly, knowing the extent to which Pacific Coast steel users are buying Japanese-made steel is important information to a domestic steel company. Likewise, it is important for an upstate New York manufacturer of room air conditioners to learn as soon as possible of a "run" on his product in Washington, D.C. Such items, which have immediate, though often fleeting, implications are called "market news" to distinguish them from other pieces of marketing information that have longer-range and continuing significance.

Marketing information is gathered in diverse ways. Executives obtain much market news rather informally through casual conversations: from reading business and trade publications, "syndicated" market news letters, and daily newspapers; from newscasts; and from reports submitted by field sales personnel. More formal information-gathering methods are used to obtain marketing information of greater long-range significance. Sales analysis techniques are applied in combing company records for information about the customers and markets. Marketing research methods are used in tapping information sources outside the company. Economic and business forecasting techniques are used to secure important information on future market conditions.

## VARIATIONS IN CLASSIFICATION OF MARKETING ACTIVITIES

Although availability of a systemized classification of marketing activities assists in studying marketing and its problems, no such classification system is universally applicable in analyzing the activities of particular companies or industries. For a cosmetics manufacturer, packaging and advertising may be so important that they deserve classification as separate marketing activities, while storage may be so unimportant as not to deserve separate classification. Each marketer should set up its own classification of marketing activities, emphasizing those important to the operation's success, deemphasizing others. Each company has its own individualized set of company and marketing goals, and the list of marketing activities is simply a compilation of those necessary to achieve these goals.

If the numbers and kinds of marketing activities required vary with the marketer, the product, and the distribution method, we may ask whether it is meaningful to classify activities performed under diverse circumstances into general groups. Certainly, for example, farmers, unlike manufacturers, cannot change the design of their products. Melon growers know that consumers would prefer seedless watermelons, but they cannot develop them personally. They can only hope that plant scientists eventually will succeed in doing so. Hence, farmers appear naturally to have little practical interest in "product design." Despite such variances, different marketers still share enough common goals and activities to justify generalizations about the marketing activities they perform.

## PERFORMANCE OF MARKETING ACTIVITIES
## AND MARKETING EFFICIENCY

Some marketing critics assert that repetition in performance of marketing activities is a sure sign of inefficiency. In evaluating this criticism, we must admit that some activities are performed at each distribution level—buying and selling, for example, may be performed several times since each middleman, interposed between producer and final buyer, both buys and sells. But, seeing this as further evidence of inefficiency, the critics suggest that marketing costs could be reduced through eliminating certain middlemen. Following this line of reasoning to its logical end, the most efficient marketing system would stress direct sales by producers to final users. In some instances, of course, as in marketing certain industrial products, direct sale is the most efficient marketing system; but in most marketing situations, direct sale is not efficient and in marketing many consumer products, it is impractical. Agricultural marketing provides numerous examples—direct distribution of potatoes or oranges by many thousands of growers would not only be prohibitively expensive but highly inconvenient for consumers, most of whom prefer to buy several food items at once and at a time of their own choosing. Even with such manufactured products as soap and flour, produced mainly by a few large companies, direct sale is impractical because consumers buy these products frequently and in small quantities so that the amount of money realized from each transaction would be insufficient to cover the costs of reaching the customer. Marketing channels for such products necessarily are complex and long, and individual marketing activities must be performed repeatedly as products move from producers to final buyers. At each distribution level, these activities are performed in specialized ways; under these conditions, shortening the marketing channel often results in *increased* costs and *reduced* efficiency. The question is not which activities have to be performed, but rather which combination of marketing institutions can perform them most efficiently. Marketing efficiency results from finding the optimum division of responsibility among the institutions performing the activities at different distribution levels.

## *CONCLUSION*

Emphasis in this chapter has been on the marketing process and the activities performed during its various phases. Little has been said about marketing individual products or the institutions engaged in marketing, except by way of illustrating the performance of various marketing activities. Marketing activities, products, and marketing institutions are all essential elements of marketing. Company and marketing goals determine which products move through what combinations of marketing institutions.

# 4

# ORGANIZING FOR MARKETING

The organization is the mechanism through which management translates its business philosophy into action. As its philosophy changes, management not only shifts its orientation and revises company goals but also makes changes in the organization. In moving toward the marketing concept, significant changes occur in the marketing organization, the company's main link with the market. In adapting operations to fit the market environment more appropriately, decisions are made on products, marketing channels, physical distribution, promotion, and prices. The marketing organization provides the vehicle and implements these decisions.

## COMPANY GOALS AND THE MARKETING ORGANIZATION

An organization is a group of people brought together to participate in a common effort directed toward accomplishing certain goals. The basic goals of a company indicate what the company wants to be, since they override and permeate the rest of its administration. Certain goals have important implications for the marketing organization.

**1.** *Desired Financial Results.* Traditionally, business enterprises are intended to be economic institutions. Generally the organizers anticipate that operations will generate profits. Once operations are underway, profits must be forthcoming on a sufficiently regular basis to permit the company's continued survival.

The profit goal is important for the marketing organization. It has implications both for the amount of sales volume that should be obtained and for maximum allowable costs. Also significant is the time span within which a target profit goal is to be reached, inasmuch as this influences tradeoff relationships between investments for current profit and those for future payoff.

**2.** *Desired Place in the Industry.* A company defines its desired place in the industry in terms of: size of operation, major function (manufacturing, wholesaling, retailing, etc.), quality and price levels for its products, and specialization or diversification of its activities. Different decisions on these variables result in different types of marketing organizations. For instance, a company that strives to have the largest sales volume in the industry requires a different type of marketing organization than one that wants to have the highest quality products.

**3.** *Disposition Toward Change.* A company's attitude toward change determines the type of employees who are attracted to it and the scheme by which they are welded into an organizational framework. Firms operating under the marketing concept opt in favor of emphasizing change rather than stability. They recognize the need for making continual adjustments in the company's operations and organizational structure in the process of adapting to changing market requirements and competitive conditions.

**4.** *Social Philosophy.* The basic goals controlling a company's relationships with the community and governmental units permeate and affect the operations of all departments and, most certainly, operations of the marketing department.

**5.** *Competitive Posture.* A company's posture with respect to its competition has implications for the marketing organization, such as whether or not it will incorporate features permitting aggressive selling and advertising.

**6.** *Desired Customer Service Image.* There is a world of difference between a company seeking long-run customer satisfaction and one emphasizing quick "one-time" sales. This facet of the company image is important to all departments producing, selling, and servicing the product line.

**7.** *Relationships with Suppliers.* The nature of a company's desired relationships with suppliers has indirect but important implications for marketing organization, since such relationships affect product quality, availability of repair and replacement parts, pricing practices, and the like.

## MARKETING ORGANIZATION AND TRANSITION TO THE MARKETING CONCEPT

How far a company moves toward adopting the marketing concept is up to top management. Such factors as executives' personalities and experience influence this decision, but the most critical is top management's appraisal of the current state and probable future intensity of competition. The more directly such environmental trends as those discussed in Chapter 2 impinge upon a company's operations, the more severe is its competition and the more crucial is adoption of the marketing concept to its survival.

### Historical Shifts in Top Management's Business Philosophy

*Production Emphasis.* When production problems were of prime importance, top management generally visualized a need for only a skeletal marketing organization. A slow rate of technological change made product changes infrequent; marketing channels were well-defined and adhered to traditional patterns; little promotion was required due to the absence of strong competition; and pricing was according to what the market would bear. Under these conditions, the marketing organization was little more than an adjunct to the factory—charged with physically distributing its output.

*Personal Selling Emphasis.* As introduction and refinement of mass production techniques caused increased factory outputs, the key problem became that of selling at the highest possible price what the factory could turn out. Advertising and other marketing activities were cast in supporting roles, being viewed as means for making personal selling more effective. Products and quantities manufactured were determined according to what the factory could produce, and the sales force was charged with selling that output. The sales organization often constituted the entire marketing organization or, at least, dominated other marketing activities such as advertising.

*Market Emphasis.* Growing numbers of top managements recognize that rather than focusing on what the factory can produce, it is more sensible to determine what consumers want and then design, manufacture, and market products capable of satisfying those wants. With this shift in orientation, far-sweeping organizational changes occur. Marketing research becomes an important component of marketing organizations, as it sees increasing use in improving market knowledge and understanding. Product research and development gain in organizational stature as consumers become steadily more sophisticated in what they will buy. At the same time, advancing technology makes it possible to tailor product specifications ever more closely to what consumers want. Advertising's organizational stature has been elevated, as development and expansion of mass media has helped make advertising a powerful element in marketing strategy even though personal selling—and the sales department—continues as the "backbone" of most marketing organizations. Similarly, changes in marketing channels, in operating methods of distributive institutions, and in physical distribution facilities have made channel and distribution decisions more important and have earned a place in a growing number of marketing organizations for specialized units dealing with these areas. Finally, in industry after industry, the competitive tempo has risen, making pricing decisions more important and sometimes causing reallocations of decision-making authority. Summing up—all types of marketing decisions are rising in importance, resulting in changed organizational structures as companies adopt or move toward adoption of the marketing concept.

### Company Organization and the Marketing Concept

Proper company organization under the marketing concept results in a total integration and coordination of all organizational units (marketing, research and development, manufacturing, financial, etc.) into a single operating system directed toward achieving company goals and, at the same time, toward serving the market and its changing wants and desires. Neither marketing nor any other organizational unit dominates. All are welded into an operating system whose components are so orchestrated that the market is served effectively while company goals are reached.

The organizational structure of a company operating under the marketing concept is subject to frequent, sometimes drastic, modifications. Shifts in environmental factors, such as technological breakthroughs by competitors or changes in distributive institutions, require not only reappraisals of the organization's appropriateness but possibly modifications. Ideally, the organization should have built-in flexibility enabling it to adapt readily to unstable conditions; the hierarchy itself should change with changing conditions, each member performing his or her specialty according to a common understanding of the company's goals.

### Organizational Responsibility for Marketing Policy Formulation

As a company reorganizes in line with the marketing concept, a hard look is taken at the ways in which responsibility is assigned for formulating marketing policies. Traditionally sales force management, advertising, marketing research, and the building and maintaining of relationships with marketing channels have been recognized as marketing activities. Traditionally, too, marketing executives have been responsible for policy formulation in these areas. But other departments, such as production and finance, have strong interests in how sales personnel are trained and operate, in the messages advertising conveys, and in the information marketing research gathers. Therefore, in the modern organizations, nonmarketing executives participate, or at least have input, in making policies for these areas of marketing.

Similarly, marketing executives help make policies in any organizational area where there are important marketing implications. One area is pricing, which often is the responsibility of the treasurer, controller, production manager, or some combination. Another is the product line, traditionally the province of production, or research and development, or both. Still another is physical distribution, often either under the production department's control or segregated into a separate department. Policies on pricing, products, and physical distribution all have important implications for marketing; by their very nature, these are interfunctional activities and, as such, marketing executives should share the responsibility for policy formulation. When a company adopts the marketing concept, every effort is made to "pull down the walls between departments." The main way to do this is to discard traditional authority and job-task relationships wherever they prevent or act as deterrents to effective coordination of the organization as an operating system.

### Integration of Marketing Activities

As marketing receives recognition as a major business function, one requiring coordination of numerous activities, top executives reexamine the ways in which these activities are incorporated in the formal organizational structure. Sales force management, advertising, and marketing research, for instance, traditionally have all been set up as separate departments reporting directly to top management. Integration, or centralization of these activities under a single high-ranking marketing executive, by improving coordination, increases marketing effectiveness. There has been a strong trend in this direction.

## INTERNAL ORGANIZATION OF THE MARKETING DEPARTMENT

Executives in small marketing departments must handle all types of problems, but in large departments dividing the work is not only desirable but also critical. In a large marketing organization, numerous executives are specialists, with technical knowledge of activities such as advertising, marketing research, and physical distribution. The chief marketing executive is responsible for dividing the work among these specialists and other subordinates.

### The Chief Marketing Executive

Increasing centralization of marketing responsibilities and growing complexity of the marketing function has led large companies to search for a new "breed" of chief marketing executive. No longer is he or she directly in charge of the sales force but delegates authority for its management to a subordinate, the general sales manager. This gives him or her more time to plan other marketing activities and to coordinate the work of the staff divisions, which have grown both in numbers and influence. Older staff divisions, such as advertising, marketing research, and credit management, now brought together under his or her direction, exert a greater total impact on marketing strategy and tactics. New staff divisions, such as product management and physical distribution, occupy important organizational niches.

### Dividing Marketing Line Authority

Line executives are those in the direct chain of command whose jobs consist mainly of managing subordinates who directly accomplish the company's objectives. In a marketing organization, the chief marketing executive is also its top line executive, and the direct chain of command runs down through the sales organization (since it is the sales personnel who ultimately and directly perform the work leading to company objectives). Generally, however, the chief marketing executive assigns the major responsibility for sales force management to a subordinate—the sales vice president or general sales manager—who then is regarded as the marketing organization's principal line executive. When the sales force is small, the principal line executive manages it directly. But as the sales force expands, eventually line authority must be divided. (See Figure 4-1.)

*Geographic Division.* When a sales force is deployed over a wide area, line authority is often divided geographically. Division of authority along geographical lines is appropriate when the market's nature or buyers' characteristics or both vary significantly from region to region; in such instances, each sales region can adapt its selling methods more closely to the needs and customs of local markets. However, the underlying reason for dividing line authority geographically is to improve the sales force's effectiveness by increasing the frequency of executive contacts with sales personnel and by simplifying and strengthening their supervision. Each subordinate sales manager devotes his or her main efforts toward improving the performances of sales personnel. Whether the subordinate sales manager is permanently based in an assigned area or not makes little difference; increases in the availability and speed of public transportation have all but eliminated the need for this requirement, which once was universal.

**FIGURE 4-1** BASES FOR DIVIDING MARKETING LINE AUTHORITY

| | |
|---|---|
| I *Geographic* | By region, e.g., southeastern United States |
| | By state |
| | By metropolitan or trading areas |
| II *Product* | Different products |
| | Different brand names |
| | Family brands |
| III *By Customer or Marketing Channel* | Industrial Market |
| | Consumer market |
| |    Direct to Retailer |
| |    Wholesalers |
| |    Agents |

***Product Division.*** Sometimes a company's products dictate the organization of its sales force. When variations among products require considerably different selling methods and technical know-how, line authority may be divided by products and separate sales forces set up for each product or product group. General Electric requires different kinds of sales personnel to sell large electrical generators and small household appliances. Generator sales personnel need technical training and must be prepared to wait years sometimes for their first order from a utility company; small appliance sales personnel need little technical training and perform routine selling work. It would be wasteful to use the more technically trained personnel to sell both types of products, so separate selling groups are maintained—each qualified to sell its particular products and each reporting to its own sales executive.

Maintaining separate sales forces for different products is expensive because it frequently results in several salespersons covering the same geographical areas. Thus, the benefits should clearly outweigh the extra cost. These benefits are greatest for companies selling broadly diversified product lines, for those reaching different markets with different products, and for those having individual products with unique selling problems.

***Customer or Marketing Channel Division.*** When customers or marketing channels for a product or group of products vary substantially, it may be appropriate to divide line authority on that basis. A power-saw manufacturer, for example, sells identical products to two very different markets: the lumber industry and the construction industry. These two markets have both different geographical characteristics (lumbering is heavily concentrated in the Northwest and Southeast, whereas construction is broadly distributed relative to population and industrial concentration) and different buying practices. Under these conditions, separate sales forces are justified.

Many marketers sell the same consumer products through multiple marketing channels. Part of the factory's output may reach consumers through wholesale distributor and independent retailer channels, another part through chain stores buying directly from the factory, and still another part through export middlemen selling to overseas markets. The type of selling required in each case is quite different, and the number and kinds of buyers varies greatly. (It takes, for example, only a few salespersons to reach all chain store buying offices in the United States, but it takes dozens or hundreds to reach all wholesalers.) Marketers using multiple channels often find it advantageous to organize separate sales forces for each channel.

***Division on Several Bases.*** Many companies use more than one basis for dividing line authority. Large sales organizations require several levels of management, and different bases of division may be used at different levels. When product differences require division of authority along product lines, the sales force may be organized accordingly, but if further subdivision is needed, it may be on a geographic basis. Thus, the resulting organization provides sales specialization in terms of both different product lines and geographical market differences.

### Division of Marketing Staff Authority

Staff people theoretically have purely advisory roles with no place in the command structure and without the right to give orders, but this clear distinction does not exist in practice. The nature of the staff executive's work gives him or her an intimate and broad view of line executives' problems that almost inevitably provides *informal* authority. Furthermore, with higher management relying increasingly on processed information, the staff authority to advise becomes the authority to *screen* and, thus, to make decisions. Generally, division and allocation of staff authority is decided according to areas of special competence.

### The Product Manager

The product manager does not fit neatly into either the line or staff categories. Especially in large multi-product companies, product managers are common, mainly because too often a simple two-way (line and staff) division of marketing authority causes some products to receive inadequate attention. Thus, no one is specifically responsible for the success or failure of particular products. It is possible for some products to receive too little or too much promotion for optimal results from expenditures, for advertising particular products not to be coordinated properly with sales activities, so that much of the effort is wasted, and for changes in consumer wants and competitors' actions with respect to individual products to go unheeded. The product manager's position was created in an attempt to fill such vacuums— in effect, he or she serves as a deputy marketing director for a particular product or product group. Normally, he or she is concerned with all phases of the planning, execution, and control of marketing activities for assigned products. The broad scope of duties makes the product manager a combined line and staff executive with respect to the assigned products.

### Organization Under the Marketing Concept

Figure 4-2 shows a typical formal marketing organization for a large company operating under the marketing concept. The organization is divided into three main parts: marketing services (mainly staff responsibilities), management of personal selling (including the line organization and staff activities closely related to sales force operations), and product management. The subdivisions on the marketing services side illustrate the broad range of staff-type responsibilities. Those under the general sales manager, who here serves as the principal line executive, are: field sales (made up of line executives managing the sales force); sales training (a staff activity); sales service (a staff activity); and physical distribution (inventory management and movement of customers' orders). Those under the pro-

**Figure 4-2** Organization Under the Marketing Concept

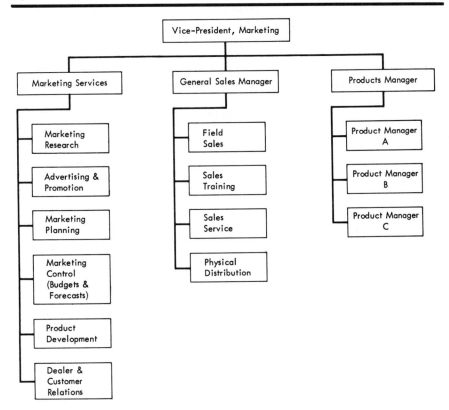

ducts manager are in charge of product groups A, B, and C—each product manager being responsible for coordinating all marketing activities (staff as well as line) exerted in behalf of his or her products.

Staff personnel are generally concentrated at the central office because many of their activities are similar for all products, marketing channels, and geographic regions. Centralization allows coordination of efforts and a pooling of financial resources so the best available personnel and equipment are brought together. Without good staff liaison at headquarters, some divisions might make decisions for their own good rather than for the good of the company; for example, long-range research projects might be omitted because of their immediate adverse effect on a division's profits. A strong central staff keeps division executives aware of broad company policies and objectives.

In large marketing organizations, it may still be necessary to provide staff assistance in field sales offices. In these instances, it must be decided whether (organizationally) to place these staff field executives under the authority of their central office staff executives or under local line sales executives. As in other organizational decisions, the solution rests in compromise among the authority, communication, coordination, and human-relations needs of the affected individuals and groups.

## CONCLUSION

As a company makes the transition to the marketing concept, management looks to the market for guidance and the entire company is geared toward serving that market. The concept of total company organization, as well as marketing organization, should be dynamic. An organization that is satisfactory today may prove inadequate tomorrow. Markets change because of changes in income, shifts in population, changes in tastes and life styles, and the like. Market changes coupled with technological advances result in a flow of new products and the continual modification of old products. Important developments in mass communciations media and in marketing channels occur from time to time. A significant change in any market factor reduces the effectiveness of an organizational structure not only for serving the market's needs but as a vehicle for achieving the company's objectives. Since market factors are forever in a state of change, continual monitoring and regular reappraisal of organizational effectiveness are imperative.

# 5

# MARKETING INFORMATION

Information is needed both to begin and to carry through the analysis of marketing problems. It is needed to conceptualize or understand a problem's nature and to predict the consequences of alternative courses of action. There are several important sources and uses of marketing information.

Marketing information comes from both internal and external sources. Internal information sources are mainly company records; examples include the operating statement, sales records, and production records. External information sources are both "outside organizations," providing general information, and those tapped by marketing research.

## THE OPERATING STATEMENT AND OPERATING RATIOS

The operating statement (profit and loss statement) is the most widely used internal source of marketing information. Marketing executives should understand the accounting concepts on which the operating statement is based and know how to use it as a tool in decision making. The operating statement is a financial summary of operating results for some period, usually a month or a year. It shows whether the firm operated at a profit or a loss and explains the quantitative relationships among sales, cost of goods sold, and expenses. These relationships are:

|        |                           |
|--------|---------------------------|
|        | Sales                     |
| Minus: | Cost of Goods Sold        |
| Equals:| Gross Margin (or Gross Profit) |
| Minus: | Expenses                  |
| Equals:| Net Profit (or Net Loss)  |

This skeleton operating statement portrays only relationships among the major operating items—sales, cost of goods sold, and expenses. Each major item is, in its turn, the result of a set of relationships existing among more detailed items of financial operating data. Table 5-1, an operating statement, shows in considerable detail these several sets of relationships, as well as the interrelationships among the major operating items.

The *Percentages* column in Table 5-1 expresses the relationship between net sales and other important items. These operating ratios are percentages of net sales, with net sales equal to 100 percent. The rationale for using net sales as the base (that is, the denominator or 100 percent) is that all costs, expenses, and profit (if any) come out of the proceeds of net sales. Thus, when an executive says that net profit is 5 percent, this means 5 percent of net sales. Similarly, when gross margin is 33 percent, this means 33 percent of net sales.

### Gross Margin Ratio

Gross margin is the difference between sales and cost of goods sold. Expressing this amount as a percentage of net sales allows comparison with previous operating periods, or with competitors' figures. The gross margin ratio may be increased or decreased: by changing the selling price per unit or by changing the cost per unit. When a marketer believes the gross margin ratio is high or low relative either to past performance or to competitors' experiences, he or she may seek to improve the ratio by raising prices, reducing costs, or both. Thus, a retailer alerted by an abnormally low gross margin ratio might reevaluate buying procedure to find low-cost suppliers, improve working capital position to take advantage of cash discounts, improve traffic control to decrease freight costs, or improve merchandise selection to command higher markups.

### Expense Ratio

The expense ratio provides the basis for evaluation of the relationship between sales, gross margin, expenses, and profit. It is concerned not with a breakdown analysis of individual expense categories but with a comparison of total expenses and other figures on the operating statement. The ratio of expense to sales varies considerably among companies, even within the same industry. For this reason, expense comparisons among companies must be made with caution. Even so, the expense ratio allows management to compare current expenses with those in other operating periods.

**TABLE 5-1** Operating Statement
For December, 198_

|  |  |  | PERCENTAGES |
|---|---|---|---|
| Gross sales |  | $105,000 | 105.0 |
| Less: Returns and allowances |  | 5,000 | 5.0 |
| Net sales |  | $100,000 | 100.0 |
| Cost of goods sold: |  |  |  |
| Opening inventory @ cost |  | $10,000 |  |
| Purchases @ billed cost | $65,000 |  |  |
| Less: Purchase discounts | 1,500 |  |  |
| Net cost of purchases | $63,500 |  |  |
| Plus: Freight in | 4,000 |  |  |
| Net cost of purchases delivered |  | 67,500 |  |
| Cost of goods handled |  | $77,500 |  |
| Less: Closing inventory @ cost |  | 16,500 |  |
| Cost of goods sold |  | 61,000 | 61.0 |
| Gross margin (or gross profit) |  | $ 39,000 | 39.0 |
| Expenses: |  |  |  |
| Advertising | $ 4,000 |  |  |
| Sales salaries and commissions | 10,500 |  |  |
| Warehousing and delivery | 9,000 |  |  |
| Administrative | 4,000 |  |  |
| General and other | 6,000 |  |  |
| Total expenses |  | 33,500 | 33.5 |
| Net profit on operations (before Federal Income Tax) |  | $ 5,500 | 5.5 |

### Sales Returns and Allowances Ratio

This ratio, like all other operating ratios, is expressed as a percent of net sales, even though sales returns and allowances are subtracted from gross sales in arriving at net sales. Analysis of sales returns and allowances ratios helps to determine whether these figures represent normal or abnormal experience. Some returns and allowances are expected because of human error and product failings, but excessive returns reflects bad merchandise or overselling.

### Net Profit Ratio

This well-known operating ratio relates most directly to the profit objective but, when used alone, it has limited value. A profit decline alerts management to possible troubles; but because profit results from a combination of sales, gross margin, and expense, evaluations of all three ratios are necessary to isolate the problems. Similarly, if management wants to increase profits, it analyzes proposed operational changes in the light of other operating ratios.

## OTHER ANALYTICAL RATIOS

Certain analytical ratios serve as everyday aids in decision making. Included are the markup, the markdown, and the rate of stockturn. These ratios are so well known, in such wide usage, and so basic to marketing decision making that they are called "marketing arithmetic."

### Markup

The amount by which an item's selling price exceeds its cost to the seller is the *markup*. When, for example, a discount house pays $14 for an electric carving knife and prices it at $21, the $7 difference is the markup. Out of the total of all such markups placed on all of the items it sells, the firm seeks to cover its expenses and earn a net profit.

Marketers think not only of a markup in terms of so many dollars and cents but also as some percentage either *of original selling price or of cost.* They often use the markup concept as an analytical ratio to express the relation between dollar markup and either the original dollar selling price or the dollar cost. If an automobile dealer pays the manufacturer $7,200 for a vehicle and prices it at $9,000, the markup percentage is 20 percent (that is, $\frac{\$1,800}{9,000}$) on the selling price and 25 percent (that is, $\frac{\$1,800}{7,200}$) on the cost.

Most sellers use original selling price rather than cost as the base, and whenever we speak of markup as a percentage, we shall mean markup as a percentage of original selling price. Keep in mind, however, that under either system of computing markup percentages, the same dollar markup is involved. In one system, markup is related to dollar selling price; in the other, to cost. To clarify the relationship between these two markup systems, consider Table 5-2 which illustrates the situation where the auto dealer bought a vehicle for $7,200 and priced it at $9,000.

**TABLE 5-2**

| PERCENTAGE BASED ON SELLING PRICE | | PERCENTAGE BASED ON COST |
|:---:|:---:|:---:|
| 20% | $1,800 Markup | 25% |
| 80% | $7,200 Cost | 100% |
| 100% | $9,000 Selling Price | 125% |

### Markdown

Merchandise does not always sell at the original selling price, and a seller may, in an effort to "make it move," mark down, or reduce the price. When a furniture store manager, for example, concludes that a fancy wall decoration is not going to sell at the $10.00 price asked in the beginning, it may be marked down to $7.50, at which price a customer buys it. The difference between the original selling price and the actual selling price is the *markdown*. The dollar markdown, then, is $2.50 in this example. Retailers customarily compute markdown percentages by using actual selling price rather than original selling price as the base.[1] Thus, when an item is marked down from $10.00 to $7.50, the $2.50 price reduction is a 33⅓ percent markdown (that is, $2.50/$7.50).

Merchants recognize that every item stocked carries some probability of having to be marked down. Such markdowns can occur either before or after sales are made. The second type of markdown (allowances to customers) appears on the operating statement; the first type does not. Both types are taken into account in setting original selling prices, for the total of original markups should be sufficiently high so that subsequent markdowns will not reduce sales below the total of cost of goods sold and expenses. The formula, then, for computing the markdown ratio is:

$$\text{Markdown \%} = \frac{\text{\$ Allowances to Customers + \$ Markdowns}}{\text{Net Sales}}$$

The markdown percentage is computed for an operating period. The accounting system provides the figures on allowances to customers and net sales, and a supplementary record furnishes the figure for other dollar markdowns taken during that period. This means, then, that some marked down items probably have not been sold and are still in stock. Entries are made in the supplementary markdown record at the time markdowns are taken, not at the time marked down items are sold.

The markdown ratio is a useful analytical tool and control device. It provides information needed for planning original markups, and it reminds management that prices must be set (sooner or later) at levels that customers are willing to pay. If the original price is too high, markdowns are inevitable; but if original selling price is realistic, markdowns are unnecessary.

The markdown ratio is used, too, as a measure of the efficiency of store buyers and retail sales personnel. Reasonably low markdowns are an indication of effective buying, realistic pricing, and good selling. When used

---

[1] The opposite seems to be the widespread practice in Puerto Rico and Latin American countries. Retailers there claim that by computing markdown percentages from original selling price they can recognize more readily the actual price markdown that was required in order to make the actual sale.

as a performance measure, management defines what it considers a "desirable" markdown ratio. Such standard markdown ratios are derived either through studies of store markdown ratios over past periods or from reports of trade associations.

### Stockturn

The stockturn rate is an analytical tool used for measuring operating efficiency. It indicates the speed at which the inventory "turns over"—the number of times the average inventory is sold during an operating period. If a retailer, for instance, starts the year with an inventory having a cost value of $20,000 and ends the year with a $30,000 inventory at cost, the average inventory at cost has been $25,000. If the cost of goods sold during the year amounted to $100,000, the business had a stockturn rate of 4, calculated as follows:

$$\text{Stockturn Rate} = \frac{\text{Cost of Goods Sold}}{\text{Average Inventory at Cost}}$$

$$= \frac{\$100,000}{\frac{1}{2}\,(\$20,000 + \$30,000)} = 4$$

This retailer, in other words, sold the average inventory four times during the year, or once every three months. If the store makes a net profit of three cents every time it sells something costing a dollar, we can say that it had a return of 12 cents (3 cents × 4) on each dollar invested in inventory.

This computation of stockturn rate is the most commonly used method. Both the numerator and denominator in the formula are cost figures readily obtainable from accounting records. There are, however, some businesses that value their inventories in terms of selling prices rather than in terms of cost. In these businesses, the following formula is used for computing the stockturn rate:

$$\text{Stockturn Rate} = \frac{\text{Net Sales (\$)}}{\text{Average Inventory @ Selling Price}}$$

There is yet a third method of computing stockturn rate: dividing sales in units by the average inventory in units. The formula for this calculation is:

$$\text{Stockturn Rate} = \frac{\text{Sales (Total Units)}}{\text{Average Inventory in Units}}$$

This formula is used in two types of situations: when the firm is handling only one main product, such as shoes or ice cream, making it practical to record sales and inventories in merchandise units; that is, in pairs of shoes or gallons of ice cream; the other when the firm's management wants to measure how rapidly its stock of a given item, such as dresses retailing at $35, is turning over—to determine whether or not inventory of the item is optimum and whether the maximum return on the inventory investment in this item is being obtained.

The stockturn rate is a yardstick for measuring operating efficiency. An increase in the rate of turnover of capital invested in inventory will increase total profits unless the net profit ratio is decreased proportionally. Thus, a higher stockturn is a much sought after goal. The stockturn rate is also used as a basis for comparing the effectiveness of branches or different outlets. The unit with the highest stockturn rate is often also the most efficiently managed but not always. Where, for instance, are the two units located? The store with the fastest stockturn rate might be across the street from the factory with the opportunity to replenish inventory daily, while the other might be 3,000 air miles away with the necessity of maintaining a large reserve inventory. Also, one store may cater to only a small market segment—for example, men only—while the other may serve the whole family, necessitating a much larger basic stock. Or, perhaps, the store with the high turnover handles only low-priced, low-margin lines. These and similar considerations should cause us to be cautious in drawing conclusions based solely on differences in stockturn rates among stores.

## SALES ANALYSIS

Sales analysis is a thorough and detailed study of a company's sales records for the purpose of detecting marketing strengths and weaknesses. Although sales records are regularly summarized in the "sales" section of the operating statement, these summaries reveal next to nothing about strong or weak features of the company's marketing efforts. Through periodic sales analyses, management gains insights on such matters as: strong and weak sales territories, high-volume and low-volume products, and the types of customers providing the most and least satisfactory sales volumes. Sales analysis is used to uncover significant details that otherwise lie hidden in sales records. It provides information that management needs to allocate future marketing efforts effectively.

For example, a manufacturer of office supplies made a detailed analysis of past sales and discovered that, of 150 distributors handling the products, 27 (or 18 percent) accounted for 70 percent of sales, and that the other 123 (or 82 percent) only produced 30 percent. Similar situations exist in most companies, a large percentage of the customers accounting for a small percentage of total sales and, conversely, a small percentage of customers accounting for a high percentage of total sales. Comparable situations are found wherever a large percentage of the sales territories, products, and orders bring in only a small percentage of total sales.

Such sales patterns do not always result in unprofitable operations, but operations are often less profitable than they might be because marketing efforts and, hence, marketing costs, all too frequently are divided on the basis of number of customers, territories, products, orders, and so forth, rather than on the basis of actual or potential dollar sales. It usually costs, for example, just as much to maintain a salesperson in a good territory as in a bad one, almost as much to promote a product that sells in large volume as one that sells poorly or not at all, and as much to have a salesperson call on and service a customer who places large orders as on another who places small orders. It is common for a large proportion of the total spending for marketing efforts to result in only a very small proportion of total sales and profits. Detecting such situations is the important task of sales analysis.

Each type of sales analysis sheds light on a different aspect of marketing operations. Analysis of sales by territories tells how much is being sold *where*. Analysis of sales by product tells how much of *what* is being sold. Analysis of sales by customers tells *who* is buying how much. All types of sales analysis relate to *how much* is being sold, but each answers this question in a different way. Although sales analysis can identify different aspects of marketing strength and weakness, it cannot explain *why* they exist. Answering the "why" question is the marketing manager's responsibility.

## MARKETING RESEARCH

Marketing research is the systematic gathering, recording, and analyzing of data about marketing problems; its purpose is to provide information useful in marketing decision making. Putting information to use in marketing decision making typically requires the tapping of both internal and external sources of data. The internal studies focus on resources and activities within the company and the external studies on the relation of the firm to its environment and, particularly, to its markets. The marketing decision-maker considers internal data in the light of information from external sources. Information revealed by external studies is considered in relation to data obtained from internal sources. Internal and external marketing studies are necessary complements of each other. In fact, the art of management may be described as taking into account simultaneously the inner workings of the firm and its interaction with external forces. This decision-making process is illustrated in Figure 5-1.

### Problem Identification and Marketing Research

Even though marketing management may have already identified the problem, it must make certain that the researcher understands its precise nature. The marketing researcher, like the marketing decision-maker, looks upon problem identification as a basic first step. Only if the researcher knows what problem management is trying to solve can he or she do an

**Figure 5-1** The decision-making process

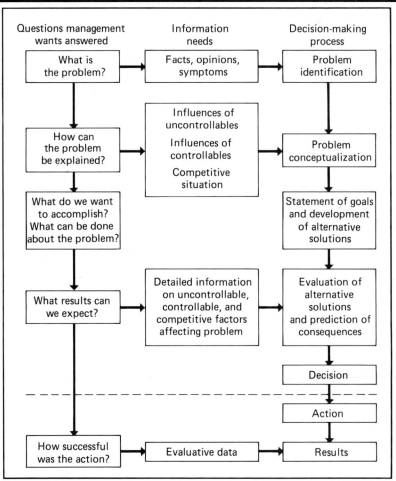

*Source:* Cundiff, E.W., Still, R.R., Govoni, N.A.P., *Fundamentals of Modern Marketing*, (Englewood Cliffs, N.J.: Prentice-Hall, Inc., 1985), p. 102.

effective job in designing a research project that will provide the needed information. Only if the problem is clearly in mind can he or she be expected to intelligently direct the resulting project—to steer it as directly as possible to predetermined informational goals (set by the nature of the problem itself) and to keep it from "going off course" on the way to those goals. Competent marketing researchers, do not undertake any study until they are certain that the executive making the request has some problem "pinned down" and until that executive communicates the problem's nature clearly. All too frequently, executives originate requests for studies that subsequently prove of little value simply because they had not probed deeply enough to identify the basic problem. In one such case—where management asked for a study of advertising effectiveness—further probing by an alert researcher revealed that a sales decline could be traced directly to the effects of a newly inaugurated distribution policy that was slowing up deliveries to retail outlets causing them to be out of stock frequently.

### Preliminary Exploration and the "Situation Analysis"

In the course of identifying the problem, the marketing researcher begins the preliminary exploration of data sources to gain insights into the problem's nature. Because the specific problem is not yet identified, there is a certain amount of groping around for information. This makes the preliminary exploration an informal and, to a large extent, unplanned investigation.

In doing a preliminary exploration, the researcher taps as many sources of readily available data as time permits. Company records (sales, financial production, and others) that might shed some light on the problem are examined. Trade and professional publications are skimmed for reports on similar situations encountered and/or researched by others. And the company's own reports of previous investigations of similar and related situations are studied. Thus, the researcher builds background for his or her own thinking. Marketing researchers refer to this phase of preliminary exploration as the "situation analysis."

### Project Planning for Marketing Research

Basically, a marketing research project is a *planned search for information*. Time spent in project planning should not only reduce the time required to conduct the project but also ultimately result in securing more reliable and meaningful information. When project planning is neglected, marketing researchers flit aimlessly from one information source to the next, choose research methods and approaches at random, and have only vague notions of the specific information needed. The earmarks of project planning in marketing research, as elsewhere, are well-defined goals, an organized effort, and a step-by-step schedule, all aimed at uncovering, reporting, and analyzing as reliable and meaningful information as it is possible to obtain in the available time.

Planning a marketing research project requires decisions on: (1) research objectives, (2) specific information needed, (3) information sources to tap, and (4) research methods to employ.

***Deciding on Research Objectives.*** After the marketing problem has been identified and the preliminary exploration finished, the first step in project planning is to set the research objectives. The preliminary exploration should have clarified the purposes for any subsequent formal research. In studying how the company spends its advertising appropriation, for instance, the researcher may have concluded tentatively that less money should be devoted to newspaper advertisements and more to radio. Thus the purpose of formal research might be to test two hypotheses:

1. The company should spend less on newspaper advertising.
2. The company should spend more on radio commercials.

The statement of research objectives should be limited to a small number of hypotheses to test or questions to answer. The number must be small, for no project can produce timely and reliable information if it is directed toward collecting too many facts. In pruning the list of objectives, the researcher should consider two questions about each "tentative" objective:

1. If we succeed in obtaining this information, of what use will it be to the decision maker?
2. If this information is of possible usefulness, is it useful enough to justify the cost of obtaining it?

***Deciding on Information Needed.*** The second key decision is determining the specific information needed to achieve the research objectives. The researcher considers the different types of information that seem pertinent to achieving the objectives and ascertains that each bit of specific information finally decided upon is relevant to achieving them. Suppose, for example, that the project being planned has the objective of answering "Should I open a self-service shoe store in Middletown, Pennsylvania?" What kinds of information are necessary to answer this question? The researcher should search out, as a minimum, the following:

1. Number of Middletown residents who are potential customers of this type of store.
2. Probable frequency and intensity of patronage. (How often and how much will members of different market segments patronize this store?)
3. Competing stores, their relative advantages, and their comparative costs.
4. Amount, kinds, and costs of persuasion (advertising, and so forth) needed for Middletown residents to patronize the store.

***Deciding on Information Sources.*** The next step is to identify the information sources. It is helpful to classify information sources as primary or secondary. A primary source is one from which information is obtained directly as, for example, through questionnaires and interviews. Primary sources include consumers and buyers, middlemen, sales personnel, trade association executives, and others. Secondary data sources are mostly published materials, such as government census publications and *Sales and Marketing Management's Survey of Buying Power.* Sometimes another type of secondary source (such as company files of marketing research and other reports) contains the desired information, although this may not be known to the decision maker needing it. Secondary data sources are repositories not of items of information gathered specifically to achieve the objectives of the research project being planned, but rather of material assembled for other purposes. Table 5-3 lists major published sources of secondary data.

The researcher should always look to the secondary sources first, for if the needed information is already available, the time and expense of gathering it from primary sources is saved. Usually, however, some information can be gleaned from secondary sources (for example, population and income statistics) but more crucial data (for example, the disposition of consumers to buy a given product under certain marketing conditions) must be obtained from primary sources. In the Middletown study on opening a self-service shoe store, for example, census publications (a secondary source) should reveal the number of residents who are potential users, and city directories (another secondary source) could be consulted to identify competitors selling shoes in the trading area. But to obtain other desired items of information, primary sources (namely, the potential consumers) would have to be tapped.

***Deciding on Research Methods.*** If all the needed information is obtainable from secondary sources, no decision on research methods is required; if, as is more likely, however, primary sources must be tapped, a decision on research methods is required. Table 5-4 outlines major factors to consider in collecting primary data.

***The Survey Method.*** In the survey method, information is obtained directly from respondents either through personal interviews or through mail questionnaires or telephone interviews. Questionnaires are used either to obtain specific responses to direct questions or to secure more general responses to "open end" questions.

The survey method has three uses: (1) to gather facts from respondents, (2) to report their opinions, or (3) to probe the interpretations they give to various matters.

In the *factual survey,* respondents are asked to report actual facts, as exemplified by questions such as: "What brand of cigarettes do you smoke?" "Where do you do most of your shopping for groceries?" "How many persons live at this address?" Even the answers to "factual" questions are subject to error because some respondents have faulty memories, are unable to generalize about personal experiences, or may give answers they believe interviewers want to obtain.

The *opinion survey* is designed to gather expressions of personal opinions, to record evaluations of different things, or to report thinking on

**TABLE 5-3** Sources of secondary data*

**I. Internal Sources**

Profit and loss statements, balance sheets, sales analyses, sales call reports, sales expense reports, inventory records, inquiries for product information, previous research reports.

**II. External Sources**

A. *Government publications*

*U.S. Industrial Outlook* provides information on industry segments including the costs of production, sales, and employment.

*Statistical Abstract of the U.S.* provides summary data on demographic, economic, and social data in the United States.

*County and City Data Book* presents statistical information on cities and counties on education, employment, income, housing, bank deposits, and retail sales.

*Census of Manufacturers and Survey of Manufacturers* provide detailed information on the production of U.S. industry by type of product.

Other governmental publications—*Census of Population, Census of Retail Trade, Wholesale Trade and Selected Services, Census of Transportation, Federal Reserve Bulletin, Monthly Labor Review, Survey of Current Business,* and *Vital Statistics Report.*

B. *Associations*

There is a wide variety of associations of manufacturers, distributors, and end users. The *Encyclopedia of Associations* lists every major trade and professional association. These associations often collect and distribute statistics and studies on their industry.

C. *Magazines*

General business—*Business Week, Forbes, Fortune, Harvard Business Review, Duns.*

Marketing—*Journal of Marketing, Journal of Marketing Research, Journal of Personal Selling and Sales Management, Industrial Marketing Management, Business Marketing, Sales and Marketing Management.*

Trade magazines—A wide variety of trade magazines exists covering specific types of products and end users. These magazines often collect valuable statistics as well as provide surveys and reports.

D. *Commercial data*

A. C. Nielsen provides data on products sold through retail stores, data on television audiences, and magazine circulation data.

Simmons provides an annual report covering the television markets, sporting goods, proprietary drugs, etc., giving detailed demographic and brand preference data.

---

*Thousands of other companies provide information either on a subscription basis or per report basis on a wide variety of topics. A sample of these companies includes Audit Bureau of Circulation, Audits and Surveys; Dun & Bradstreet; Standard Rate and Data; Starch, Frost and Sullivan; and Predicast.

**TABLE 5-4** Decisions on the collection of primary data

---

WHAT TYPE OF RESEARCH DESIGN SHOULD BE USED?
— Survey
— Observation
— Experimentation
— Test marketing
— Simulation

WHAT METHOD OF COLLECTING THE DATA IS MOST APPROPRIATE?
— Personal interview
— Telephone interview
— Mail interview
— Indirect interview

WHAT TYPE OF INSTRUMENT SHOULD BE USED?
— Questionnaire
— Mechanical instrument

WHAT TYPE OF SAMPLING PROCEDURE IS MOST APPROPRIATE?
— Sample size
— Probability sample
— Nonprobability sample

---

particular matters. Opinion surveys share the potential errors of factual surveys and, in addition, by forcing immediate answers to questions on subjects that the respondents may have not thought about lately, may produce answers not accurately reflecting real opinions.

In the *interpretative survey,* the respondent acts as an interpreter as well as a reporter. Interpretative data are gathered by using such questions as "Why do you use Brand X spray deodorant? and "What feature of the new *Thunderbird* appeals to you most?" A limitation of the interpretative survey is that respondents' answers often reflect an inability consciously to interpret personal feelings, motives, and attitudes.

The survey method is most accurate and reliable when used to gather factual data, less so when used to record opinions, and least so when used to gain insights into respondents' interpretations.

***The Experimental Method.*** Patterned after the procedure in scientific research, the experimental method as used in marketing research involves carrying out small-scale trial solutions to problems while simultaneously attempting to control all relevant factors except the one being studied. An advertiser, for example, may run two versions of a proposed advertisement (Ad A and Ad B) in a city newspaper, with half of the issue carrying Ad A and the other half Ad B. This "split run" test might be used to determine the most effective advertisement in one or more market areas, which might then be placed in newspapers in other markets, or in national media.

The main assumption in the experimental method is that the test conditions are essentially the same as those encountered in the broader market. Of course, test conditions are never quite the same as parallel conditions in the broader market. Nevertheless, a well-designed experiment, even though it cannot replicate total market conditions, can provide guidance and information for decision making.

*The Observational Method.* Here, marketing research data are gathered not through direct questioning of respondents, but by observing and recording consumers' actions. So, for example, in studying the impact of a department store's mass display of shelving paper, observers, stationed unobtrusively, record the total number of people passing by a display, the number stopping, the number picking up and examining the product, and the number making purchases. In another study, whose purpose was to determine which types of consumers buy what brands of home remedies, researchers made inventories of the contents of household medicine cabinets. In a third study, researchers used concealed tape recorders and posed as customers to evaluate selling techniques used in florist shops.

The main advantage of the observational method is that it records respondents' expressed actions and behavior patterns. Its principal shortcoming is that its design does not provide for detection of buying motives and other psychological factors since, in its pure form at least, this method involves simply "watching or listening or both," with no attempt at probing the reasons lying behind actions and behavior patterns.

*Gathering Primary Data Through Sampling.* In gathering data from primary sources, most marketing research projects use sampling. A sample is only a portion of the "universe" from which it is drawn; therefore, studying the characteristics and attitudes of the members of a sample, rather than of all members of the relevant universe, not only makes possible completion of a study in less time but results in lower research costs. Limitations of time and money are the main reasons that marketing research usually studies samples rather than whole universes.

All samples used in marketing research fall into one of two classes: probability and nonprobability. The distinction between these classes lies in the way items are selected for inclusion in the samples. Probability samples result from a process of random selection whereby each member of a universe has a *known* chance of being selected for the sample. Nonprobability samples result from a process in which judgment (and, therefore, bias) enters into the selection of the members of a universe included in the sample. Judgment also is involved in using probability samples (in deciding, for instance, on a particular sample design), but the actual selection of the individual items for inclusion is made solely through a probability mechanism as, for example, a table of random numbers (eliminating the human bias otherwise entering into the selection).

There are two kinds of error in samples: nonsampling and sampling. Samples contain both kinds of errors. Complete censuses contain only nonsampling errors. This, however, does not mean that census results are necessarily any more error-free than sample results. It means only that there is one kind of error in a census and two kinds in a sample. Sampling errors in probability samples are more easily evaluated because it is possible to measure them. This procedure is described in most marketing research texts.

Common sense tells us that the larger a sample, the greater the chances for reliable research results. However, sampling errors are the only errors that can be reduced by increasing sample size. And because the statistical formulas for computing sampling errors apply solely to probability samples, only in their case can we obtain statistical measures of the adequacy of sample size. The amount of sampling error considered acceptable (and, hence, the acceptable sample size) depends on management's willingness to assume risk, the money available for the project, and the basic nature of the research. In summary, the steps in the marketing research process are outlined in Table 5-5.

TABLE 5-5 Steps in the marketing research process

1. **Identify problem**
2. **Undertake preliminary exploration**
3. **Plan and conduct the research**
   a. *Establish research objectives*
   b. *Determine informational needs*
   c. *Collect secondary data*
   d. *Collect primary data*
      (1) Select research design
      (2) Select collection method
      (3) Design and test questionnaire
      (4) Select sample
      (5) Collect data
4. **Analyze and interpret data**
5. **Present results to management**

## *CONCLUSION*

Even though marketing decisions always involve uncertainty, they should be based to the extent possible on relevant information from both internal and external sources. Ultimately, every marketing decision is made in the hope that it will contribute to long-term profitability. The operating statement summarizes the relationships among financial factors affecting net profit and, thus, is the source for such marketing data as the markup and the stockturn rate. Reworking of original records through sales analysis is another source of information for the decision maker. Marketing research is designed to generate a flow of ideas and information from external sources—data on the uncontrollable environmental factors, the competitive situation, and factors over which mangement has some control (products, marketing channels and distribution, promotion, and prices).

# 6

# BUYER BEHAVIOR

Marketing management's basic problem is to adjust the forces under its control within an environment composed of diverse and ever-changing forces outside its control. We call these forces, respectively, the *controllables* and the *uncontrollables*. Controllables are directly influenced by the individual company's decisions and actions; they include products, marketing channels, physical distribution, promotion, and prices. The uncontrollables are those phenomena—competitive, scientific and technological, economic, sociological, psychological, and political and legal—that the individual company can influence only indirectly, if at all. Marketing management seeks to manipulate the controllables in terms of the uncontrollables in ways that contribute to meeting such company goals as profit, position in the industry, and desired public image. Management, in other words, taking the uncontrollables into account, blends the controllables into an overall marketing strategy (often called "the marketing mix") in order to achieve company goals. Collectively, the uncontrollables make up the environment in which the company operates, and the controllables are the means by which it adapts to that environment.

Numerous uncontrollables influence the behavior of buyers. Of particular importance are the economic, psychological, and sociological uncontrollables.

## ECONOMIC THEORY OF BUYER BEHAVIOR

Economic theorists were the first to advance formal explanations of buyer behavior. Economists visualize the market as made up of homogeneous buyers who act in a predictably similar fashion, and the economic process as the matching of homogeneous segments of supply with homogeneous segments of demand. Economic theory describes the individual human as a rational buyer who has perfect information about the market and uses it to obtain optimum value for the buying effort and money. Price is regarded as the strongest motivation. The individual compares all competing sellers' offerings and, since all are alike in every respect, buys the one with the lowest price. Above all, economic individuals' behavior is rational. Under these circumstances, buying choices are predictable and yield maximum value.

In some situations the model of the economic individual helps us understand and even predict consumer buying behavior. It explains why many a housewife selects the food store with the most or best "weekend specials" for her Friday shopping trip. It explains why a special price on Brand X may attract a customer who normally buys Brand Y. It also explains why a consumer, having decided to buy a new Ford station wagon, visits several Ford dealerships to get the best trade-in and price.

However, decision making by individuals is far too complex and too involved to reduce to the simplistic model of the economic individual. Although this model may explain, for example, why a buyer chooses one Ford dealer over another, it does not explain why the decision was to buy a Ford instead of a Chevrolet, a station wagon instead of a sedan, or a V-8 instead of a six. In order to analyze buyer behavior, we must consider both economic and noneconomic factors.

### Markets Are Heterogeneous

In striving for a realistic explanation of buyer behavior, we must discard one assumption that pervades the concept of the economic individual—that markets are homogeneous. Heterogeneity, not homogeneity, characterizes markets. The entire notion of market segmentation (described in Chapter 1) is based on the realization that not all buyers are alike, that they differ in numerous and distinctive ways. Furthermore, this heterogeneity is evident on both the supply (sellers') and demand (buyers') sides of every market. Essentially, then, the overall marketing problem of the total economy is to match heterogeneous segments of supply with heterogeneous segments of demand.

One way to explain consumer buying is in terms of what consumers are trying to do. Essentially, they are engaged in building assortments, in replenishing or extending inventories of goods for use by themselves and their families. The consumer buyer enters the market as a problem-solver. Solving a problem, either on behalf of a household or on behalf of a marketing organization, means reaching a decision in the face of uncertainty. In the double search which pervades marketing, the consumer buyer and the marketing executive are opposite numbers. The consumer buyer looks for products in order to complete an assortment, while the marketing executive looks for buyers who need his or her products.

This explanation is consistent with those economic theories that explain competition among sellers by emphasizing innovative competition, product differentiation, and differential advantage. The position occupied by every firm engaged in marketing is in some respects unique. Each firm is differentiated from all others by the characteristics of its products, its services, its geographic location, or any combination of these features. Each firm's survival requires that it present, to some group of buyers, a differential advantage over other suppliers. Any marketing organization makes sales to a core market composed of buyers who prefer its product or service, and to a fringe market made up of buyers who find it acceptable. This interrelationship and interdependence is illustrated in Figure 6-1.

**Figure 6-1** The core market concept for a specific industry

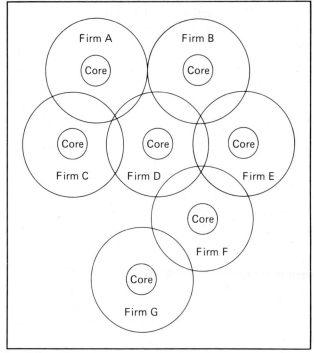

*Source: Cundiff, E.W., Still, R.R., Govoni, N.A.P., Fundamentals of Modern Marketing,* (Englewood Cliffs, N.J.: Prentice-Hall, Inc., 1985), p. 49.

## SOME ECONOMIC FACTORS INFLUENCING
## PERSONAL CONSUMPTION SPENDING

Numerous economic factors, important to the marketing man, influence consumers in the ways they spend their incomes for personal consumption. In this section we examine the "uncontrollable" economic factors; that is, those that individual firms cannot influence to any significant extent.

### Disposable Personal Income

Goods and services are produced for purposes of consumption; purchasing power is used to convert production into consumption; and disposable personal income (that is, what people have left to spend or save after they have paid their taxes) represents *potential* purchasing power in the hands of consumers. In most years, however, people do not spend all of their income. Disposable personal income (in the total economy) exceeds the total of spending for personal consumption. Disposable personal income, in other words, is used both for personal consumption spending and for saving.

To facilitate analysis of the way people allocate changes in their total incomes between spending and saving, economists employ two important concepts: the *marginal propensity to consume* and the *marginal propensity to save*. If disposable personal income should rise by $10 billion, businessmen would be interested in learning what proportion consumers might spend and what proportion they might save. Suppose that out of the $10 billion of "marginal" income, consumers spend $9 billion and save $1 billion. The proportion spent (9 ÷ 10), or 90 percent, is the marginal propensity to consume. The proportion saved (1 ÷ 10), or 10 percent, is the marginal propensity to save.

*Personal consumption spending tends both to rise and fall at a slower rate than does disposable personal income,* but in inflationary periods, such as in the 1970s, and well into the 1980s, spending sometimes rises faster than income. Generally, however, in years of higher income, a lower proportion is spent and a higher proportion is saved. In years of lower income, the proportion spent tends to increase while that saved declines. The concepts of marginal propensity to consume and to save take into account the rates of change, and that is why analysts consider them valuable.

### Size of Family, Size of Family Income,
### and Changes in Family Income

Size of family and size of family income affect spending and saving patterns, but little research has been reported on these relationships. One study made many years ago disclosed that in urban families with lower incomes, average personal consumption spending exceeded income. It also showed that the average propensity to consume tended to decline rather rapidly as income rose above the poverty level.[1]

[1] See: *Study of Consumer Expenditures, Incomes, and Savings* (Philadelphia: Wharton School of Finance and Commerce, University of Pennsylvania, 1956), Vol. 18.

A second study, made a little later, provided some insights on spending behavior relative to household gross income (i.e., income before taxes). It confirmed what business executives had long assumed: average annual household spending rises with increases in gross income per household; those with above-average incomes are above-average spenders, those with below-average incomes are below-average spenders. But contrary to what is commonly assumed, this study found that the number of people in a household appears directly related to the size of its annual income. As the number of people in a household increases, annual household income rises—perhaps because more members have incomes and/or because people with larger incomes can afford larger families.[2]

Findings such as these are important to the marketing analyst. They imply that significant changes occur in a family's spending and saving pattern as it moves from one income bracket to another. They also indicate that changes in the distribution of all the families in a population, relative to income brackets, may bring about significant changes in marginal propensities to consume and to save.

### Consumers' Income Expectations

The incomes that consumers expect to receive in the future have some bearing on their present spending patterns. In particular, spending for automobiles, furniture, major appliances, and other "big ticket" items tends to be influenced by consumers' optimism or pessimism about future income. Consumers' expectations of higher or lower income have a direct effect on spending plans.

### Consumers' Liquid Assets

Consumers' buying plans are influenced, especially those for "big ticket" items, by the size of their holdings of liquid assets; that is, cash and other assets readily convertible into cash: for example, balances in checking and savings accounts, shares in savings and loan associations, deposits in credit unions, and holdings of government bonds and readily marketable stocks and bonds. Even though a consumer may actually buy with current income, the freedom with which he or she spends is influenced by his accumulation of liquid assets. Retired and unemployed individuals may use liquid assets to buy everyday necessities. Other consumers may use liquid assets to meet major medical bills and other emergencies.

### Consumer Credit

Availability of consumer credit strongly influences the pattern of consumer spending. Through credit, making it possible to buy now and pay later, a consumer can command more purchasing power than that repre-

---

[2] *The Life Study of Consumer Expenditures,* Vol. 1, 1957, pp. 18–21.

sented by his current income. Thus, availability of credit has been a key factor in the rapid growth of the markets for mobile homes, boats, camping trailers, and the like.

Personal debt includes all short- and intermediate-term consumer debt, other than "regular" charge (i.e., "nonrevolving") accounts, and excludes mortgage and business debt. Personal debt, thus defined, is equivalent to installment credit; i.e., the consumer pays off his debt in a number of installments. Generally speaking, more than half of all spending units have such debt. The size of income is directly related to the amount of credit a consumer can obtain; lower income groups tend to have either no debt or smaller debts than higher income groups. Since 1975, the volume of install- ment consumer credit has been approximately five times the volume of noninstallment credit.[3]

### Discretionary Income

A family with money left over after buying such necessities as food, clothing, shelter, and transportation, has discretionary income. During 1980, for example, families with disposable personal incomes under $20,000 gener- ally had little or no discretionary income. But, as families moved above $20,000 there was extra income to use for other purposes. They could buy better food and drink, or better furniture, or they could take a small flyer in the stock market, or they could spend it all on one big fling, such as a trip to Europe.

By the time families move above the $25,000 income level, about half of their income is discretionary, and the decisions are not between purchas- ing certain items or others but rather of choosing an entire life style. The skilled laborer with a $25,000 income can choose to live in a working class neighborhood and save a large portion of his income, or he can choose to live like a junior executive. It is estimated that in 1985 over half of all disposable income was discretionary.

Even small fluctuations in income cause sharp repercussions in con- sumers' purchases of durables. This can be traced partly to the fact that consumers are able to postpone or speed up their purchases of such durables as automobiles, furniture, and major appliances. If a family is temporarily short of income, it can always use the old refrigerator for another year or so. Or if the family finds itself suddenly with more discretionary income, it may decide to replace the refrigerator this year instead of next. The quick re- sponse of durable goods expenditures to income changes relates also to the wide use of installment credit in financing such purchases. Consumers are more willing to increase installment debt when income is rising and are more reluctant to incur additional indebtedness when income is declining. Lenders are also more agreeable to debt creation in prosperous times. Purchases of

---

[3] *Federal Reserve Bulletin*, April 1978, p. A42.

nondurables and services, which are much less postponable than purchases of durables, are far less dependent on changes in income.

## PSYCHOLOGICAL FACTORS AFFECTING CONSUMER DEMAND

There have been three major approaches to the development of a psychological theory of human behavior: the experimental, the clinical, and the Gestalt. Experimental psychology has concentrated upon physiological tensions or body needs as motivational forces and has experimented with both human beings and animals. In clinical psychology, the basic physiological drives are examined as they are modified by social forces. Gestalt psychology, often called *social psychology,* regards the individual and his environment as an indivisible whole and considers individual behavior as being directed toward a goal or goals. Each approach adds to our understanding of human behavior, but thus far no single psychological theory of consumer motivation is completely adequate or satisfactory in explaining buyer behavior. Consequently marketing has borrowed those theoretical concepts that seem most applicable.

### Learning Theory

Studies of learning and the related areas of recognition, recall, and habitual response have furnished marketers with several keys to understanding consumer behavior. Concepts borrowed from learning theory help in answering such questions as: How do consumers learn about products offered for sale? How do they learn to recognize and recall these products? By what processes do they develop buying and consuming habits?

The current trend in psychological thinking is to look at the total experience of the individual and to consider learning as a process in which total functions are altered and rearranged to make them more useful to the individual. Particular external stimuli do not always activate predictable responses, because motives and other factors internal to the individual also affect responses. What does this mean for the marketer? Simply that the buyer is influenced not only by external stimuli—for example, the marketer's promotion—but also by internal factors. What basic factors influence learning? Many psychologists answer "repetition, motivation, conditioning, and relationship and organization."

*Repetition,* necessary for the progressive modification of psychological functions, must be accompanied by attention, interest, and a goal—if it is to be effective. Mere repetition of situations or stimuli does not promote learning; advertisers who depend on repetition alone waste both their efforts and advertising dollars.

The individual's *motivation* is the most important factor in initiating and governing his or her activities. Activity in harmony with one's motives is satisfying and pleasing; other activity is annoying at best and frustrating at worst. When, in a given situation, an individual has several motives, they may either reinforce each other, which promotes learning, or be in conflict, which hinders learning. Human motivation is a topic of great interest to marketing professionals, especially those preparing advertising and sales presentations. But neither marketers nor the psychologists have thus far been able to reach more than partial agreement about what constitutes even the most common or basic motives.

*Conditioning* is a way of learning in which a new response to a particular stimulus is developed. For example, seeing just any glass bottle does not evoke any standard response but seeing one particular type of bottle makes most Americans think of Coca-Cola. Through long advertising effort and continual exposure of this symbol, the Coca-Cola Company has conditioned the American public to recognize its bottle. The conditioned response, however, establishes a temporary rather than a permanent behavior pattern and, if it is not frequently reinforced by the original stimulus, the conditioned response eventually disappears. Furthermore, research indicates that all persons do not respond equally well to conditioning, nor are their responses generally predictable.

*Relationship and organization* are factors facilitating learning. Or, to put it another way, learning effectiveness is enhanced if the thing to be learned is presented in a familiar environmental setting. Thus, a salesperson more effectively demonstrates a vacuum cleaner by using it in the customer's home and showing the dirt it has picked up than by describing its capacity and cleaning power in a store. The prospective buyer is interested in the machine's performance specifications only as they directly relate to the task of cleaning his or her own carpets. Thus, sales messages should relate the products to the consumer's needs and interests, if they are to attract the consumer's attention and lay the groundwork for purchase.

### Retention and Forgetting

There is significance for the advertiser in the psychological explanation of retention and forgetting. Retention is explained in terms of impressions left in the nervous system as a result of learning. Forgetting, or "negative retention," develops with the deterioration of these impressions. The more meaningful the material learned—that is, the more the learner understands it—the greater the rate of retention and the lower the rate of forgetting. Retention curves for both meaningful and unmeaningful materials, plotted as functions of time, drop most rapidly immediately after learning and then gradually decline until the material is almost or entirely forgotten. This phenomenon is important with respect to long–run promotion and advertising campaigns. Messages should be spaced closely enough to fortify the learning process. If they are too far apart, information learned from earlier messages will have been forgotten and must be relearned.

### Some Concepts from Clinical Psychology

The principal motivation-research techniques can be traced to concepts developed by clinical psychologists. Among the most important are the concepts of the unconscious, rationalization, projection, and free association.

*The Unconscious.* This concept originated with Sigmund Freud, the founder of psychoanalysis. According to Freud, the mind contains ideas and urges—some conscious and some beneath the threshold of consciousness but all influencing behavior. The fact that people are not usually consciously aware of their motives explains why consumers are often unable to articulate their real reasons for buying or not buying. Recognizing the existence of the unconscious mind, motivation researchers use indirect approaches, such as depth interviewing. More conventional research approaches, such as direct questioning, have been unsuccessful in providing data sufficiently reliable to justify predictions of consumer behavior. Practical marketers, of course, have long known that there are often differences between what people say they will buy and what they actually do buy.

*Rationalization.* This concept relates to the mental process of finding reasons to justify an act or opinion that is actually based on other motives or grounds than those stated, although this may or may not be realized by the rationalizer. In advertising, rationalization often may be capitalized upon by providing readers or listeners with a plausible, acceptable reason for buying in situations where they may be unwilling, consciously or unconsciously, to admit the real reason. The prevalence of rationalization in our society explains why such direct questions as "Why did you buy this?" or "What were your reasons for buying?" so often fail to uncover the real buying motives. Where rationalizing is a factor in consumer behavior, indirect research approaches, such as depth interviewing, are appropriate.

*Projection.* This concept concerns the reaction that occurs when a person, seeing someone facing a certain problem or situation, assumes the other person's reactions would be the same as his or her own. In other words, he or she ascribes his or her own motives to the other person. Putting the projection concept to practical use, motivation researchers have designed projective techniques (for example, the "stimulus picture") that provide a means for uncovering consumers' hidden or unconscious motives and attitudes.

*Free Association.* The principle of free association, which traces to Freud and is used extensively in psychoanalysis, has also been put to use by motivation researchers in their development of indirect research techniques. One application of the principle of free association is found in depth interviewing where many of the techniques take the form of word–association tests, in which respondents are asked to give the first word that comes to mind for each in a list of unrelated words. Given the word *rain,* for example, the respondent might reply *drip.* Among the many marketing applications of the word–association tests are those of screening possible names for new products, measuring the penetration of advertising appeals, and approximating the market shares of different competitors.

### Need Satisfaction and Buyer Behavior

Psychological studies indicate that human activity, including buying behavior, is directed toward satisfying certain needs. Not every individual acts in the same way in the effort to fulfill these needs; the actions of each not only depend upon the nature of the needs themselves but are modified by the individual's particular environmental and social background. The motivation for any specific action derives from the tensions built up to satisfy basic needs, needs that frequently lie beneath the threshold of consciousness. Whatever action the individual takes is directed toward reducing these tensions.

Although clinical psychologists have not agreed on a single list of basic needs, the different lists available show more agreement than disagreement. In one list, Maslow enumerates basic needs in their order of importance for most people. According to him, an individual normally tries to satisfy the most basic needs first and, satisfying these, he is then free to devote his efforts to the next one shown on the list. The Maslow list is as follows:[4]

**1.** *Physiological Needs.* The needs to satisfy hunger, thirst, sleep, and so forth. These are the most basic needs, and until they are satisfied, other needs are of no importance.

**2.** *Safety Needs.* In modern society, these needs are more often for economic and social security rather than for physical safety.

**3.** *Belongingness and Love Needs.* The need for affectionate relations with individuals and a place in society is so important that its lack is a common cause of maladjustment.

**4.** *Esteem Needs.* People need both self-esteem, a high evaluation of self, and the esteem of others in our society. Fulfillment provides a feeling of self-confidence and usefulness; nonfulfillment produces feelings of inferiority and helplessness.

**5.** *Aesthetic Needs.* These may not appear to be present among many individuals because of their failure to satisfy more basic needs, but among some the need for beauty is strong.

Often the marketing success of a brand depends on its ability to satisfy several needs at once; motivation research techniques are available to identify the strength or weakness of a product in terms of the needs it fulfills.

[4] H. Maslow, *Motivation and Personality* (New York: Harper and Brothers, 1954), pp. 80–85.

The concept of basic needs and the theory that individuals normally try to satisfy them in some order are very important.

### Buying Motivations of Industrial Users

Industrial users are more "rational" in their buying than are ultimate consumers. Industrial users buy to fill the needs of their organizations, and these needs normally are of a practical nature. But it is nonetheless true that organizations are composed of individuals, that one or more individuals do the buying, and that they all have personal needs that sometimes become enmeshed with their roles as buyers. Thus, even industrial purchases may be made on "emotional" bases, as in the case of the purchasing agent who buys from a certain supplier because the salesperson is a good friend.

### Imagery

Images are the formalized impressions residing, consciously or unconsciously, in the minds of individuals with regard to given subjects. Patterns of buying behavior are influenced by the images consumers have of different products, particular brands, companies, retail outlets, and of themselves. Because images affect consumer buying behavior, marketers take them into account in drafting promotional plans and programs. Differences among individuals, products, brands, and the like result in different images, and motivation research is used not only to identify the nature of images but to detect the implications for marketing action.

*Self-Image.* The self-image is the picture a person has of himself or herself—the kind of person he or she considers himself or herself to be and the kind of person that he or she imagines others consider him or her to be. Different people have different kinds of self-image, and this gives rise to market segmentation along psychological lines. For instance, the woman who sees herself primarily as a good housewife and mother exhibits a different total pattern of buying behavior from that shown by the woman who sees herself as a social leader or professional careerist. A basic tenet of motivation research is that in many buying situations an individual prefers to buy those products and brands whose images appear consistent with the individual's self-image. However, the power of the self-image as a buying influence varies from individual to individual and even within the same individual as different buying decisions are made at different times.

*Brand Image.* The brand image, another stereotype, results from all the impressions consumers receive, from whatever sources, about a particular manufacturer's brand. In the minds of consumers familiar with a particular brand, there tends to be considerable consistency in the brand image or, as it is sometimes called, the "brand personality." But for competing brands, there are usually, in the minds of consumers, distinctive images. Similarly, retail stores exhibit distinct images or personalities, as do corporations.

Consumers' appraisal of the distinctiveness of a brand's physical attributes not only affects the brand image but has important implications for marketing. When consumers believe the brand is physically different from competing brands, the brand image centers on the brand as a specific version of the product. Depending on whether the marketer considers the image favorable or unfavorable, physical attributes of the product may be retained or changed, and marketing strategy may be directed toward reinforcing or altering the image. By contrast, when consumers believe a brand has no differentiating physical attributes, the brand image tends to be associated with the personalities of the people who are thought to buy it.

Through long-continued use of particular advertising and selling appeals, many brands have acquired definite images. In numerous cases, a brand image has developed without the management intending it. Whether or not a particular brand image was shaped deliberately, management should identify its nature. Otherwise, ignorance of the brand image may result in poorly planned promotional programs. If the image is favorable, for example, inconsistent sales and advertising appeals are likely to be ineffective and may confuse or alienate existing customers. Before introducing a new brand to the market or an established brand to a different market, management should determine the sort of image it wishes to build.

### Cognitive Dissonance

When a person makes an important decision, dissonance or discomfort almost always occurs because the person making the decision knows that it has certain disadvantages as well as advantages. After making the decision, then, the person tends to expose himself or herself to information that he or she perceives as likely to support the choice and to avoid information that may favor the rejected alternative.[5]

This theory is evidently intended to apply only to decisions involving post-decision anxiety, but it seems reasonable that it should also hold for situations involving predecision anxiety: a buyer may panic as the time of decision arrives and either rush into buying as an escape from the problem or delay it because of the difficulty of deciding among alternatives. In marketing, an important goal both of advertising and personal selling is to reduce cognitive dissonance on the part of buyers and prospects. Customers suffering cognitive dissonance may need reassuring that their decisions are or were wise ones. This can be accomplished by providing information that permits them to rationalize their decisions.

[5] L. Festinger, A Theory of Cognitive Dissonance (Evanston, Ill.: Row Peterson and Company, 1957).

## SOCIOLOGICAL FACTORS AFFECTING CONSUMER DEMAND

Sociologists view marketing as involving the activities of groups of people motivated by group pressures as well as by individual desires. Their studies have emphasized the significance of reference groups, the individual's concept of social role, the diffusion process, social class, and culture as influences on human behavior. These studies have demonstrated the importance of social factors in analyzing and influencing consumer behavior.

### Reference Groups and the Diffusion Process

The people an individual regularly associates with exert strong influences on his or her behavior. He or she must conform at least partially to their standards of behavior to gain group acceptance. An individual's behavior also is influenced by groups with whom he or she has little regular contact, but with whom he or she identifies closely. Both types of groups are called reference groups, which include family and peer groups, social groups, and others, such as religious or fraternal organizations.

*Primary Groups.* These groups, fundamental in determining the social nature of the individual, are groups of people involved in intimate, face-to-face contact and cooperation. The most pervasive and traditionally the most influential primary group is the family, but with the emergence of the modern small, two-generation family, much of this influence has passed to other primary groups, particularly peer groups. Peer groups are composed of individuals who spend considerable time together and are of fairly common age and social background. Among children, these are often play groups; among adults, they include neighborhood and community groups. Other groups with varying degrees of socializing influence are religious, educational and political institutions, and work groups.

Each individual may hold membership in several different primary groups. At work one may be part of a close-knit friendly group of co-workers. As a church member, one may or may not have close personal contacts with other members. As a member of social or fraternal organizations, one may be a part of still other primary groups. Any of these groups might be classified as peer groups if they are sufficiently homogeneous. Purely social groups are most likely to qualify. The peer group has the greatest influence on the individual as a consumer because the group's general interests and mode of life are most nearly like his or her own.

*Significance to Marketing.* Knowledge of reference groups and their influences makes it easier to explain why consumers behave in particular ways and—more important to marketers—to predict their behavior. It explains, for example, why two groups of young people in the same community—one, high school seniors, and the other, college freshmen—adopt different styles of dress or other behavior even though they are nearly the same age and come from similar family backgrounds. Even within a college freshman group, different reference groups dictate wide variations in dress and behavior. Even the same individual behaves differently at different times as he or she identifies with different reference groups. A young executive, for example, may dress and act conservatively when on the job and in other contact with business associates, but off the job, he or she may be a sports car racing buff and behave and dress very differently.

*Individual's Concept of Social Role.* The way a person sees his or her role in social groups is important in explaining his or her motivation. A "rugged individualist" may enjoy establishing a reputation as one who sets his or her own patterns of behavior—within existing group norms of acceptable conduct. Individualism was a common mode of behavior in the nineteenth century, but it is now rare. Group behavior is much more important. Group behavior requires conformity to group norms. The group–oriented individual is anxious to fit into the behavior patterns of his or her peers. What they do, the individual must do. This does not imply, however, that the individual's pattern of behavior is frozen. Group norms may change, and the individual adjusts his or her behavior to reflect these changes. The group–oriented individual is seldom motivated by the traditional appeals of "being an innovator" or "leading the pack." To be motivated to action, one must first be persuaded that the suggested action is accepted by one's peers as the proper thing to do.

*Influentials.* An influential is a person who serves as an opinion leader of a group. Such opinion leaders are not confined to any one social class; they are found at all levels of society. Outwardly, influentials and those they influence (i.e., others in the same social groups) are very much alike—similar incomes, occupations, family backgrounds, and so on. An individual's influence is related to: (1) who one is, (2) what one knows, and (3) whom one knows.

An unmarried girl may be a "fashion leader" because of "who she is"; an older woman her group's "cooking expert" because of "what she knows"; and a man his group's "political leader" because of "whom he knows," not only in the group but outside it.

Influentials play key roles in marketing. If an influential tries or uses a product, his or her followers are prone to do the same. Marketers, therefore, often target their promotional efforts to reach influentials and, through them, reach their followers by word-of-mouth or other subtle influences exerted by the influentials.

*The Diffusion Process.* The social process of spreading information about new products or services to persuade consumers to accept them is known as *diffusion*. Studies of the diffusion process reveal that most users do not adopt an innovation simultaneously. The first group to adopt an innovation is made up of a small number of "innovators." They are soon copied by another group, who, though not venturesome enough to try an innovation first, want to be among the early users. Gradually, members of other groups adopt the innovation until it finally reaches market saturation. For a dramatically new product, such as television, the entire process may take ten years or more. It is important to identify target market segments at each stage in the diffusion process. In the initial phases of market introduction, for instance, effort and money may be wasted if the marketer tries to cultivate the entire market at once. Figure 6-2 illustrates the diffusion process and provides one estimate of the share of the population falling within each group.

The various adopter groups exhibit marked differences. The innovators are usually the youngest and have the highest social status and wealth; they are frequently cosmopolites and have professional, business, and personal contacts outside their own immediate social circles. Those in the early adopter groups are generally influentials (i.e., opinion leaders), but their contacts are restricted largely to their own local groups; they enjoy high status within their own social groups and are usually younger than those in the groups following. Those in the early majority group are the most deliberate; they will not consider buying a new product until a number of their peers (innovators and early adopters) have done so. Those in the late majority have below-average income and social prestige and are older than members of earlier groups. Laggards have still lower incomes and social status; by the time they buy a new product, the earlier groups often are already trying something newer.

**Figure 6-2** Classification of adopter groups

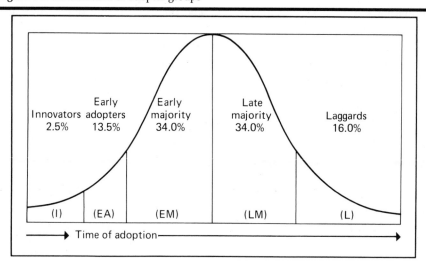

### Social Classes

Every society classifies its members according to some social hierarchy. All have people who occupy positions of relatively higher status and power. Most sociologists divide American society into three broad, roughly defined classes: the upper, middle, and lower classes. W. Lloyd Warner, on the basis of studies in three American towns, set up a hierarchy of six social classes: upper upper, lower upper, upper middle, lower middle, upper lower, and lower lower.[6] Under Warner's system the class status of each person is ascertained by asking equals, superiors, and inferiors to rank the person. This dependence on the ratings of others has been the main criticism of the Warner system. Ordinary citizens do not think in terms of this complex hierarchy and, when asked to classify their fellow citizens into the six groups, they show little agreement with others who are asked to do the same thing.

*Status Symbols.*   Despite difficulties in classifying individuals by social class, most sociologiests agree that the twin urges for self-expression and self-betterment take the form of aspiring to higher status. Sociologists explain this phenomenon by holding that (1) people express their personalities not so much in words as in symbols (for example, mannerisms, dress, ornaments, possessions); and (2) most people are increasingly concerned about their social status. Different products vary in their status symbol value, and these values may change. The automobile was once the major status symbol, but many now assert that it has been replaced by the house and its furnishings. The status symbol concept is a valuable one for marketers, for when they recognize that they are selling symbols as well as products, they view their products more completely. The marketer should understand not only how the product satisfies certain needs but how it fits into modern culture.

### Culture

Every culture evolves unique patterns of social conduct. Analysis of the patterns helps in explaining the buying behavior of individuals. Many aspects of American culture are unique, including the roles of ethnic groups, religion, women in society, leisure time, and fashion, as well as the population composition itself.

*Ethnic Groups.*   The United States is often called a "melting pot" of cultures and peoples, but this blending has not been complete. An identifiable American national culture *has* emerged, but it has not equally permeated all portions of society or all geographic regions. There is, for example, an African influence not only in the Deep South but wherever black people have moved in large numbers, a Mexican influence in much of the

---

[6] W. L. Warner and P. S. Lunt, *The Status System of a Modern Community* (New Haven: Yale University Press, 1942), pp. 88–91.

Southwest, a Scandinavian influence in Minnesota and the Pacific Northwest, and a Cuban and Puerto Rican influence in such cities as Miami, Chicago, Washington, New York, and Philadelphia. Although ethnic differences decrease with each succeeding generation, their continuing existence helps explain differences in consumer motivation and behavior that would not exist in a country with a population of common cultural heritage.

*Religions.* Whereas the predominant religions in some nations stress passive acceptance of life and man's role, the Christian and Jewish religions, which comprise the basic religious heritage of American society, emphasize the perfectibility of people and their environment and, hence, encourage them to improve themselves and their way of life. Therefore, the production and consumption of goods are acceptable activites because they contribute to these goals. Within the American Judaeo-Christian religious pattern, however, there are many individual sects and creeds; and although they share similar feelings about the overall social roles of production and consumption, consumption patterns of selected foods, beverages, and apparel vary considerably among them.

*The Role of Women.* Well over half of adult American women work and have incomes of their own; increasingly sophisticated labor-saving appliances provide the remainder with more time free from domestic responsibilities and, hence, more time for shopping. American women have either sole or major responsibility for making many kinds of purchases and exert increasing influence on all buying decisions. As the women's movement has grown increasing numbers of women take active rather than passive roles in society. This is of great significance to marketing, especially in the choice of advertising themes.

*Leisure Time.* Increasing numbers of people have greater amounts of leisure time, and this is reflected in changes in values and the "way of life." Instead of buying an expensive car to impress friends, a consumer may economize on a car in order to buy a boat, shop tools, or fishing equipment. New homes are planned to simplify participation in leisure time activities. People have ceased being producers for much of their lives and have become active consumers for the products and services that go along with increasing leisure. The old Puritan dictum that "For Satan finds some mischief still for idle hands to do" is being overthrown, but the Puritan influence still remains. People refer to "active" leisure rather than just "leisure"—the "active" dissassociating leisure from the guilt-loaded idea of loafing.

*Fashion.* The role of fashion in American society has been growing in importance. With widespread ownership of television sets, not to mention rising circulations of magazines and newspapers and the increasing mobility of consumers, fashion news is disseminated in minimum time. The time span covered by the appearance of a new fashion, its adoption by a few pacesetters, its rise to popularity, and its subsequent decline is becoming progressively shorter. At the same time, expansions in discretionary income permit consumers to spend more in their attempts to satisfy the desire for change. Since there are increasing numbers of group-oriented people and fewer individualists, more importance has been placed on conforming to fashion changes.

*Population Composition.* Most of the population growth in metropolitan areas is in the suburbs rather than in the cities themselves. This trend has marketing significance because the suburbanite often represents a very different market than the city dweller. The suburb retains much of the character of a small town—thus, neighborhood and local social groups strongly influence individual consumption patterns.

The population composition of the central core cities has been changing to a predominately low-income and poverty-level group of consumers. At the same time, an increasing proportion of central city residents are members of minority groups—from 1960 to 1980, for instance, New York's black population doubled. Low-income and ghetto groups are often served by marketing instutions different from those serving others. One countertrend should be mentioned: the "back to the city movement," a social phenomenon evident in certain large cities that can be traced to increased living inconveniences resulting from the extreme sprawl of suburban areas.

## CONCLUSION

There have been three main approaches to an explanation of buyer behavior: the economic, the psychological, and the sociological. Classical economists explained buyer behavior in terms of financial self-interest. "Economic person" acts rationally to maximize financial gains, and this has continued as a foundation of economic theory. But this explanation provides little comfort to business executives who are confronted daily with instances of apparently irrational consumer behavior. Hoping for a more satisfactory explanation, executives next turned to psychology. Psychologists explain individual behavior in terms of basic needs common to all people. Psychological explanations of human motivation have helped, but there were still, from the standpoint of business, fuzzy areas where there were no satisfactory answers. Finally, executives turned to sociologists for added insights, and it is now recognized that consumers, as social creatures, are strongly influenced in their buying by the social environments of which they are parts. All three behavioral sciences—economics, psychology, and sociology—have been important contributors to the explanation of buyer behavior.

# 7

# PRODUCERS, MIDDLEMEN, AND FACILITATING AGENCIES

Part II (Chapters 7 through 13) focuses on the institutions that perform marketing activities. These institutions serve important roles as components of marketing channels that, formally defined, *are paths traced in the direct or indirect transfer of ownership for products as they move from producers to final buyers.* Every marketing channel contains one or more of these ownership transfer points; at each point there are always marketing institutions of some sort playing roles as sellers, buyers, or both.

During a product's marketing, legal title changes hands at least once, this bare minimum occurring when producers deal directly with final buyers and there are no intervening middlemen. Most commonly, however, legal title to the product passes from the producer to and through a series of middlemen before the consumer or industrial user finally takes possession. Ownership transfers may be direct, as when the producer sells the product outright to a wholesaler, retailer, or other buyer; or ownership transfers may be indirect, as when an agent middleman does not take title but simply negotiates its transfer from a seller to a buyer or vice versa. From the producer's standpoint, such a network of institutions used for reaching a market is a *marketing channel.*

## SOME IMPORTANT DEFINITIONS

Before examining individual types of wholesalers and retailers and their operating characteristics, we need definitions for the following terms:

*middleman, merchant, agent, retailer, wholesaler, retailing,* and *wholesaling.* These words, of course, form part of nearly everyone's everyday vocabulary but, when used in a marketing context, they carry more precise meanings than in common usage.[1]

### Middlemen

Middlemen specialize in performing activities directly related to the purchase and sale of goods as they flow from producers to final buyers. As the name, "middleman" suggests, such institutions are situated in a marketing channel at points somewhere between the producer and final buyer. Producers regard middlemen as extensions of their own marketing organizations because if there were no middlemen, their own organizations would have to carry on all negotiations leading up to sales to final buyers. Final buyers—ultimate consumers and industrial users—consider middlemen as sources of supply and points of contact with producers.

### Merchants and Agents

Middlemen fall into two broad classifications: merchants and agents. A *merchant takes title* to (i.e., buys) *and resells merchandise.* An *agent negotiates* purchases or sales or both, *but does not take title to the goods in which it deals.* Thus, the chief distinguishing characteristic is whether the middleman takes title to the goods it handles. If it does, it is a merchant. If it does not, it is an agent. Also, the merchant always both buys and resells, whereas the agent *may* specialize in negotiating only buying or only selling transactions.

### Retailer and Wholesaler

Middlemen may also be separated into two other major categories: retailers and wholesalers. The principal basis for distinguishing retailers and wholesalers relates to whether the business sells in significant amounts to ultimate consumers. If it does, it is a retailer. If it does not, it is a wholesaler.

A *retailer* is a merchant, or occasionally, an agent whose main business is selling directly to ultimate consumers. It is distinguished by the nature of its sales rather than by the way it acquires the goods in which it deals. It usually sells in small lots, but this condition is not essential. The dealer who sells furniture and floor covering for the initial outfitting of a large home, for instance, may make a sale of several thousand dollars, but it is still a retail sale if the buyer (i.e., the homeowner) is an ultimate customer.

*Wholesalers* buy and resell merchandise to retailers and other merchants and to industrial, institutional, and commercial users, but do not sell in significant amounts to ultimate consumers. Notice that this definition

---

[1] Unless noted otherwise, the definitions in this section and the remainder of Part II are those compiled by the Committee on Definitions of the American Marketing Association. See: Definitions Committee. *Marketing Definitions* (Chicago: American Marketing Association, 1960).

does not specify that the wholesaler must deal in large-size lots, nor does it require that it habitually make sales for purposes of resale. Most wholesalers *do* sell in large lots, but many do not. Similarly, most wholesalers do sell for purposes of resale, but there are many who sell directly to industrial users. The one essential distinguishing feature of the wholesaler is that it must be a middleman who usually does not sell to ultimate consumers.

### Retailing and Wholesaling[2]

*Retailing* consists of the activities involved in selling directly to the ultimate consumer. It makes no difference who does the selling; but to be classified as retailing, selling activities must be *direct* to the ultimate consumer. Retailers, of course, are engaged in retailing, *but so is any other institution that sells directly to ultimate consumers.* Manufacturers engage in retailing when they make direct-to-consumer sales through their own stores, by house-to-house canvass, or by mail order. Even a wholesaler engages in retailing when it sells direct to an ultimate consumer, although its main business may still be wholesaling. *If the buyer in a transaction is an ultimate consumer, the seller in the same transaction is engaged in retailing.*

*Wholesaling* involves selling to buyers other than ultimate consumers. These buyers may be wholesalers and retailers who buy to resell. They may be industrial users (manufacturers, mining concerns, or firms in other extractive industries), institutional users (schools, prisons, or mental hospitals), commercial users (restaurants, hotels, or factory lunchrooms), government agencies or farmers buying items for their agricultural operations. Wholesaling is carried on not only by wholesalers, but by manufacturers, other producers, and other business units that make sales to buyers who are not ultimate consumers. *If the buyer in a transaction is buying for resale or to further its business operations, the seller in that transaction is engaged in wholesaling.*

## PRODUCERS

In any market channel, the producer is the first seller in the sequence of marketing transactions that occur as the product moves toward its market. Such producers include enterprises engaged in manufacturing, in mining and the extractive industries, in farming, and in provisions of services. Of these, manufacturers and marketers of services normally have the most power to influence the total sequence of transactions involving their products.

### Manufacturers and Service Enterprises

How much power a given manufacturer or service enterprise has to influence the sequence of transactions depends on the opportunity for differ-

---

[2] The Committee on Definitions of the American Marketing Association does not provide a definition for "wholesaling."

entiating the product from those of competitors and on the enterprise's success in capitalizing on the opportunity. If the product or service can be differentiated and final buyers (ultimate consumers or industrial users) can be convinced that differentiating features make it a better buy than competing items, the marketer can gain a significant marketing advantage. The automobile manufacturer, for example, has considerable opportunity to differentiate his product in appearance, performance, and operating characteristics. The manufacturer of common nails, by contrast, has little opportunity to make the product much different from those of competitors.

Capitalizing on a product or service differentiation opportunity requires more than convincing final buyers of the superiority of the manufacturer's product or service. It must be possible for final buyers to buy the item at prices they can pay. Middlemen vary in their support of the manufacturer in promoting and selling the product. Variations also exist in the costs of using different middlemen, and this affects the price that final buyers pay. Balancing the need for support with associated costs, the manufacturer or service enterprise tries to put together a distributive network that gives final buyers access to outlets handling the product or providing the service, at prices they consider reasonable. If the product can be differentiated in ways important to final buyers, the "channel captain" (manufacturer or service enterprise) can exercise considerable discretion in selecting members for its "channel team"; that is, it has considerable power to control the sequence of transactions as the item moves to market. If little opportunity exists for product differentiation, the manufacturer or service enterprise is not a channel captain and has little power to control this sequence of transactions, and the sequence may be controlled instead by middlemen or by final buyers. The firm attempting to control the marketing channel pays primary attention to the market—the final buyers of its product. Starting with the market, a manufacturer, for instance, details the sequence of steps required to supply prospective buyers with its product.

The manufacturer whose product can be differentiated seeks to exercise some control over the order in which his product changes hands as it goes to market. Again, the manufacturer usually should devote his primary attention to the market—the final buyers of his product. Starting with the market, the manufacturer attempts to detail the sequence of steps required to supply it with his product. Even before this, however, the marketer has identified and evaluated final buyers' needs and the strength of market demand and, in its research and product development effort, should have designed a product that meets these needs.

The sequence of steps required for moving the product to market, of course, may or may not call for the services of middlemen at one or more distribution levels. Even after he decides on this sequence—that is, the marketing channel—the marketer often devotes considerable effort to assuring that the planned series of transactions takes place. Through its advertising and other promotional activities, for instance, a manufacturer works to build the demand to the point where final buyers insist that suppliers stock and sell the product. Or, as another example, the manufacturer uses advertising to final buyers to direct prospective customers to outlets where the product is sold. In these and similar ways, a marketer seeks to assure that its distribution network functions according to plan.

### Other Producers

Enterprises not engaged in manufacturing, such as mining concerns, other extractive industries, and farmers, have less power to influence the total sequence of marketing transactions involving their products. They usually can do very little about differentiating their outputs to meet final buyers' needs more closely. Furthermore, it is difficult for them to stimulate demand. Demand for the mining company's output, for instance, derives from the demand for products manufactured by its customers. Demand for aluminum depends upon the demand for products fabricated by customers of aluminum mining companies; that is, products such as aluminum beach chairs, pots and pans, golf carts, and siding and sash used in building construction. It might even seem logical, then, for the mining company to direct its efforts toward stimulating the demand for its customers' products. Individual mining companies, however, often are too small to finance promotional programs of the required magnitude.

The situation confronting farmers is similar to that of the mining company, for unless they sell their crops through cooperatives, they are generally unable to support the extensive promotion needed to exert a significant influence on demand. Moreover, demand for farm products commonly derives from the demand for products of processors of agricultural commodities. When certain food processors, for instance, began making oleomargarine out of "100 percent pure corn oil" and successfully promoted the new product's health benefits to consumers, increases in demand for corn followed increases in demand for corn oil margarine. Furthermore, unlike most manufacturers who find it easy to drop or add products as demand changes, many grain farmers, orchardists, or cattlemen, are limited by their land, equipment, and experience to one product. They are unable to do much about adjusting the nature of their outputs to fit the market's changing needs and preferences.

Different types of producers enjoy different degrees of power in controlling the flow of their product through marketing channels to final markets. In general, manufacturers have the most power and are able (within certain limits) to use channels containing the type and number of transfer points that they regard as most appropriate for the product and market. Farmers and producers in the extractive industries cannot direct the flow of their products to market. But their products do eventually get to market even though the flow generally is more involved and round-about than with most manufactured products. Marketing channels serving the extractive industries tend to develop in an unplanned way, the way a river "cuts" its own course.

### Producers' Cooperative Marketing Association

Hoping to improve the efficiency with which their output is marketed, some producers, chiefly in agriculture but sometimes in other extractive industries, organize and operate producers' cooperative marketing associations. These associations represent the collective effort of small producers who desire more control over distribution of their output in the hope of reducing distribution costs and favorably influencing demand. Such cooperative endeavors tend to put their members more on a par with manufacturers as far as marketing channels are concerned.

The agricultural cooperative marketing association, with its relatively large size and the specialized attention its management gives to marketing can, if it chooses, bypass one or more levels of middlemen present in more conventional marketing channels. Some cooperatives succeed in eliminating only the assembler or broker of agricultural products. Others extend their marketing operations even to maintaining sales offices in important marketing areas, as is done by Sunkist Growers, Inc., a cooperative marketer of California and Arizona citrus fruits. Most agricultural cooperative marketing associations are set up primarily to handle the packing and grading of their members' crops, usually managing to perform these activities at lower costs than members would incur individually. Some, such as Sunkist Growers, affix brands to the product and conduct massive promotional programs designed to build and maintain consumer recognition for the brand and to expand its demand. Thus, the cooperative marketing association often succeeds in providing its members with enhanced power in controlling the flow of their product through marketing channels to final buyers.

*Use of Pooling.* One of the operating practices unique to cooperative marketing associations is "pooling." This is the practice of mixing the outputs of members and, after deducting average expenses, paying them the average price received during the marketing season, usually on the basis of established grades. Among the arguments advanced for pooling are that: (1) it is difficult or impractical to keep each member's output segregated in storage and en route to market; (2) shipments are made at different times during the marketing season at different prices for comparable qualities and grades of produce.

*Use of Cash Advance.* The producers' cooperative marketing association gives its members cash advances when they deliver their crops to the packing house. As sales are made, members receive further payments. Final distribution of the remaining proceeds of sales are often delayed until six to nine months after closing the pool. Some cooperatives do not use cash advances, instead issuing warehouse receipts to members; these can be used as collateral for loans from commercial banks.

*Formal Membership Contracts.*   Most cooperative marketing associations require members to execute written formal membership contracts. This helps to assure the association of a continuous volume of business and enables management to draft firmer plans for future operations, especially where such plans involve financial obligations and commitments. At one time, provisions of membership contracts were stringent, often giving the association the right to enforce specific performance by injunction. The recent trend has been toward more liberal contracts as associations have relied more on their performance to hold members' loyalty.

*Purchasing Services.*   Many producers' cooperative marketing associations provide members with purchasing services. They buy such items as seed, fertilizers, tools and implements, and gasoline and oil for resale to members, and a few deal in consumer goods. Some, such as AGWay, not only market crops grown by its farmer-members, but also operate "stores" to supply members and others with items used on farms, as well as such diverse goods as grass seed, lawn mowers, automobile tires, and food for wild birds.

## MARKETING FACILITATING AGENCIES

Many institutions make significant contributions to the process of marketing but are not classified as marketing middlemen because they neither take legal title to goods nor negotiate purchases or sales. These *marketing facilitating agencies* assist in performing one or more marketing activities but neither take title nor negotiate purchases or sales. Examples include banks, railroads, storage warehouses, commodity exchanges, stockyards, insurance companies, industrial design consultants, graders and inspectors, advertising agencies, firms engaged in contract marketing research, cattle loan companies, furniture marts, and packers and shippers. Below we have listed marketing activities together with examples of marketing facilitating agencies which may assist in performing each:

| | |
|---|---|
| 1. Marketing information | Marketing research firms |
| 2. Product decisions | Industrial design consultants, graders and inspectors |
| 3. Marketing channels | Merchandise marts Stockyards Commodity exchanges |
| 4. Physical distribution | Public warehouses Railroads, truck lines, air and ocean carriers |

|            |                            |
|------------|----------------------------|
|            | Freight forwarders         |
|            | Packers                    |
| 5. Pricing | Banks and loan companies   |
|            | Credit bureaus             |
| 6. Promotion | Advertising agencies     |
|            | Advertising media          |
|            | Incentive campaign agencies |

Marketing facilitating agencies are *not* marketing middlemen. Facilitating agencies neither affect ownership transfers nor negotiate them, whereas marketing middlemen always perform one or both activities. Even though certain facilitating agencies (for example, stockyards and advertising agencies) sometimes *assist* in getting buyers and sellers together (creating a market), they neither negotiate nor effect ownership transfers.

## *CONCLUSION*

Analysis in this chapter focused on the broad classes of institutions engaged in marketing. Among the basic terms defined were *middlemen, merchant, agent, retailer, wholesaler, retailing, wholesaling,* and *marketing channel.* Analysis of the producer's role as seller in the first of the sequence of ownership transfers occurring as the product moves toward its market emphasized the factors affecting their power to influence and control the make-up of the marketing channel. Certain operating practices of producers' cooperative marketing associations—pooling, cash advances, membership contracts, and purchasing services—also were explained. The roles played in, and contributions made to, the process of marketing by different marketing facilitating agencies were also discussed.

# 8

# WHOLESALERS:
# MERCHANT AND AGENT

Wholesaling is a big industry, both in number of establishments and total sales volume. In the United States 383,000 wholesale establishments (342,000 wholesalers and 41,000 manufacturers' branches) annually transact over $1.258 trillion in sales; from 1943 to 1977, the number of wholesale establishments rose by over 75 percent (See Table 8-1.) Sales in constant dollars showed only a moderate increase.

Merchant wholesalers are the most numerous wholesale middlemen, and they transact more business than any other type. The 1977 *Census of*

**TABLE 8-1** U.S. Wholesalers: establishments and sales, selected years, 1954–1977

| YEAR | NUMBER OF ESTABLISHMENTS | SALES (BILLIONS) |
|------|--------------------------|------------------|
| 1977 | 289,000 | $1,258.4 |
| 1972 | 348,200 | 695.2 |
| 1967 | 311,000 | 459.5 |
| 1963 | 308,000 | 358.4 |
| 1958 | 287,000 | 285.7 |
| 1954 | 250,000 | 234.0 |

*Source:* U.S. Department of Commerce, Bureau of the Census, *Statistical Abstract of the United States, 1982–83*, 103rd Edition, p. 820.

*Business* reported that of the 342,000 wholesale establishments in the United States, 307,000 (or 90 percent) are merchant wholesalers, transacting over $675 billion in sales each year. Merchant wholesalers buy and resell goods on their own account; that is, they take title to the products they handle and convey title directly to those with whom they deal. In consumer goods marketing, their principal customers are retailers, but they also sell to industrial users and to institutional and commercial users. Merchant wholesalers are also active in industrial marketing as intermediaries between supplying manufacturers and industrial users; here they are known as *mill supply houses, mining supply distributors, machine dealers,* and *oil well equipment houses.*

Table 8-2 shows the 1977 sales of merchant wholesalers by kind of business. Machinery, equipment, supplies, wholesalers, and motor vehicles—automotive equipment wholesalers were the most important durable goods wholesalers, accounting for 32 percent of total durable goods sales. (See Table 8-3.) In nondurable goods, groceries and related products, although still the most important category, accounted for only 31 percent of the total, down from 41.7 percent in 1972; this reflects the increasing vertical integration in grocery marketing. (Figure 8-1 classifies wholesalers by ownership.)

**TABLE 8-2** Sales of merchant wholesalers by kinds of business, 1977

| KIND OF BUSINESS | SALES (MILLION) |
| --- | --- |
| Total sales (excluding farm products, raw materials) | $572,213 |
| Durable goods, total | 285,729 |
| Motor vehicles, automotive equipment | 54,139 |
| Electrical goods | 31,763 |
| Furniture, home furnishings | 30,763 |
| Hardware, plumbing, heating equipment, supplies | 22,425 |
| Lumber, construction materials | 26,166 |
| Machinery, equipment, supplies | 82,052 |
| Nondurable goods, total | 356,559 |
| Groceries and related products | 110,743 |
| Beer, wine, distilled alcoholic beverages | 23,386 |
| Drugs and allied products | 10,867 |
| Papers, paper products | 15,473 |
| Other nondurable goods | 48,623 |
| Farm products (raw materials) | 70,071 |
| Merchant wholesalers, grand total | $642,285 |

*Source:* U.S. Department of Commerce, Bureau of the Census, *Monthly Wholesale Trade Report,* December 1977, p. 2.

wholesalers generally pride themselves on the strong promotional support they provide for the restricted number of manufacturers' brands they handle. They do this by concentrating on relatively few items. It is possible for the specialty grocery wholesaler's salespersons to "push" every item handled on every sales call and to perform such activities as erecting special displays, handling in-store product demonstrations, and arranging for distribution of samples. Sales personnel of general line grocery wholesalers, by contrast, cannot give special "push" to more than a handful of the many thousands of items in stock or to any one manufacturer's brand.

The narrowness of the specialty wholesaler's merchandise offering, together with the strong promotional support for all items handled, causes it to concentrate on market areas where there are numerous retail outlets. Selling only a few items and strongly promoting each one, it can make economical use of sales personnel only where there are numerous retailers and relatively little travel time between stops. The specialty wholesaler's salesforce make frequent calls on retailers, but because this makes smaller retail inventories possible, the average order size is small.

The combining of high call frequency and low average order size restricts the opportunity for specialty wholesaling to areas where retail outlets are close together and numerous, as in the heavily industrialized and thickly populated parts of New England, the Middle Atlantic states, the Midwest, and the Pacific Coast. In other areas (such as in most of the Rocky Mountain states and throughout much of the South), where population is sparse, cities and towns far apart, and retail outlets widely scattered and few in number, few specialty wholesalers exist.

### Classification by Method of Operation

Merchant wholesalers perform many marketing activities for their suppliers and customers. Those who perform all or most of the activities generally associated with wholesale trade are *service wholesalers*. (These activites are: buying and assembling, selling, storage, transportation, marketing risk bearing, marketing financing, and marketing information.) General merchandise and general line wholesalers perform these activities and, therefore, are service wholesalers. Some specialty wholesalers perform only a few of these activities; others perform more. Depending on the extent of its service, a specialty wholesaler may be either a service wholesaler or a limited function wholesaler who performs only a few of the normal wholesaling activities. All merchant wholesalers—limited function as well as service wholesalers—take title to the goods they handle and resell to those with whom they deal. Thus, *all* perform the buying and assembling and selling activities. The main types of limited function wholesalers are discussed below.

*Truck Wholesalers.* Combining selling, delivery, and collection in one operation, truck wholesalers (also known as "wagon jobbers") carry only a limited stock, although the selection within that stock may be very complete. Thus, the nature of a truck wholesaler's merchandise offering also make it a specialty wholesaler. Truck wholesalers call mainly on retailers, although some, such as in the grocery trade, also sell to restaurants, hotels, and other food service establishments. Because the items handled are often perishables or semiperishables, truck wholesalers make frequent calls on customers. Their ability to make fast and frequent deliveries is their main appeal to both customers and manufacturers.

*Rack Jobbers.* The rack jobber markets specialized lines of merchandise to retail stores and provides certain special services. The merchandising policies of most rack jobbers make them also specialty wholesalers. Rack jobbers evolved after World War II to serve supermarkets, which, in increasing numbers, were adding nonfood lines. Rack jobbers serving supermarkets and other grocery retailers specialize in one or both of two lines—toiletries and housewares. Managers of retail stores served by rack jobbers are relieved of merchandising problems in handling "sundry items," and can concentrate their merchandising efforts on major lines. The rack jobber may or may not furnish its own display racks, but, basically, all that the retailer must provide is selling space, which the rack jobber stocks with a selection of items priced for sale. Occasionally rack jobbers consign merchandise until the retailer sells it, the retailer paying only for the goods it sells (and, incidentally, for "shoplifted" items) and retaining a portion of the profit for itself. Through aggressive merchandising and effective displays, rack jobbers have built up large volumes of nonfood sales in grocery stores. Manufacturers of nonfood lines find that rack jobbers provide an effective means of achieving low-cost distribution through retail food stores.

*Cash-and-Carry Wholesalers.* Cash-and-carry wholesalers pursue the same service policy that characterizes cash-and-carry retail operations. Whereas service wholesalers send their salesreps to retailers to solicit orders, later deliver these orders, and grant credit to retailers, cash-and-carry wholesalers require retailers to come to the warehouse, "pick" their own orders, pay cash, and carry away their purchases. By restricting services and lowering operating costs, the cash-and-carry wholesaler is able to price lower than service wholesalers. Price is what attracts retailers to the cash-and-carry wholesaler. But, because retailers must perform additional services for themselves, they often find that by the time the order gets to the store, its cost is every bit as high as if it were purchased from a service wholesaler. However, cash-and-carry "departments" are an economical means for service wholesalers to reach many small retailers who buy in lots too small to justify the wholesaler's sending salesreps, providing delivery, and extending credit, but since travel time and distance are important, they operate mainly in large cities.

*Drop-Shipment Wholesalers.* A drop-shipment wholesaler does not physically handle the goods but leaves storage and transportation to the manufacturers whom it represents. When goods are ordered, the manufacturer ships them directly to the retailer but bills the drop shipper at factory prices. Subsequently, the drop shipper collects from the retailer. This distribution system cuts transportation and storage costs. It eliminates double hauling (that is, from the factory to the wholesaler and then on to the retailer) and costs for handling the goods in a wholesaler's warehouse.

However, customers buying through drop shippers often order in comparatively small lot sizes and, because freight rates are higher for small lots than for large lots, higher freight rates offset some of the savings from eliminating double hauling. The retailer, to make economical use of drop shipments, must order in larger than normal quantities and allow for longer periods for goods in transit. These adjustments are necessary inasmuch as most retailers are located farther from the manufacturers' plants than from the wholesalers serving as alternative supply points. Ordering in larger than normal quantities forces the retailer to invest additional funds in his inventory. Despite these unattractive features, however, retailers often find cost savings sufficient to justify drop shipments, especially for standard, fast-selling items that sell regardless of season.

Drop-shipment wholesalers are also important in industrial marketing. They are important distributors of sand, clay, coal, and lumber—all commodities of low value, relative to transportation costs incurred in their distribution, and all involving situations where any interruption of deliveries causing breaks in customer's production operations lead to significant cost increases. Industrial users purchase these items in such large quantities and with such great regularity that it pays to have several shipments in transit at any one time, each spaced to arrive before it is needed and always allowing some margin of safety for late arrivals. Thus, the industrial user manages to "work around" the long period when drop shipments are in transit. Furthermore, customers generally buy these commodities in lots large enough to obtain freight rates as low as service wholesalers.

*Mail-Order Wholesalers.* Mail-order wholesalers sell entirely by mail. They substitute mail-order catalogs and order forms for a sales force and pass on to retailers the savings in the form of lower prices. This limited function wholesaler is mainly active in selling staple consumer items such as hardware and dry goods. With successive improvements in transportation and communication, the importance of mail-order wholesalers has declined. One basic weakness of this type of operation is that it does not provide the manufacturer with a good substitute for strong promotional push by sales personnel. Moreover, its success rests on retailers' willingness to take the initiative in placing orders, something not always done, especially when competitors' sales forces call personally on retailers.

## AGENT MIDDLEMEN

*Agent middlemen*—most of them in wholesaling rather than in retailing—assist in negotiating sales or purchases or both on behalf of their principals (buyers or sellers or both). Usually the agent does not represent both buyers and sellers in the same transaction. Agents ordinarily are paid commissions or fees. Agent wholesalers differ from merchant wholesalers as they do not take title to the merchandise and perform only a few wholesaling activities. The 1977 Census reported 35,000 agent middlemen in the United States with annual sales in excess of $130 billion. This amounted to approximately 10 percent of the wholesale establishments and 10 percent of wholesale sales.

Agent wholesalers operate in many fields, but individual agents concentrate on such lines as foods, grain, copper, steel, machinery, electronic supplies, or textiles. The main agent wholesalers are brokers, commission houses, manufacturers' agents, selling agents, resident buyers, and auction companies. (See Table 8-4.)

### Brokers

A *broker* is an agent who represents either buyer or seller in negotiating purchases or sales without having physical control over the goods. The broker is more often the agent of the owner seeking a buyer than of a buyer searching for a source of supply. Each broker tends to specialize in arranging transactions for a limited number of products, enabling the broker to be well-informed about market conditions.

Acting strictly as an intermediary, the broker has limited powers as to prices in terms of sale, and it possesses little or no authority to bargain on behalf of its principal. The broker's main service is to bring buyer and seller together. Representing either the seller or the buyer, the broker relays the buyer's offer to the seller and the seller's counteroffer to the buyer and continues this process until the terms are satisfactory to both parties, and the exchange takes place. The broker never has direct physical control over the goods but sells by description or sample. Whenever the broker arranges a sale, the seller ships the goods directly to the buyer. The broker receives its commission from the principal who sought its services.

Brokers are most used by producers who find it uneconomical to establish sales forces of their own or long-term relationships with other types of agent wholesalers. Although an individual producer may use the same broker year after year, each transaction is considered completely apart from every other. There is no obligation on the part of either the broker or the seller to maintain their relationship in future transactions. Small canners whose outputs are too small to justify promoting brands of their own and whose entire pack is put up in two or three months often rely on brokers. Similarly, farmers harvesting one major crop find brokers economical.

Sometimes large manufacturers use brokers to extend the distribution

**TABLE 8-4** Major types of agent middlemen

| TYPE OF AGENT | DURATION OF RELATIONSHIP | KIND OF MERCHANDISE | SERVICES PERFORMED |
|---|---|---|---|
| 1. Broker | Each individual transaction | Farm products Canned goods | Negotiating between buyer and seller |
| 2. Commission house | A harvest season | Fresh produce | Sells at best available price Collects payment |
| 3. Manufacturers' agent | Long term | Noncompeting related lines of consumer durables, industrial goods | Acts as district sales office in an exclusive territory |
| 4. Selling agent | Long term | Textiles | Acts as marketing department |
| 5. Resident buyer | Indefinite | Apparel, white goods, fashion merchandise | Source of interim supply at major market |
| 6. Auction house | Each transaction | Tobacco, live stock | Sells at market price |

of their products. Brokers serve as key middlemen in arranging initial product distribution among other middlemen. Thus, a broker may be instrumental in opening up a new market for the producer or in gaining access to outlets not previously stocking the product.

### Commission Houses

A *commission house* is an agent who exercises physical control over and negotiates the sale of goods belonging to principals. The commission house has broad powers as to prices, methods, and terms of sale, although it must obey its principals' instructions. Generally, it arranges delivery, extends credit, collects, deducts its fees, and remits the balance to its principal. Thus, except that it does not take title, the commission house performs activities very similar to those of service merchant wholesalers—more so than any other agent wholesaler.

Most commission houses are active in the distribution of fresh fruit and produce. The relationship of the commission house and its principals covers a harvest and marketing season. A truck farmer, for instance, signs a seasonal agreement with a commission house in a market center; as the crop is harvested, it is shipped to the commission house. The commission house is authorized to sell each shipment on arrival at the best price obtainable without checking back with the farmer. Although legal title to the goods never passes to the house, it sells in its own name, bills buyers, extends credit, makes collections, deducts its fees, and remits the balance to the truck farmer. The farmer might prefer to hold the crop off the market at times and bargain for higher prices, but perishability makes delays in selling costly. The commission house's operation is geared for rapid sale of perishable commodities, and this is the main reason this type of agent is important in agricultural marketing.

### Manufacturers' Agents

Four main features characterize the operations of a *manufacturers' agent:* (1) it has extended contractual relationship with its principals, (2) it handles sales for each principal within an exclusive territory, (3) it represents manufacturers of noncompeting but related lines of goods, and (4) it has limited authority as to prices and terms of sale. Some manufacturers' agents have physical control over an inventory, but most do not. Ordinarily, the manufacturers' agent arranges for shipments directly from the factory to the buyer. Because its main activity is selling, the agent fields a sales staff large enough to provide adequate coverage of its market area. It sells at prices or within a price range stipulated by its principal and receives a percentage commission based on sales.

Manufacturers' agents are used either when a manufacturer finds it uneconomical to have its own sales force or when it is financially unable to do so. Some manufacturers, for instance, find that certain market areas do not provide enough business to justify assigning their own sales personnel. Yet manufacturers' agents, each representing several principals, operate profitably in the same areas. It is common for manufacturers to use their own sales force in areas with large sales potential and manufacturers' agents elsewhere. Other manufacturers use agents to open up new market areas, then replace them with their own sales personnel as sales volume grows. Still others, particularly small manufacturers with narrow product lines, use a network of manufacturers' agents to avoid altogether the problems and expenses of maintaining their own sales forces. Manufacturers also find manufacturers' agents useful in selling in foreign markets because of their familiarity with local customs and markets.

Manufacturers' agents are most important in the marketing of industrial goods and such consumer durables as furniture and hardware. In industrial goods marketing, such as in the marketing of electronic components, agents employ sales representatives who have considerable technical competence and who contact industrial users directly. In marketing consumer durables, sales personnel employed by manufacturers' agents generally call on and sell to retailers. Many furniture manufacturers rely on manufacturers' agents to sell their entire outputs. In both industrial and consumer goods marketing, the manufacturers' agents because of close contacts with markets advise manufacturers on numerous matters, including styling, design, and pricing.

### Selling Agents

A *selling agent* operates on an extended contractual basis, negotiates all sales of a specified merchandise line or its principal's entire output, and usually has full authority as to prices, terms, and other conditions of sale. Thus, it differs from the manufacturers' agent in that it is ordinarily not confined to a given market area, has more authority to set prices and terms of sales, and is the sole agent for the lines it represents.

Some selling agents render financial assistance to principals. This practice traces back to early selling agents who were much stronger financially than their principals. Many textile mills, for instance, started up with the financial backing of selling agents who saw this as a way to increase their own business volumes and hence their commissions. Today, selling agents do not provide investment capital for principals, but many help principals finance current operations. Because many modern selling agents have higher credit ratings than their principals, it is common for them to endorse their principals' short-term notes at banks and other lending institutions. Occasionally, too, a selling agent assists its principal financially either by making direct loans on accounts receivable or by guaranteeing these accounts so that a lender will advance needed funds. There is, however, a trend away from this type of financing activity by selling agents. The trend has accelerated with the growth of "factors," who specialize in discounting accounts receivable—that is, in making short-term loans with accounts receivable as the collateral.

The manufacturer who uses a selling agent, in effect, shifts most of the marketing task to an outside organization. This frees the manufacturer to concentrate on production and other nonmarketing problems. Because the selling agent is in close contact with buyers, it often guides the manufacturer on styling, design, and pricing matters. Often, too, it assists with or takes over sales promotion and even specifies the features that the principal builds into the product and how much to manufacture. Since the selling agent works for a straight commission, the principal's selling costs vary proportionately with sales made, and no fixed selling costs are incurred. For all these reasons, small manufacturers with neither the managerial talent nor the financial strength to market their own products use selling agents.

The manufacturer who uses a selling agent should realize, however, that it is "placing all its marketing eggs in one basket." The selling agent is the manufacturer's only contact with the market, and the bulk of the bargaining power rests with the agent, not with the manufacturer. Recognizing this, selling agents may resort to price cutting instead of exerting a reasonable effort to sell at established prices. The manufacturer, cut off from the buyers by the selling agent and having dealt only through this intermediary, is literally "over the barrel." If it is weak financially and needs loans that cannot be obtained without the selling agent's help, it may not be able to break with the selling agent in order to obtain another agent. The moral is clear: If the manufacturer is going to use a selling agent, its first choice should be a good one.

### Resident Buyers

A resident buyer differs from most other agent middlemen in that it represents buyers only. Specializing in buying for retailers, it receives its compensation on a fee or commission basis. The resident buyer operates in lines such as furniture and apparel where there are well-defined market centers to which retailers travel to make their selections. Resident buyers maintain offices in market centers and whenever retailers cannot make the trip to market, they serve as retailers' contacts with the sources of supply.

Resident buyers are independent of their principals. They should not be confused with resident buying offices, maintained in such market centers as New York, which are owned by out-of-town stores. Nor should they be confused with central buying offices maintained by chain-store organizations. The resident buyer is an independent agent specializing in buying for principals who are retailers.

### Auction Companies

As its name indicates, an *auction company* uses the auction method of catalogs and competitive bidding by prospective buyers to sell its principals' products. Auction companies are important in selling products of varying quality and those that cannot be efficiently graded—situations frequent in agricultural marketing. In the fresh fruit and vegetable trade, auction companies are in central markets—that is, in important distribution points. In marketing livestock and agricultural crops such as leaf tobacco, auction companies are located in producing areas and at shipping points. An auction company has physical control over the lots consigned to it, arranges for their display, conducts the auction, makes collections from buyers, and remits the proceeds, less its commissions to principals.

The auction method of selling leaf tobacco dates back to Civil War days. Until then tobacco leaf was spread on sidewalks for display, and growers had no option whatever but to accept prices offered by buyers. This caused the Virginia legislature to give some attention to the marketing situation, resulting first in provisions whereby tobacco was graded by professionals on the basis of intrinsic value and later in establishing warehouses using auction selling.

### Other Agents

Other agent middlemen evolved to serve special marketing needs. Whenever enough buyers or sellers need some special marketing service, there are always enterprising individuals who set up in business to provide it. There are *export and import agents* in leading port cities who serve the needs of principals seeking foreign markets or overseas sources of supply. There are *purchasing agents* who independently specialize in locating sources of supply for industrial buyers. They all have the same basic economic purpose—to bring buyers and sellers together in return for fees or commissions.

## *CONCLUSION*

Merchant wholesalers are not only the most numerous wholesale middlemen; they also transact more dollar sales than any other type of wholesale middlemen. General merchandise wholesalers have gradually declined in relative importance, and general line wholesalers continue as important suppliers to small-scale independent retailers and as convenient sources of items bought in small quantities by industrial users. Specialty wholesalers have expanded their operations significantly, especially in market areas where retail outlets are both close together and numerous. The service wholesaler classification overlaps the general merchandise and general line wholesaler categories entirely and the specialty wholesaler category partly. Limited function wholesalers (that is, those merchant wholesalers who do *not* perform all or most of the activities normally expected in the wholesale trade) include truck wholesalers, rack jobbers, cash-and-carry wholesalers, drop shipment wholesalers, and mail-order wholesalers, each of whom has unique operating characteristics fitted to the distribution needs of certain producers in reaching certain customers. Merchant wholesalers constitute important links in the marketing channels of many marketers, consumer and industrial products.

Agent wholesalers constitute an important sector of the wholesaling structure and perform valuable services both for producers searching for markets and for buyers seeking sources of supply. Individual types of agent wholesalers tailor their operations to uniquely fit them to the marketing needs of their principals. Table 8-4 summarizes the operating characteristics of the major types of agents. Brokers serve small producers unwilling or unable to maintain their own sales forces, large producers wishing to extend their distribution or desiring help in the introduction of new products, and buyers seeking suppliers. Commission houses gear their operations especially to the marketing of perishables, thus serving growers who otherwise may have only the remotest contact with ultimate markets. Manufacturers' agents make it possible for producers to market products in areas that would be unprofitable to cultivate directly. Selling agents enable their principals to shift most of the marketing task to an outside organization. Similarly, other types of agents have operations geared to meet the special marketing needs of their principals and clients.

# 9

# SMALL- AND LARGE-SCALE
# RETAILERS

*Retailing,* by definition, consists of the activities involved in selling directly to ultimate consumers: thus, retailing exists in all consumer goods marketing channels. Retailers are the most numerous of all marketing institutions, and wherever there is more than a handful of people there are retailers. In 1977 there were more than 1,800,000 retailers in the United States, with total sales of $723 billion. (see Table 9–1.) Each adjusts to needs of the market through merchandise selection, size of operations, pricing, location, and selling methods—as well as through other operating policies and practices. There is tremendous variety among retail institutions, as they range all the way from the corner grocery to the multibillion dollar corporate chain, as shown in Figure 9–1. But regardless of the specific class of retail institution, the basic economic purpose is that of buying and assembling the products of manufacturers and other producers and reselling to ultimate consumers.

Although we tend to think of retailing as being confined to "fixed" retail locations, retailing takes place wherever an ultimate consumer and seller get together. In fact, "fixed" retail locations are a relatively recent development. Retailing in ancient times was carried on mostly by traveling peddlers or from temporary stalls situated in town or village markets. The outdoor public market is still a feature of the American retailing system (though a relatively unimportant one), and the peddler has evolved into the house-to-house selling organization.

**TABLE 9–1** Retailers: Number of establishments and total sales, selected years, 1948–1977

| YEAR | NO. OF ESTABLISHMENTS (THOUSANDS) | SALES (BILLIONS) |
|------|------------------------------------|-------------------|
| 1977 | 1,855 | $723.1 |
| 1972 | 1,780 | 457.4 |
| 1967 | 1,763 | 310.2 |
| 1963 | 1,708 | 244.2 |
| 1958 | 1,795 | 200.4 |
| 1954 | 1,722 | 170.0 |
| 1948 | 1,770 | 130.5 |

*Source:* U.S. Department of Commerce, Bureau of the Census, *Statistical Abstract of the United States*, 1982–83, 103rd Edition, p.801.

**Figure 9–1** Retail store sales, by kind of business, 1980 and 1981

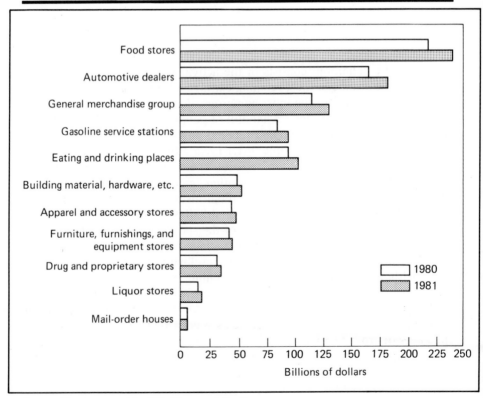

*Source:* Chart prepared by U.S. Bureau of the Census.

## HOUSE–TO–HOUSE SELLING

Modern house-to-house salesmen are descended from the "Yankee peddlers" who, on foot, on horseback, and then in wagons, traveled from farm to farm and from settlement to settlement, selling a variety of manufactured articles to pioneers and frontierspeople. Today's house-to-house salesperson differs from the peddler in two important ways. First, he or she is seldom a completely independent operator. Most house-to-house salespeople are either semi-independent agents or employees of large manufacturers or distributors using this retailing method. Among them are such well-known organizations as Avon Products (cosmetics and toilet articles), Wearever Aluminum (cooking utensils), Tupperware (plastic housewares), and the Fuller Brush Company (cleaning and household articles). Second, today's house–to–house sellers tend to restrict their offerings to a small number of articles within a single merchandise line. They may specialize in encyclopedias, lawn and garden stock, vacuum cleaners, china, cosmetics, or household cleaning materials. The salespeople employed by the large house-to-house organizations are almost equally divided among men and women, more than half working part–time. Thus, it is not unusual for a direct-selling company to have from 5,000 to 10,000 salespeople, nearly all working on a commission basis. Avon Products is said to have more than 350,000 people, mainly women, selling part–time in its world–wide operation.

House-to-house selling eliminates the expenses of retail store operation, but it is by no means a low-cost retailing method. It requires travel and personal contact and the substantial costs of recruiting, maintaining, and managing sales staffs large enough to transact profitable sales volume. These costs lead the direct-selling companies to handle either fairly high-priced items or articles that are sold in assortments, in both cases to build up the average order size. Some, such as Avon Products, strive to make more effective use of representatives' time by establishing steady customers. Others, such as Tupperware, use "party-plan selling," or bringing a group of potential buyers together in one of their homes for a product demonstration, so that several orders may result. The commissions paid house-to-house salespeople usually range from 25 to 40 percent.

The total costs of house-to-house selling run to approximately 60 percent of sales. This estimate includes not only sales commissions but costs of supervision and administration, clerical work, shipping, credit, and promotion and advertising. This is high-cost retailing, but companies using house-to-house selling normally do not have to allow for wholesalers' and retailers' margins, and fixed selling and administrative expenses are low. Whether house-to-house selling is an expensive distribution method depends on the manufacturer's alternatives. If they involve the use of wholesalers and retailers and the maintenance of a full-time permanent staff of salaried salespeople, house-to-house selling may be economical in comparison.

There are times when house-to-house selling is the best solution to a manufacturer's marketing problems. Sometimes it is the only way that a radically different new product can be introduced, particularly by a company with limited finances. For example, the early manufacturers of vacuum cleaners found it almost impossible to secure distribution among conventional retailers who had difficulties in convincing consumers of the merits of the product. By demonstrating their cleaner's superior cleaning power in the home on the housewife's own carpets, these manufacturers were quickly able to overcome sales resistance. Once vacuum cleaners had been generally accepted by consumers, regular retailers could be used. However, one successful manufacturer, Kirby, never abandoned this method of selling its vacuum cleaners. There are other products, too, such as sewing machines and rug cleaners, that seem to sell more easily when demonstrated in the home. Still other products, such as encyclopedias and Bibles, that most consumers do not shop for in retail stores, can be sold house-to-house.

## INDEPENDENT STORES

An *independent store* is a retailing business unit controlled by its own individual ownership or management. Although there are both large and small independent stores, most large-scale, independently owned stores are classified under headings such as supermarkets, department stores, and discount houses. We consider as independent any individually owned or managed retail business unit, small or large, which cannot be readily classified as a supermarket, department store, or discount house. This definition sidesteps the academic problem of distinguishing small-scale from large-scale retailers. How does one decide where "small" ends and "large" begins? The sales-volume yardstick is used most but number of employees, square feet of floor space, and inventory dollar size have all been tried. One difficulty with all these measures is that the dividing line must still be chosen arbitrarily; furthermore, the idea of just what "large" means keeps changing. In the 1940s a grocery store with $250,000 in annual sales was considered rather large, but by the 1980s such a store was considered small. Thus, the criteria for largeness are constantly being revised upward. But, because at any given time some retailers are smaller than others, in the following discussion we refer to independent retailers as being relatively "small" or "large."

### The General Store

The *general store* is one of the oldest types of independent retailers. It is a relatively small retailing business, not departmentalized, usually located in a rural community, and primarily engaged in selling a general assortment of merchandise—the most important of which is food. Its more important subsidiary lines are notions, apparel, farm supplies, and gasoline. These stores were important in farming and frontier sections until in the 1920s the spread of other types of retailing and the increased ownership of automobiles gave consumers greater shopping mobility, causing general stores gradually to decline. Some general stores, however, still operate in sparsely populated areas of the West and South.

### Other Small Independent Retailers

Today, most small independent stores are concentrated in fields where it is "relatively easy to set up in business." This usually means that no great amount of capital is needed or that easy financing is available. This probably is the main reason why there have been so many small independent gasoline retailers—a fairly small investment in inventory "turned over" rapidly results in a sales figure many times the value of the inventory. Until the early 1970s, many petroleum refiners offered generous financial assistance to individuals who wanted to open their own stations, but this policy changed with the energy crisis.[1] Many small retailers, of course, are well-financed, but they are the exceptions.

Small independent retailers meet strong competition from large retail chains, supermarkets, discount houses, and department stores. The small independent generally buys its inventory from wholesalers or other middlemen, rather than directly from producers, so the merchandise costs are higher than those of large, direct-buying competitors. Thus, it often has to charge higher prices (to cover costs) than its competitors.

Small independents must use something other than price in their efforts to attract trade. The more successful usually find some way to differentiate their stores in customers' minds. It may consist of nothing more than personalized service and friendly relations with customers. Or the independent may stay open longer hours than larger competitors and may offer such extra services as credit and delivery. A convenient location, too, may be attractive to customers. As long as substantial numbers of ultimate consumers continue to consider such things important, small independent stores are likely to remain on the retail scene.

### Large Independent Retailers

Large independent stores are most important in retail fields where corporate chains, department stores, and other integrated retail institutions either have no operating advantages or are at a competitive disadvantage. In retailing women's clothing, for instance, the independent store buys most of its merchandise directly from manufacturers, the same source from which the chain women's clothing store and the women's clothing departments of the department store must buy. Whereas the chain may buy larger quantities

[1] After the energy crisis of the 1970s, it became evident that the number of gasoline stations was excessive and many independents were squeezed out by petroleum company-owned stations.

than the independent, the resulting quantity discounts are generally too small to permit it to use the "lower price" appeal effectively.

Of even greater significance is the fact that *most* items of women's clothing are not all standardized, either in appearance or construction. In large towns and cities, several women's clothing outlets may handle the same manufacturer's line, but because they normally handle very few identical garments, the consumer has little opportunity to shop around and compare prices. In small towns, there is even less likelihood that competing retailers will represent the same manufacturers, or sell identical garments if they do, so that it is virtually impossible for the consumer to make direct price comparisons. This is what makes merchandise selection especially important in the successful retailing of women's clothing. Whereas the local independent can offer dresses and sportswear that are "in tune" with the consumer preferences in its own locality, chain organizations with their centralized buying procedures find it hard to adjust their buying patterns to fit the unique preferences of local markets. Other lines that offer similar competitive advantages to the independent retailer are men's clothing and furniture.

Some large independent stores are successful because their owners have specialized knowledge that enables them to "run rings around" larger competitors. Examples abound in the retailing of such goods as Oriental rugs, musical instruments, and sports equipment. Large numbers of consumers hesitate to buy such items in the absence of what they consider "professional advice." Chain stores and department stores sell these items, but they usually have less well-informed personnel than do independent specialty stores.

Another group of large independent retailers has succeeded in building local reputations as "quality stores." Some handle large assortments of related merchandise, for example, men's or ladies' apparel, and pride themselves on featuring the latest fashions. Others deal in lines such as jewelry where consumers consider the "store image" almost as important as merchandise quality. Independents often find it easier to build prestige reputations than their chain-store or department-store competitors. Furthermore, many independent quality stores are old and well-established; it is not easy for competitors to acquire quality reputations locally in a few months or years.

### Competitive Advantages of Independent Stores

In comparison with their competitors, successful independents, both large and small, possess significant advantages. Probably most important is that they can more easily adapt to the unique needs of the communities in which they do business. Furthermore, there is no question but that the owner-managers of a good many successful independent stores are more able and more aggressive than the hired managers of department store and chain store units. Also many consumers tend to be loyal to locally owned and operated stores and look askance at stores controlled from out of town.

## LARGE–SCALE INTEGRATED RETAILERS

The large-scale or "mass" retailers achieve their growth in several ways. First, some grow by increasing the physical size of the operating unit to cater to a large number of customers. As a store becomes larger, its power to attract customers increases because of the greater variety of merchandise offered for sale; moreover, up to a certain size, its costs per dollar of sales tend to decrease. Beyond the optimum size, costs increase at a faster rate than sales. The maximum size of a retail establishment also is limited by the geographical extent of its market. For example, a department store whose market is limited to a single trading area does not have the growth potential of a mail-order retailer whose market area may be as broad as the reach of the Postal Service or United Parcel Service. Retailers also can expand by acquiring additional stores in different market areas. Multiple outlets may be operated in any of three ways: (1) branch-store operation with the parent store servicing the branches' merchandising and operating needs; (2) the outlets may operate independently, tied to the parent organization solely on a financial basis; or (3) a central "management" office may handle all aspects of the retail stores' operations.

A third way of achieving retail growth is through integration. An integrated marketing institution reduces marketing costs by eliminating, simplifying, or consolidating various marketing activities. When a retailer bypasses a wholesaler to buy directly from a producer, some part of that wholesaler's activities are taken over by the retailer. If the retailer performs these activities more efficiently than the wholesaler, costs are reduced accordingly. Most large-scale retailing operations grew through some combination of larger outlets, additional outlets, and integration.

## MAIL-ORDER HOUSES

### Rise of the Mail-Order House

A number of developments contributed to the founding and growth of mail-order retailing. Montgomery Ward and Sears Roebuck, founded in 1872 and 1886, respectively, both owed much of their early success and rapid growth to the completion of the transcontinental railroads and improvements in postal service, including the advent of rural free delivery. These developments in transportation and delivery, coupled with the comparative isolation from retail centers of the then predominantly rural population of the United States, set the stage for an enthusiastic reception for mail-order merchandising. General stores, formerly the chief source of supply for the farm population, found themselves hard pressed to meet either the prices (achieved through integration of wholesaling and retailing) or the extensive merchandise offerings of the mail-order houses.

### Mail-Order Retailing of General Merchandise

Both Montgomery Ward and Sears Roebuck confined themselves solely to mail-order operations until the 1920s. In 1921 Montgomery Ward (and in 1925 Sears Roebuck) opened their first retail stores. These stores were hastened by the spectacular growth in automobile ownership and by considerable improvements in rural roads that helped transform many rural consumers into small-town shoppers and lessened the relative attractiveness of mail-order buying. Furthermore, the nation's population was rapidly shifting from predominantly rural to predominantly urban. The managements of Ward and Sears were alert to the marketing significance of these changes, hence their decisions to open retail outlets in urban centers. Today the bulk of the sales of both concerns comes from their retail stores, although mail order still accounts for sizable proportions of their business. Indeed, the retail stores of both companies feature "catalog order desks," which solicit orders for delivery by their mail-order operations. In some locations, too, both Sears and Ward maintain "catalog order stores" at which consumers are invited to place mail orders either in person or by telephone.

Mail-order houses such as Ward, Sears, Spiegels, and Penney offer wide assortments of articles within a large number of merchandise lines. They buy directly from the producer, often contracting for a large share or even all of a producer's output. Many small manufacturers are completely dependent on one or the other of the large mail-order houses for distributing all they produce. Most of the 20,000 sources of supply for Sears, for instance, are small manufacturers. Indeed, the company is on record as stating that "It prefers to work with smaller factories, which concentrate on production, and look to it for a substantial part of their distribution."[2] In the case of Sears, such small manufacturers are the main suppliers of Sears' own brands—Kenmore, Homart, Craftsman, Silvertone, J.C. Higgins, Charmode, and others.

The large general mail-order houses are only one facet of mail-order retailing. More limited selections of merchandise are also "retailed directly" by mail-order retailers, who are often small manufacturers of shirts, men's and women's apparel, toys, bird houses and feeders, and rugs. Some of these manufacturers distribute catalogs to consumers that tend to emphasize expensive top-of-the-line clothing and giftware. Other mail-order retailers use direct-mail promotional literature and small advertisements in magazines and newspapers. Mail-order retailing is an important distribution

---

[2] "How Sears Stays on Top," *International Management,* Vol. 23, April 1968, p. 61.

method, too, for many growers of trees, shrubs, plants, and seeds, who distribute their catalogs to home-owners throughout the country.

Mail-order retailing is used also by the many "of-the-month" clubs. These clubs typically provide their so-called members with preselected merchandise, thus relieving them of the need for choosing from a large number of alternatives. *Book-of-the Month Club,* for instance, informs its members of monthly selections, which must be *rejected* if they do not wish to receive them. Those not sending in rejections will automatically receive monthly selections and be billed accordingly. Club members, therefore, find it easier to accept rather than reject selections and to continue rather than discontinue their memberships. Because of these features, the clubs are often said to provide automatic distribution for products chosen as monthly selections. Most of the clubs are true middlemen, for they make their purchases from producers and resell them to consumers. The book clubs are the longest established in their field, but similar organizations engage in mail-order retailing of such items as food, fruit, toys, gifts, and foreign imports.

### Current Trends of Mail-Order Retailing

Mail-order retailing has experienced considerable growth in recent years as a result of changes in consumer needs and habits. Working wives have very limited time for shopping, and they welcome the opportunity to conserve their time by shopping by mail. A great many new mail-order retailers have come into existence to serve this need. These retailers focus primarily on affluent two–income households, and their catalogs emphasize expensive top-of-the-line clothing and giftware.

## DEPARTMENT STORES

### History and Growth

The department store was a European, not an American, retailing innovation. the Bon Marché and other Paris department stores came into existence and flourished during the period of the Second Empire (1852–1871). Leading American retailers of the 1850s and 1860s regularly included Paris and other European market centers on buying trips and observed the operating methods of their stores. Thus the idea was transplanted to the United States. Among the American firms to begin operating as department stores during this period were R. H. Macy (New York), Jordan Marsh (Boston), Marshall Field (Chicago), Scruggs-Vandervoort-Barney (St. Louis), Meir & Frank (Portland, Oregon), City of Paris (San Francisco), Thalhimer Brothers (Richmond), and Rich's (Atlanta). Not all of these would have qualified as department stores when they began; most started out as other types of business and converted later to department-store operations. By the close of the 1870s, department stores were well-established in nearly every major U.S. city and in many smaller cities and towns.

Department stores have been a major retailing institution in major cities throughout the world for over 100 years, and they still fill an important role in the sales of shopping goods. In 1981 department stores sales in the United States were $103.6 billion, approximately 10 percent of total retail sales. Their share of the market twenty-five years earlier was approximately the same.

### Nature of Operations

Formally defined, a *department store* is a large retailing business unit that handles a wide variety of shopping and specialty goods—including women's ready–to–wear and accessories, men's and boys' wear, piece goods, small wares, and home furnishings—and which is organized into separate departments for purposes of promotion, service, and control. Thus, the two main features of the department store are a broad merchandise offering and departmental organization. Responsibility for buying and selling is decentralized to individual departments, each carrying different lines of goods and each under the control of a merchandising executive called a *buyer or department manager*. Buyers are relatively free to operate their departments as they see fit, provided they operate within budget restrictions and their operations produce profits considered adequate by the store's top management. In addition to exercising general supervision over merchandising operations, the store's central administrative organization operates and maintains the physical facilities, provides such services as credit and delivery for the customers, and assists the merchandising department in such activities as advertising and promotion.

Originally, department stores relied on the great breadth of their merchandise offerings to attract customers. Gradually, however, the more aggressive stores, seeking to build their trade, broadened the range of services offered to customers. Today it is a rare department store that does not provide such customer services as charge accounts, installment plans, and home delivery. Some offer such services as elaborate restaurants and tearooms, gourmet boutiques, and fashion shows. A few of these services are self-supporting; others are not. But even though some services may show an "accounting-type" loss, they generally are maintained because of their proven power to "pull in" customers.

By its very nature, the department store is a "horizontally integrated" retail institution. It brings together under one roof a range of merchandise offerings comparable to the combined offerings of many stores specializing in single or fewer merchandise lines. Although this "exposition-like" character is the source of much of the department store's drawing power, it is not without its disadvantages, particularly in purchasing. Some departments do enough business to justify direct buying from sources of supply, but many do not. The small-volume departments, particularly in individually owned stores, often are unable to buy in large enough lots to qualify for the quantity discounts offered by manufacturers and, hence, must frequently resort to buying through wholesalers and agents, which results in rather high merchandise costs.

### Department-Store Buying Groups

Because of the advantages they encounter in purchasing, some independently owned department stores have joined buying groups. Member stores cooperatively own, maintain, and use the services of resident buying offices located in market centers such as New York and Chicago. Through consolidation of the orders of member stores, the buying office is able to achieve considerable savings by buying lots larger than any member could buy individually. Furthermore, the combined bargaining power often results in lower price quotations by suppliers. A secondary though important activity of the resident buying office involves providing member stores with current information relating to prices, availability of new items, and fashion trends.

### Department-Store Ownership Groups

Many previously independent department stores have been absorbed into ownership groups. Most department-store ownership groups were put together originally by financiers rather than by merchandisers. They were intended to result primarily not in improved operating efficiency but in immediate profits for the organizers, who, as financial middlemen, were most interested in profiting from the flotation of new issues of common stock. But over time, central managements of the ownership groups lost their solely financial orientations and began to emphasize the improvement and standardization of operating policies and procedures. One early development was the centralized buying offices which enabled stores in the group to buy many standard stock items and some fashion goods at lower costs. Nevertheless, many types of merchandise are still bought by stores individually. Among these are high-fashion items, where speed of procurement and direct contact with the producer is important, and articles needed to satisfy purely local demands. Top management of the department-store ownership groups have also worked toward greater uniformity in nonmerchandising activities, such as the standardization of personnel policies and store-operating systems and records.

Each store in an ownership group plans its merchandise offerings to cater to classes of trade in its own selling area. Because the inventory is mainly shopping goods (items customers "shop around for" and compare before buying) and specialty goods (items customers will spend considerable time searching for), and because consumer preferences for such articles vary considerably from one area to another, most department stores, whether or not they belong to ownership groups, find it difficult to standardize the merchandise offerings of stores in different locations. Furthermore, stores in the same ownership group often attract different classes of trade in different cities. The uniqueness of the merchandise offering and the trade catered to results in each store's having a distinctive image. Thus, most department-store ownership groups continue to operate stores under the names they had when they were independently owned. Allied Stores Corporation, for instance, operates among others, Jordan Marsh in Boston, Titche-Goettinger in Dallas, the Bon Marche in Seattle, Dey Brothers in Syracuse, and Joske's in San Antonio and Houston. Federated Department Stores operates among others, Filene's in Boston, Shillito's in Cincinnati, the Boston Store in Milwaukee, Bloomingdale's in New York, Abraham & Straus in Brooklyn, Burdine's in Miami, and Bullock's in Los Angeles. Each of these stores has quite a distinct image in its own trading area.

## CHAIN-STORE SYSTEMS

Fundamentally, a *chain-store system* is a group of retail stores of essentially the same type, centrally owned and with some degree of centralized control of operation. This definition is broad enough to include not only the well-known A & P and Radio Shack "chains," but also Penney's and Sears' retail stores and the different department-store ownership groups. Thus, basically, the distinguishing feature of a chain-store system is that it owns and controls a group of stores. The department-store ownership group is one type of chain-store system, the retail J. C. Penney stores are another, and the K-Mart stores represent still another type. However, if only by virtue of long-established and customary usage, the term "chain-store system" normally refers to a multi-unit retailing operation that cannot be categorized as a department-store ownership group or the retail outlets affiliated with a mail-order house, and where there is some central control over merchandising. Table 9–2 shows the types of merchandise in which chains are important.

Chain store systems, made up of eleven or more stores, collectively have accounted for an increasing share of the nation's total retail sales in the fifteen years between 1966 and 1981. In 1966, chain stores accounted for 26.4 percent of total retail sales; by 1981, they accounted for 35.8 percent of total retail sales. (See Table 9–3.) Most important in the sale of nondurable goods, for example, they accounted for 87.7 percent of total sales in department stores.

### Strengths from Horizontal Integration

Certain strengths of the chain-store system lie in the fact that it is horizontally integrated (that is, it operates multiple stores). With the addition of each new store, the system extends its "reach" to another group of prospective customers. Also, each store added means greater sales volume and, consequently, increased opportunity to effect economies through buy-

**TABLE 9–2** Sales of chain store systems in various retail fields, 1981

| KIND OF BUSINESS | CHAIN STORE SALES IN 1981 (BILLIONS) | AS A % OF TOTAL RETAIL SALES IN 1981 |
|---|---|---|
| Durable goods stores | $ 27.2 | 10.2% |
| Tire, battery, accessory dealers | 3.6 | 17.9 |
| Nondurable goods stores | 345.2 | 48.5 |
| Apparel and accessory stores | 18.8 | 39.3 |
| Women's apparel, accessories | 8.0 | 44.3 |
| Shoe stores | 4.1 | 61.0 |
| Drug and proprietary stores | 17.8 | 53.9 |
| Food stores | 115.1 | 48.4 |
| General merchandise group | 106.0 | 83.1 |
| Department stores | 90.9 | 87.7 |
| Variety stores | 6.6 | 73.3 |
| Total U.S. retail sales | $372.4 | 35.8 |

*Source:* U.S. Department of Commerce, Bureau of the Census, *Statistical Abstract of the United States, 1982–83*, 103rd Edition, pp.802–803.

**TABLE 9–3** Total sales of retail stores and chain-store systems (with eleven or more stores), selected years, 1966–1981

| YEAR | SALES OF ALL RETAIL STORES (BILLIONS) | TOTAL SALES OF CHAIN STORE SYSTEMS (BILLIONS) | CHAIN STORE SALES AS A % OF TOTAL RETAIL STORES |
|---|---|---|---|
| 1966 | $ 303.9 | $ 80.3 | 26.4% |
| 1968 | 339.3 | 94.6 | 27.9 |
| 1970 | 368.4 | 117.2 | 31.8 |
| 1974 | 541.0 | 169.4 | 31.3 |
| 1975 | 588.1 | 183.1 | 31.1 |
| 1976 | 657.4 | 199.6 | 30.3 |
| 1977 | 725.2 | 244.2 | 33.6 |
| 1978 | 804.7 | 283.8 | 35.3 |
| 1979 | 894.3 | 309.4 | 34.9 |
| 1980 | 951.9 | 338.0 | 35.5 |
| 1981 | 1,038.8 | 372.4 | 35.8 |

*Source:* U.S. Department of Commerce, Bureau of the Census, *Statistical Abstract of the United States, 1982–83*, 103rd Edition, pp.802–803.

ing in larger-sized lots. It also means that the cost of central administration and of providing highly specialized merchandising, buying, and promotional services can be spread over more stores. Thus, such costs are reduced for each store in the system. Furthermore, other economies are effected through standardization of store systems and procedures and adoption of uniform personnel policies. These strengths, all due primarily to horizontal integration, are reflected in lower costs for the merchandise handled and in generally lower operating expenses than those incurred by most independent retailers.

### Merchandising and Operating Economics

Relative to most of its competitors, particularly independent stores, the chain manages to realize significant savings in merchandising and operating expenses. Some are secured through eliminating or limiting such customer services as credit and delivery. Others are obtained by limiting the variety of merchandise available by stocking, for example, only three different brands of canned peas in each of two sizes rather than three brands in four sizes.

Other economies are realized through application of the basic merchandising philosophy of the chain, which is to squeeze the maximum sales out of each dollar invested in inventory. The chain, in other words, gears its operation so that it has a small inventory relative to the size of its sales volume. One aspect of applying this philosophy relates to decisions on composition of the inventory; the chain seeks to maximize the number of items which have a short shelf life (the fast sellers) and to minimize the number of those that have a long shelf life (the slow movers).

The chain attempts to build a large sales volume by pricing its merchandising lower than many of its competitors with a comparatively lower profit per item sold. Successful application of this merchandising philosophy results in a large sales volume relative to size of the inventory. The chain stresses high sales volume and low unit profits, while many competitors are satisfied with low sales volumes and high unit profits.

### Buying Policy

Because the chain-store system is a high-volume operation, it ordinarily gets its merchandise directly from producers or through their agents. Rarely does a chain buy from merchant wholesalers, for the system is usually able to buy in larger quantities than wholesalers can, and with larger discounts. Thus, by operating its own warehouses, the chain-store system effectively becomes its own wholesaler. Chain-store systems, therefore, are also vertically integrated institutions; they take over and perform for themselves marketing activities that would otherwise be performed by separate wholesale institutions.

### Weaknesses

Most weaknesses of the chain-store system stem from its horizontal integration and its merchandising philosophy. Centralized decision-making often means that individual chain units cannot react to changing local conditions as quickly as alert local competitors. When individual chain units lag behind the independents in making new products and brands available—and they frequently do—centralized purchasing is usually at fault. Furthermore, in keeping with the high sales volume and low-profit merchandising philosophy, the chain economizes on other costs and typically dispenses with such services as charge accounts and delivery. In doing this, it concedes to competitors the patronage of consumers desiring these services. Moreover, because of its integrated nature, the chain has many stores and requires many managers. Recruiting, training, and retaining managers in the numbers needed present formidable tasks. Individual chains, of course, have found ways to deal with or minimize these inherent weaknesses; nevertheless, such weaknesses together with the "impersonal and cold" character of most chains serve to offset many competitive advantages chains have over independents.

### Distribution of Convenience Goods

Chain–store systems are important links in the distribution system for many convenience goods—those goods that consumers generally want to buy frequently, immediately, and with minimum shopping effort. Both large and small manufacturers of grocery and drug products, for instance, know that their brands cannot be made sufficiently available to large masses of consumers unless chain outlets stock them. Manufacturers of many items sold through department stores or variety stores find that if they are to achieve the sales volumes necessary for mass production, they need chain-store distribution.

Holding out to producers of convenience goods the tempting prize of widespread and high-volume retail distribution at a relatively low selling cost, skilled chain-store buying specialists drive hard bargains. They push for and usually obtain the lowest possible prices and the most advantageous promotional allowances (which are payments made by manufacturers for advertising and otherwise promoting products at the retail level). Chains handling convenience goods generally expect most suppliers to promote their own products with heavy consumer advertising to minimize the "in-store" selling effort needed. In the case of products that do not lend themselves to such promotion, the chain often prefers to handle its own "store" brands, packed for it either under contract by outside manufacturers or by "captive" (that is, owned by the chain) canning or processing plants.

### Distribution of Shopping Goods

Chain-store systems are also important retailers of shopping goods, which are items that consumers select and buy only after doing some "shopping around." Chains are extremely active, for instance, in the retailing of men's and women's apparel, dry goods, and shoes. In contrast to many of their independent competitors in these lines, however, shopping-goods chains tend to concentrate on low-priced and fast-selling items. In other words, chains that specialize in shopping goods seek items that resemble convenience goods as closely as possible. To obtain them, chains often have to forgo handling high-fashion merchandise in favor of more staple items. Because of this, as well as because of the need for large sales volumes, shopping-goods chains generally cater to middle–and lower–income consumer groups.

Shopping-goods chains commonly have manufacturers under contract to supply them with goods according to the chain's own specifications. The supplying manufacturers need not be especially large, only large enough to assure the chain that they can produce enough to fill its requirements. Some shopping-goods chains are the retail arms of the manufacturers who own and control them. Bond Clothes, a retailer of men's and boys' clothing, makes its own suits and coats. The Thom McAn stores are operated by Melville Shoe Corporation. Other manufacturers, such as Hart, Shaffner, and Marx, sell part of their output through their own retail outlets and the rest through other types of retailers. But even when chain-store systems are controlled by manufacturers, there is a need for outside sources of supply. Thus, a manufacturer-controlled shoe chain, such as Thom McAn, retails not only shoes but related items, such as hosiery and shoe polish, bought from "outside" sources.

## COOPERATIVE ACTION BY INDEPENDENTS

### Retailer-Owned Cooperatives

The *retailer-owned cooperative* is an enterprise owned and controlled by independent retailer-stockholders who wish to have the advantage of large-scale buying to compete with chains. Often, too, the cooperative members adopt a uniform name, store front, and sign and engage in cooperative advertising. The net effect is an organization in the image of a chain-store system. When retailer-owner cooperatives give sufficient emphasis to group promotion, their members generally become strong competitors of chain-store outlets.

### Wholesaler-Sponsored Groups

In other instances, wholesalers take the initiative in organizing independent retailers into voluntary groups. Each retailer affiliating with a voluntary group owns and operates its own store but is associated with the sponsoring wholesaler for buying and merchandising purposes. The wholesaler-sponsor often makes its main contribution and justifies its role through providing promotional assistance and management advice. Retailer cooperatives and voluntary groups have become very important distributors of convenience goods and their largest volume is in the food industry. In some cases, their buying power equals or exceeds that of the chains.

### Consumer Cooperatives

A *consumer cooperative* is a retail business owned and operated by ultimate consumers to purchase and distribute goods and services primarily to the membership. There are some large consumer cooperatives in the United States, but their total impact on American retailing has been neglibible. They have failed to be as successful in the United States as in Europe because other types of retailing institutions grew up here and provided the strongly competitive setting that kept retailing profits low. In Europe, the high and often exorbitant profits of retailers furnished the stimulus for consumers to band together to open their own retail stores. While the consumer cooperative movement was expanding in Europe, chain stores and their competitors in the United States were learning how to provide quality merchandise at low prices.

Most United States consumer cooperatives are in the grocery retailing field mainly because their organizers have been impressed with the large part that food purchases play in total consumer spending. Consumer cooperatives have experienced rough sledding in the retail grocery field, where the chains and supermarkets have so dramatically demonstrated the importance of large size, adequate financing, well-planned inventory, and efficient management. Consumer cooperatives have more chance for success when they handle merchandise lines other than groceries. For instance, they have been highly successful in operating college and university bookstores.

## *CONCLUSION*

The competitive strength of the independent retailer varies considerably from one line of retailing to another. In the retailing of many convenience goods such as food and drugs, independents account for only a small portion of total volume, and these independents obtain their competitive advantage through convenience of location or the offering of additional services. In other retailing lines where chains and other mass retailers can gain little price advantage through volume buying and where the independent can often adjust more nearly to the needs of this market, independents frequently account for important shares of the market.

Mail-order houses, department stores, chain stores, and cooperatives share certain common characteristics besides large sales volumes. All seek the benefits of vertical integration through shortening the marketing channel. Their large size generally also contributes to efficient management and broad selections of merchandise. Large-scale integrated retailers, however, have one inherent weakness that partially offsets their advantages—their size often makes them inflexible competitors in comparison with independently owned and managed retail stores.

# 10

# OTHER RETAIL INSTITUTIONS
# AND DEVELOPMENTS

The successful retailer learns to identify his potential customers and to provide the merchandise and services they want and desire. The wide range of differences among consumers helps to explain the complexity of the retail structure. The dynamic character of American society makes it essential for retailers to be constantly prepared to modify and improve existing ways of doing business. Most retailers must either "innovate or perish." New and experimental forms of retailing institutions open their doors each year. A few succeed, but many fail—either from inefficiency or from inability to satisfy the consumers' needs. The successful ones, however, make their impact on older retail institutions in the ever–increasing competition for consumer patronage. Among the more recent arrivals on the American retailing scene are such innovative forms as supermarkets, discount houses, automatic selling, and planned shopping centers.

## SUPERMARKETS

The first supermarkets appealed to the consumer by offering lower prices than their chain-store competitors. The low prices were made possible by high turnover, low markups, low rents, and minimal services. Supermarkets first appeared in the early 1930s during the depth of the Great Depression. The pioneer supermarkets often began in vacant warehouses and through use of mass merchandise displays and heavy advertising succeeded in transacting what were then tremendous volumes of business. They featured low prices and operated on a cash-and-carry basis. That the stores were physically unattractive was of little importance; widespread unemployment and lack of purchasing power made the low-price appeal unusually attractive.

The first operators of supermarkets were independents, but by 1937 nearly all leading food chains were building supermarkets as fast as they could find suitable locations—and closing up three or four of their existing smaller stores to make way for each new supermarket. By this time, of course, the "cheapy" supermarkets that had located in vacant warehouses were rapidly giving way to more attractive supermarkets on sites more convenient to customers. As this new retailing concept caught on, with more and more businessmen recognizing the great profit possibility of supermarket operation, the revolution in food retailing gathered steam. Almost half a century later (in 1985) supermarkets were still growing, both in numbers and in dollar volume.

The basic characteristics and operating philosophy of the supermarket are indicated in its definition: a large retailing business unit selling mainly food and grocery items on the basis of low-margin appeal, high turnover, wide variety and assortments, self-service, and heavy emphasis on merchandise appeal. Supermarkets were devised originally as food-retailing businesses, and they continue to base most of their operations on the mass selling of food and grocery items. However, in order to widen their merchandise appeal and at the same time improve their profit potentials, increasing numbers of supermarkets add such nonfood lines as drugs, household utensils, hardware items, and garden supplies. This trend toward "scramble merchandising," together with the spreading habit of many consumers to shop only once or twice a week for groceries, has enabled the supermarket to increase the dollar value of the average order sold each customer on each trip to the store. To stimulate store traffic, the supermarket typically promotes its low prices through heavy advertising and mass merchandise displays; many also feature premium and trading stamp plans. Because the supermarket needs a high sales volume for profitable operation, large merchandise stocks are placed on the selling floor to achieve maximum merchandise exposure. Readily accessible reserve stocks and adequate check-out counters along with check-cashing facilities and a parking lot large enough to handle peak volumes of business also make for high volume.

Many buying practices of supermarkets are routine. Certain staples and nationally advertised items are carried by nearly all supermarkets. The responsibility for buying varies with the company's size and organizational structure. Large supermarket chains have specialized buyers whose function is to bargain with and make purchases from suppliers and store managers who requisition such items from warehouses. In smaller companies, a single executive often negotiates and makes all purchases. Managers of produce and meat departments often have authority to do their own buying. Supermarkets affiliated with retailer cooperatives and voluntary groups generally make most of their routine purchases through the wholesaling units of such organizations. Ordering and shelf-stocking of certain items, such as crackers and cookies, often are handled by manufacturers' salesreps under supervision of the owner, manager, or other individual responsible for buying. The ordering and stocking of nonfood lines often are taken care of by rack jobbers with minimum supervision by supermarket personnel.

## DISCOUNT HOUSES

A discount house is a retailing business unit that features consumer durable items and soft goods, competes on a low-price basis, and operates on a relatively low markup with a minimum of customer service. Most discount houses today are full-line, limited-service, promotional stores that closely resemble and actually are department stores. One of the early developments was the "closed door" or membership discount house that supposedly catered only to homogeneous groups such as union members, government employees, or teachers,and this approach is still used by some discounters. However, the term "discount house" is used increasingly to refer to any retail establishment whose main promotional emphasis is on selling nationally advertised merchandise at prices below those of conventional dealers. Table 10–1 describes the major categories of discounters.

In the late 1940s and early 1950s, then, circumstances were ripe for the establishment and growth of discount houses. Traditional appliance outlets such as department stores and small-appliance dealers had grown accustomed to high markups—often 35 to 40 percent of the retail price—and they were also used to selling at manufacturers' full "list" (or suggested) prices. Furthermore, appliance manufacturers had promoted their brand names to a point where the consumer was no longer concerned whether the retailer would guarantee the quality of the product. Discount-house operators found that they could sell appliances and other consumer durables profitably at prices as much as 30 percent below those of conventional outlets. The conventional retailers first maintained their own total sales and profits and for a few years did not put up much of a competitive battle. By the time they realized they had to meet or undercut discount-house prices, discount houses had already won strong customer loyalty.

By the early 1960s, the selection of merchandise offered by discount houses had broadened appreciably. To the original lines of hard goods, broad lines of soft goods—including clothing for men, women, and children, linen and bedding, and giftwares—had been added. Today, soft-goods lines normally occupy at least half of the selling floor space in the typical large discount house. The early hard-goods discount houses depended strongly upon brand, attracting customers by offering well-known brands at discount prices. Since brands are far less important in soft-goods lines, the newer discount houses with broadened lines of merchandise find it more difficult to

**TABLE 10–1** Kinds of retailers and some leading retail organizations engaged in discounting

1.  The Pre-pioneers(who were discounting before the discounters)
    Klein Department Stores, Inc.
    Ohrbach's
2.  The Pioneer Discounters
    Vornado, Inc.
    Spartan Industries
    Gibson Products Company
3.  Department Store Operators
    Allied Stores Corp.—Almart Stores
    J.C. Penney Company—Treasure Island Stores
    Mangel Stores Corp.—Shoppers Fair
    Federated Dept. Stores—Richway
4.  Variety Store Operators
    K-Mart
5.  Corporate Grocery Chain Stores
    Grand Union—Grand Way Division
    Stop and Shop—Bradlee's Division
    Kroger
6.  The Catalog Discounters
    Service Merchandise Company
    Unity Buying Service, Inc.

prove that their prices are really lower. They must instead build consumer confidence in their pricing structures.

Discount houses buy their merchandise stocks both indirectly from wholesale distributors and directly from manufacturers. Early in their growth, they did nearly all their buying from distributors. Sometimes, so-called "legitimate" retailers, not wanting to compete on a price basis, put pressure on distributors to stop supplying the discounters. When their supplies were cut off, discount houses would buy from other retailers, either legitimate or discount types, on a cost-plus basis, or work out exchange arrangements with other discount houses whose supplies had not yet been cut off.

As discount houses grew larger and became important outlets for many consumer durables and as chains of discount houses such as E.J. Korvette were organized, more and more manufacturers began to make direct sales to them. Discount houses now have as many direct-buying privileges as the largest chains. Although discount houses like chains are "hard" buyers, they are also "fast" buyers. Manufacturers appreciate a "fast" buyer when they find themselves with unexpectedly large inventories that more conventional retail outlets seem incapable of moving. In fact, one of the most distinguishing characteristics of the large, broad-line discount houses today is their strong emphasis on specially priced "distress" merchandise offered on a "one time" basis.

### Comparison of Supermarkets and Discount Houses

The supermarket and the discount house have a great deal in common. Both rely on the appeal of low prices, wide variety and assortments, self-service, and the handling of well-known brands of merchandise. Both seek to keep their prices down by combining operating expense economies with a high-volume business in fast-selling items. However, the supermarket is, by definition, a large retailing business, whereas the discount house may be any size—from very small to very large.

The larger discount house is the one most resembling the supermarket; as a matter of fact, some large discount homes feature grocery departments and offer tough competition to supermarkets. Because a discount house, like a supermarket, must transact a large total sales volume if it is to offer low prices, many operate their grocery departments at no profit or even a loss, considering them mainly a means of getting people into the store and of obtaining the required overall level of sales. Nearby supermarkets have found it difficult to match the discount house's "nonprofit" grocery policy—tough competition indeed!

## AUTOMATIC SELLING

Automatic selling or, as it is more commonly known, "automatic vending" involves the sale of goods or services to ultimate consumers through coin-operated machines. Whereas most automatic vending machines are still coin-operated, machines that will make change for one-dollar bills exist and are seeing expanding use. This procedure for changing currency is overcoming a long-time disadvantage of automatic vending—the inability to serve customers who do not have proper change. Automatic selling is not really a new retailing method; the Tutti-Frutti Company installed chewing-gum machines at elevated railroad stations in the 1880s. Historically, the major portion of vending-machine volume has come and still comes from soft drinks, cigarettes, and candy. Two of every 100 packs of cigarettes and more than one of four soft drinks are sold through vending machines.

Among the many attempts made to use vending machines for products other than soft drinks, candy, and cigarettes, those with packaged milk and ice cubes have been most successful. But many others have failed. Filene's, a Boston department store, once installed machines in the Boston Greyhound bus terminal selling goods ranging from men's hose and ties to ladies' panties and babies' rattles. After two years the experiment was abandoned as a failure. The Grand Union supermarket chain has conducted a round-the-clock supplementary vending operation for certain grocery staples on an experimental basis.

In 1966, a new type of vending machine designed to serve as a complete off-hours convenience food store was introduced. This machine which could stock as many as 100 items, both refrigerated and nonrefrigerated, would take orders involving a number of items, receive currency, and make change. They were being placed on an experimental basis in such locations as service stations where customers could have access at any time.

Although automatic selling still accounts for only a small percent of all retail sales—only $3.95 billion out of an estimated $733 billion total in 1972—vending machines are becoming increasingly important as outlets for many types of products. The National Automatic Merchandising Association estimates that there are 6,100 vending machine operators in the United States operating more than 6.5 million machines, selling products that literally range from soup to nuts. Vending machine volume expands with each new technological improvement in machine design and operation. The first coffee vending machine, for instance, was installed in 1946 and in 1958, such machines were selling coffee at an annual rate of $189 million. N.A.M.A. states that the average person spent about $22.50 during 1967 on purchases from these machines. The association predicted that annual vending volume would double again by 1970 (rise to the $9 billion level). It had already more than doubled (from $2.1 billion to $4.5 billion) from 1958 to 1967. Actually this estimate may be too conservative because judging from the rapid progress automation is making in other fields technological advances in vending machines are likely to come with increasing frequency in the years ahead.

## SHOPPING CENTERS

A *shopping center* is a group of commercial establishments, planned, developed, owned, and managed as a unit, with off-street parking provided on the property (in direct ratio to the building area) and related in location, gross floor area, and type of shops to the trade area served. Shopping centers are classified according to their size, which is determined by the trading area served and which, in turn, determines the kinds and variety of stores included.

### Neighborhood Centers

The *neighborhood center* is the smallest and most common type of shopping center. A supermarket is usually its focal point with the smaller stores geared to supply convenience goods and services (drug and hardware stores, beauty and barber shops, laundry and dry cleaning establishments, gasoline stations) to some 7,500 to 20,000 people living within six to ten minutes driving distance. Neighborhood centers may have only a dozen stores but the total area occupied, including parking space, is likely to range from four to ten acres. Generally, a neighborhood center is well-located if there are no strong competitors within about two miles.

### Community Centers

The *community center* is a larger operation and usually features a variety store or a small department store in addition to the supermarket and other small stores also found in the neighborhood center. Thus, the community center provides merchandise that includes shopping goods, such as clothing and home furnishings as well as convenience goods. The community center serves a market of from 20,000 to 100,000 persons and occupies from ten to thirty acres. According to experts a community center should not have strong competitors within a radius of three to four miles.

### Regional Centers

The *regional center* is the largest of all. Two or more large department stores provide its main drawing power that is further enhanced by 100 or more smaller stores. Some regional centers, though not all, include one or two supermarkets to add further to total shopping attractiveness. Shoppers, therefore, may select from a very wide range of goods. Regional centers are usually set up to serve 100,000 to 250,000 people living within a radius of five to six miles. Such centers more closely resembling central city shopping districts than the smaller centers are slowly but surely changing consumer shopping habits, because they reduce the need or urgency to shop in the central city. Regional centers have increasingly become competitive with each other as their number expands. Research has indicated that driving time to the center is highly influential in determining consumer shopping preference.

### Implications for Central City Shopping Districts

Because of their relatively generous parking facilities, easy accessibility by automobile, and nearness to the suburban, middle-income market, regional centers have virtually replaced the central city's downtown shopping district in most cities. It is estimated that there were roughly 375 regional shopping centers in 1981. Central city merchants press for measures to alleviate traffic congestion and for improved parking facilities, but they are not likely ever to match the convenience of the outlying shopping centers. However, an outlying center cannot equal the strategic location of the downtown area to serve a vast region, nor can it match the central city's vast range and selection of goods and services. It is not economically feasible, for instance, for regional centers to include stores selling many items bought mainly by the "carriage trade": bracelets and earrings in the $30,000 price class, fur pieces and coats selling at thousands of dollars, grand pianos, and collections of rare books. Few regional centers serve a large enough number of people who might want to buy such items; whereas central city shopping districts in most large cities because they draw trade from a much wider area, are fully capable of supporting such retail stores. Additionally, such items fall into the specialty goods classification; consumers are willing to make a special effort to locate stores that sell such items.

### Implications for the Manufacturer

For the manufacturer, the main significance of the planned shopping center lies in the fact that it is an integrated retail unit. Consumers view the center as a single large shopping convenience and not as a conglomeration of individual stores, each going its separate way. Recognizing this, shopping center developers sometimes restrict the classes of merchandise individual stores are permitted to handle. But in large centers controlled competition among stores handling similar merchandise lines is allowed. Thus, a manufacturer of lighting fixtures accustomed to selling its line through both hardware stores and department stores encounters three different distribution situations in shopping centers: (1) in some, the line is restricted to the hardware store, (2) in others, it is restricted to the department store, and (3) in still others, both the hardware store and the department store are free to handle the line. This same manufacturer may even find instances where shopping center branches of department stores are not permitted to handle its line even though the parent stores have stocked it for years. The great need for information about such situations explains why manufacturers should maintain close contact with their dealers operating or planning to operate stores in shopping centers. In addition, the extensive use of self-service in shopping centers has caused many manufacturers to redesign product packages and add more information to the labels. And with the growing importance of regional centers, manufacturers have been led to reexamine their advertising practices especially with respect to media aimed specifically at the trading areas of shopping centers.

### Franchising

A *franchise* is a conditional right given to a retailer to market the franchise company's products or services under the franchiser's banner. The recent and rapid growth of franchising leads some to regard it as a new retailing concept, but franchising started early in the twentieth century. Until the 1960s, franchising accounted for a small share of total U.S. retail sales, but during that decade many new industries, particularly service industries, adopted the franchising concept and its total impact increased enormously. By 1976 there were more than 445,000 franchised retail outlets in the United States whose total sales (some $212 billion) accounted for nearly one-third of all U.S. retail sales. Franchising has expanded greatly in fields such as prepared foods, dry cleaning, and equipment rentals. But automobiles and gasoline are still the two most important products sold mainly through franchised dealerships, and fast foods is third. (See Table 10–2.)

TABLE 10–2 Some franchising companies that achieved rapid growth during the 1960s and 1970s

Robo-Wash—automatic car wash
Western Auto—automobile parts and accessories
Budget Rent-a-Car—car rental
Snap-on Tools—auto repair tools and equipment
Long John Silver's—fish and chips
Dunkin' Donuts—doughnut shop
McDonald's Hamburgers—hamburgers and soft drinks
International House of Pancakes—pancakes
Colonel Sanders Kentucky Fried Chicken—chicken dinners
Burger King—hamburgers and drinks
Dairy Queen—soft ice cream, sandwiches, and soft drinks
Shakey's Pizza Parlor—pizzas and soft drinks
Mr. Steak—restaurants specializing in steak dinners
Arby's Restaurants—roast beef sandwiches
One Hour Martinizing—fast cash-and-carry dry cleaning
Culligan Soft-Water Service—water conditioning service
Mary Carter Paint Company—paint and painting supplies
Manpower, Inc.—temporary office help at low cost
General Business Services—bookkeeping and tax service for all small business
A to Z Rentals—tools and household equipment
Convenient Food Mart—convenience food stores
Aero-Mayflower—moving and trucking service
Servicemaster—carpet and furniture cleaning
Howard Johnson—restaurants and motels
Wendy's Old Fashioned Hamburgers—hamburgers

Franchise retailing is attractive to the franchising company mainly because it is a way of having many of the advantages of its own outlets without having to finance them. If a manufacturer sells its products through completely independent dealers, generally it has little or no control over their promotion or how they are retailed. If the same manufacturer, however, sells through franchised dealers, it retains control over marketing practices and can specify retailing procedures. This aspect of franchising can be an advantage for both parties, since a large manufacturer can afford to hire experienced professionals to design highly effective retail operating systems and procedures.

## THE "WHEEL OF RETAILING" HYPOTHESIS

Changes in retailing evolve rather gradually over the years. According to the "wheel of retailing" hypothesis, advanced by M. P. McNair, new forms of retailing institutions generally gain a foothold on the retail scene through emphasizing price appeal made possible by low operating costs inherent in the new form of institution. Over time the new institutions upgrade their facilities and services necessitating added investments and higher operating costs. At some point they emerge as high-cost, high-price retailers, vulnerable to newer forms of retailers who, in turn, go through a similar metamorphosis. Mail-order houses and department stores, for example, originally were low-cost retailers soliciting business mainly through price appeal, but eventually the "wheel" turned and they became vulnerable to chain store systems, discount houses, and other newer institutions. As another example, conventional supermarkets in the late 1960s encountered new competition from the new "food discount stores," which in line with the "wheel" notion were featuring "lower prices" made possible by lower operating costs due to stripped-down service.

## *CONCLUSION*

Five fairly recent innovations in retailing have appeared and spread in an effort to serve the changing needs and buying habits of the American consumer more effectively and more efficiently. Supermarkets pioneered in introducing such operating policies and procedures as cash-and-carry retailing, self-service, convenient check-cashing facilities, scramble merchandising, and adequate and easy customer parking. Discount houses found ways to cut operating expenses and to offer consumers brand-name merchandise at prices lower than at more conventional outlets offering extensive customer services. Advances in automatic selling made it possible for consumers to buy an expanding number of items, mostly convenience goods, at more locations and with fewer restrictions as to times of purchase. Shopping centers have progressively reduced but probably will never eliminate entirely the need or urgency of consumers to shop in central city areas. A fifth method of retailing, franchising, has drastically increased in importance during recent years. The process of evolution and change in the forms of retailing institutions and in the nature of their operations can be expected to continue in the twin drives to serve the consumer more effectively and with increasing efficiency.

We have placed particular stress in Chapters 7 through 10 on the dynamic nature of marketing institutions. In the past 200 years the rate of institutional change has greatly accelerated. The general store and the general merchandise wholesaler, for instance, evolved, reached their peaks of importance, and gradually have almost faded away. The department store, the mail-order house, and chain-store systems appeared, scored great successes, and then settled back as significant but not dominating features of the retail scene. Newer institutions, such as the rack jobber, the supermarket, the planned shopping center, and the discount house probably have not yet grown to full maturity. Traditional institutions such as the general line wholesaler and the independent store have had to modernize their operating methods in order to stay in business.

Many of these changes in marketing institutions and their operating characteristics represent a continuation of long-range trends; a few represent a reversal of previous trends. They have come about in almost all cases as the result of attempts to adjust operating methods more closely to the often changing needs and expectations of the market. The process of institutional evolution and change can be expected to continue, perhaps at an even more rapid rate. Only those institutions capable of making adjustments to the dynamic characteristics of markets are likely to survive for long.

# 11

# PRODUCTS

---

A product is both "what a seller has to sell" and "what a buyer has to buy." It is more than a mere physical commodity, since any enterprise with something to sell, tangible or not, is selling a product. A laundry, for instance, sells the service of cleaning clothes and is just as surely engaged in selling a product as the retail stores that originally sold the clothes it cleans. Any firm that "has something to sell," in fact, sells services as part of that something, even though we may think of it as dealing in tangible goods rather than services *per se*. Furthermore, "what a buyer buys" is an item that he expects to provide certain physical and psychological satisfactions.

Formally defined, then, a *product* is a bundle of utilities consisting of various product features and accompanying services. The bundle of utilities (i.e., the physical and psychological satisfactions that the buyer receives) is provided by the seller when it sells a particular combination of product features and associated services. When a man buys a suit from a clothing store, for example, he buys not only the garment itself but the clerk's assistance and advice, the store's alteration service, the prestige of the store's and maker's labels, perhaps "charge and delivery" services, and the privilege of returning the item for refund or allowance should it not yield the expected satisfaction. The clothing store sells not only men's suits but related services that customers regard as bundles providing both physical and psychological satisfactions during consumption.

In marketing, "good" is used as a synonym for "product." This is in line with both long-standing business usage and well-established academic practice. In the following discussion, as throughout this entire book, "good" and "product" are used interchangeably.

## CONSUMERS' GOODS AND INDUSTRIAL GOODS

Depending upon the use for which it is destined, each good is classed as either a consumer or an industrial good. Consumers' goods are destined for final consumption by ultimate consumers and households. Television sets, perfumes and lipsticks, and boxed candy are all consumers' goods. Industrial goods are destined for use in the commercial production of other goods or in connection with carrying on some business or institutional activity. Iron ore, machine tools, and electronic computers are all industrial goods.

Actually, not many goods can be classified *exclusively* as consumer goods or industrial goods. Typing paper, for example, is used both for business and personal correspondence and, therefore, is both a consumer and industrial good. Depending upon the circumstances surrounding its use, the same article can be either a consumer or an industrial good.

Why is this apparently artificial distinction important? Because consumers' and industrial goods are bought not only for different purposes but—of greater marketing significance—their purchasers characteristically take different approaches in making buying decisions. Consequently, marketing situations and problems also vary, depending upon whether the item is marketed as a consumer or an industrial good.

## CONSUMERS' GOODS

The variety of consumers' goods is almost endless, literally ranging from A to Z—apples to zippers—and including such diverse items as candy bars, home swimming pools, grand pianos, and frozen TV dinners. So many different consumers' goods exist that it is clearly impractical to analyze each individually. Several classification systems have been devised to facilitate marketing analysis, but the "traditional" classification presented below is the most widely used.

### "Traditional" Classification of Consumers' Goods

Sometime prior to 1923, Professor Melvin T. Copeland of the Harvard Business School, a pioneer marketing teacher, set up what is now known as the "traditional" system for classifying consumers' goods. Copeland based his classification on differences in consumer buying attitudes and behavior. Under his system, three classes of consumers' goods are identified: convenience, shopping, and specialty.

*Convenience Goods.* Items the consumer buys frequently, immediately, and with minimum shopping effort are *convenience goods.* Examples include: cigarettes, candy and chewing gum, magazines and newspapers, gasoline, drugs, and most grocery items. Note that these are all nondurables; that is, they are consumed or "used up" rapidly. Hence, consumers buy them frequently and normally neither postpone their purchases nor make them much in advance of the consumption time. Note, too, that, in buying convenience goods, habit dominates the consumer's behavior. Through force of habit, it is easy for consumers to make buying decisions. In buying cigarettes and gasoline, for example, they know which brands they prefer, and the retail outlets where they can be bought. Little or no conscious deliberation is required. The typical consumer minimizes the time and effort devoted to buying convenience goods.

In buying most convenience goods, the consumer rarely bothers to compare competing offerings on the bases of price and quality. "It isn't worth shopping around for" expresses the typical consumer's attitude. However, if the price or quality of a convenience good, such as of a certain brand of bread, gets too far out of line with competing brands, many consumers revise their buying decisions. The consumer's possible gains in such situations outweigh the costs in time and effort.

Seeking to minimize shopping time and effort, the consumer buys convenience goods at "convenient" locations. A "convenient" location may be near home, on the way to work, or near the place of work. Recognizing that consumers will not go far out of their way to buy, marketers of convenience goods make them available for sale in numerous and diverse outlets.

*Shopping Goods.* Items the consumer selects and buys after making comparisons on such bases as suitability, quality, price, and style are *shopping goods.* Whenever a substantial number of consumers habitually make such shopping comparisons before they select and buy an item, it is considered a shopping good. Examples of goods that most consumers appear to buy in this way include millinery, furniture, rugs, dress goods, women's ready-to-wear and shoes, and households appliances. Before buying these items, consumers shop around and compare different stores' offerings. Notice that the typical shopping good is bought infrequently, is "used up" slowly, and that consumers often are in positions to defer or advance the purchase date. Thus, they can afford to devote considerable time and effort to the buying decision. In other words, consumers believe that the possible gains from making shopping comparisons exceed the costs in terms of time and effort.

Not every consumer uses the same bases of comparison in buying shopping goods. In some cases, a consumer shops primarily to find something "suitable"; for example, the person who looks for drapes to match a particular carpet or upholstery fabric. In shopping for clothing, some women consider style the most important factor, whereas others are mainly "price shoppers." In shopping for children's shoes, these same women may consider quality the most important basis for comparison. The bases of comparison and their relative importance vary both with the product and the shopper.

Branding is much less important for shopping goods than for convenience goods. In some instances, the consumer undoubtedly is willing to pay more for a branded shopping good; but the more definitely a good is a shopping good, the less he is willing to pay for the prestige of the brand name.

Typically, consumers devote considerable time and effort to the buying of shopping goods, so shopping goods marketers can manage with fewer retail outlets than can convenience goods marketers. The shopping goods marketer places great emphasis on having its goods for sale in outlets where consumers are likely to look for such items rather than on having them available in every store.

**Specialty Goods.** There are items for which significant numbers of consumers are habitually willing to make a special purchasing effort. Specialty goods must possess unique characteristics or have a degree of brand identification or both. Examples of items usually bought as specialty goods are stereo components, fancy foods, stamps and coins for collectors, and "prestige" brands of men's suits. The consumer already knows the product or brand wanted and is willing to make a special purchasing effort to find the outlet handling it. In reaching the buying decision, consumers do not compare the desired specialty good with others, as in the case of shopping goods. However, as specialty goods are often in the luxury price class, consumers may take considerable time in deciding to start the special search required.

Specialty goods are found in low as well as high price ranges. For instance, to obtain a stamp collection's missing stamp worth a dime or quarter may require nearly as much purchasing effort as to locate the rarity worth hundreds of dollars, Although less money is involved in one case than in the other, both prices are high relative to those of other articles without such unique characteristics. Consumers exert special purchasing efforts to locate such items, and *prices* are secondary considerations in buying decisions.

However, an item does not have to be difficult to locate to make it a specialty good. The consumer who wants to buy Bayer Aspirin and will not accept a substitute can find the brand in nearly all drugstores and most grocery stores. An item is a specialty good if many buyers are willing to make a special purchasing effort, not that they always have to. Marketing practices of many manufacturers of specialty goods make it unnecessary for consumers to exert special purchasing efforts. They make their brands easy to locate, thus making it easy for consumers to buy.

## INDUSTRIAL GOODS

Industrial users exhibit more uniform patterns of buying behavior than do ultimate consumers. Different industrial buyers are remarkably alike in the ways they go about making buying decisions for similar products. The automobile manufacturer's approach to the buying of machine tools, for example, closely resembles those taken not only by competitors but by other buyers of machine tools. Industrial goods, therefore, readily lend themselves to a classification system based on the uses to which they are to be put. There are four major categories: (1) production facilities and equipment, (2) production materials, (3) production supplies, and (4) management materials.

### Production Facilities and Equipment

This category includes installations, minor equipment, and plants and buildings.

*Installations.* These are major items of capital equipment (such as factory turret lathes and commercial laundry dryers) essential to an industrial user's operations. Buying an installation involves investment of a comparatively large sum, so buying decisions generally require approval of both top management and the department head concerned. Because of this "multiple influence" on purchase decisions, a seller of installations commonly must convince several individuals before actually getting the order, the negotiating period often extending over considerable time. Some installations are designed and manufactured especially to buyers' specifications; for example, installations used in cane sugar processing and refining; salespeople selling such items need technical backgrounds or training or both. Because of the characteristically high unit value, most installations are sold directly to industrial users by the manufacturers.

*Minor Equipment.* This subcategory includes pieces of equipment (such as work benches, lift trucks, and hand tools) that the industrial user uses in producing its product or service. Buying procedures are routine, ordinarily consisting simply of the industrial user's purchasing executive ordering according to specifications set by the department requesting the item. Because of the relatively high purchase frequency, marketers of minor equipment make certain that their sales reps call frequently on prospects. Listing in industrial catalogs, trade journal advertising, and direct-mail promotion make up the usual program for maintaining representation at the buyer's plant between sales calls.

*Plants and Buildings.* These are necessary to an industrial user's operation and represent sizable capital investments. Thus, the plants and buildings subcategory somewhat resembles the installations subcategory; however, it also resembles the minor equipment subcategory since plants and buildings are supplementary to, rather than directly used in, the production of the industrial user's output. Plants and buildings are not usually marketed as complete units, though some construction engineering firms specialize in such projects. In all major respects, industrial users approach the buying (or constructing) of plants or buildings in the same way that they go about buying installations.

### Production Materials

This category includes raw materials, semimanufactured goods, and fabricating parts.

*Raw Materials.* These are the basic products of farms, mines, fisheries, and forests that enter into the production of more finished goods. Buying procedures for raw materials vary, depending upon the proportion their costs bear to total production costs and upon market conditions. If raw materials cost represents only a small part of total production costs, the suppliers are middlemen and the buying procedures routine. But when raw material cost accounts for a large part of a finished good's total cost, high-ranking purchasing executives deal directly with raw material producers. Similarly, if a raw material's market is characterized by stable supply and price conditions, relatively low-level executives use routine purchasing procedures. But when raw material supplies and prices vary erratically, highly skilled and high-ranking executives do the buying and seek to adapt procurement procedures to changing market conditions.

*Semimanufactured Goods.* These are items—such as steel, glass, and lumber—that are one industry's end product and another's basic manufacturing material. Compared with raw material prices, semimanufactured good prices are relatively stable, so their purchase is more routine. Since most producers of semimanufactured goods are large companies, they sell direct to large industrial users. Where semimanufactured goods are also sold to numerous small industrial users, marketing channels contain one or more levels of middlemen.

*Fabricating Parts.* These are manufactured goods which, without any substantial change in form, are incorporated into or assembled into a more complex and finished product. Storage batteries, spark plugs, and tires for an automobile are examples. Industrial users buy fabricating parts, made to their own specifications, directly from the manufacturers. Single sales contracts are negotiated for periods of several months to a year, and the relationship between seller and buyer is generally a long-term one. These negotiations are directed by high executives of both buying and selling companies.

### Production Supplies

These products are essential to industrial users' business operations but do not become part of finished products. Included are such items as fuel oil, coal, sweeping compound, and wiping cloths. Purchase of production supplies is a routine responsibility of the industrial user's purchasing executive, who usually buys them through middlemen rather than directly from makers. But where an item is used in large quantities, as a public utility uses coal in steamplant generation of electricity, long-term purchase contracts, similar to those used in buying fabricating parts, are directly negotiated by top-ranking executives of buying and selling firms.

### Management Materials

This category covers office equipment and supplies. Pieces of office equipment of high value, such as electronic computers and data-processing systems, are usually leased rather than bought outright but, in either case, decisions are reached in essentially the same way as those on production installations. Purchase or lease of major office equipment items involves substantial sums; hence, decisions require approval of both top management and the department head concerned, and the purchasing department merely handles the needed "paper work."

Typewriters, desk calculators, and similar pieces of equipment are bought by the purchasing department as needed, on requisitions originating in the "using" departments, often with brands and models being determined by preferences of typists and clerks. Pencil sharpeners, staplers, and other low-unit value articles of office equipment, as well as such office supplies as stationery and typewriter ribbons, are bought routinely—the purchasing department taking the initiative in ordering and generally carrying a stock on hand.

## PRODUCT LIFE CYCLES

Products, like people, have a certain length of life during which they pass through certain stages. From the time a product idea is conceived, during its development and up to its market introduction, a product is in various prenatal stages (i.e., it is going through various product development phases). Its life begins with its market introduction, it goes through a period during which its market grows rapidly, eventually it reaches market maturity, afterwards its market declines, and finally its life ends.

### Industry Product Life Cycle

Figure 11–1 is a visualization of a product life cycle for an industry (i.e., firms marketing directly competing items). Three curves are shown: (1) total market sales (this is the "industry product life cycle"), (2) total

**Figure 11–1** The industry product life cycle

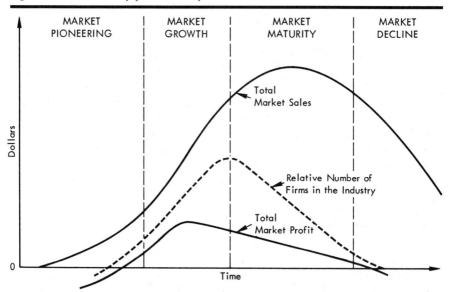

market profit (notice how this declines while sales are still rising), and (3) the relative number of competitors (notice how this continues to go up for a time after profits have turned down).

The exact path traced by the product life cycle varies. For some, like the "hula hoop," the product proves a fad and has a short life cycle, perhaps only a month or so. For others, such as plumbing fixtures, life cycles span decades. In between are most products with life cycles ranging from a few months (e.g., fashion apparel) to several years (e.g., washing machines and home freezers). All products are at some stage in their life cycles at any particular moment in time.

Life cycle curves also exist for each company's individual products Figure 11–2 shows a life cycle curve for a product's sales by the company doing the innovating. During the "market pioneering" stage of the industry product life cycle, one company—the innovator—may be the whole industry. But by the "market growth" stage, the innovator shares the market with several competitors. Hence, while Figure 11–1 is an industry curve, its market pioneering stage represents one or, at most, a few companies. Only coincidentally does the shape of an individual company's product life cycle resemble that of the entire industry since, after the market pioneering stage, the industry cycle is a composite of several companies' experiences. Furthermore, managerial action can cause a particular company's product life cycle to vary from that of the "typical" company in the industry—e.g., management may drop a product at any time, thus terminating its life cycle insofar as that company is concerned.

**Figure 11–2** Product life cycle—innovating company

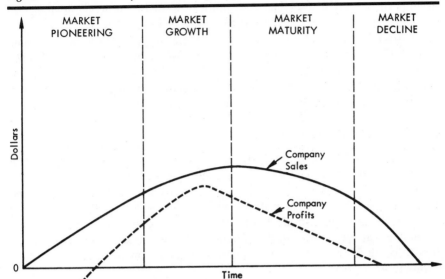

The market pioneering stage is one of heavy promotion, of securing initial distribution, and of ironing out product difficulties. Insofar as possible, marketing channels are kept adequately stocked with the product. But, if the product is destined for success, the innovator generally finds that demand exceeds what can be brought to market. Advertising and promotion are directed toward development of primary demand for the product.

During the market growth stage, competition increases rapidly, and manufacturing and distribution efficiency are important keys to marketing success. Competing firms use selective demand advertising, each emphasizing its own brand's advantages. At first personal selling is directed toward getting new outlets and keeping them stocked but later shifts to "selling against the competition." Competition ultimately becomes severe enough that if buyers cannot easily find particular brands, they readily accept substitutes.

During the market maturity stage, stiffening competition forces profits lower: prices come down and marketing expenditures rise. Sales continue to increase but at a decreasing rate, eventually leveling off with market saturation. Supply exceeds demand for the first time, making demand stimulation essential, and competitors heavily promote their brands, emphasizing subtle differences. Because of the squeeze put on profits and growing similarity of competing brands, dealer support becomes increasingly critical while most dealers now refuse to stock more than a few brands. During later phases of this stage, replacement sales dominate the market. Industry sales tend to stabilize, causing the competitive structure to solidify.

The market decline stage is characterized by either the product's gradual displacement by some new innovation or by an evolving change in consumer buying behavior. Industry sales drop off and the number of competitors shrinks. With production overcapacity, price becomes the main competitive weapon, and drastic reductions occur in advertising and other promotional expenditures. Under these conditions, most managements shift their attention to other products, gradually phasing out the declining product as its outlook grows increasingly bleak.

## PRODUCT INNOVATION

Throughout modern industry, product innovation receives increasing emphasis and attention. The underlying reason is that markets are highly dynamic. What was a profitable product yesterday may not be tomorrow. Furthermore, successful new products command substantially higher profit margins than mature or declining products. Successful new products are profitable—at least for a while—mainly because it takes time for competitors to come up with their own versions, enter the market, and eventually compete on a price basis.

Most companies face the inevitable choice of product innovation and improvement or of gradually fading from the market. Most wagon and buggy manufacturers saw their market disappear as the automobile replaced the horse. Yet, Studebaker, a wagon maker, recognized the need for change and successfully shifted to auto manufacturing and, much later, finding itself no longer able to compete profitably in the automobile market, moved into other product fields.

### Need for Product Objectives

A company advances toward its overall objectives mainly through acceptance of its products in the marketplace. Therefore, product objectives, derived directly from the company objectives, give direction to product innovation. They summarize the characteristics products should have in order that the company will actually "be in the business it wants to be in." Product objectives, of course, apply to all products, both new and old.

Under the marketing concept, a company's product objectives are oriented toward the customers and their wants. They state explicitly that the company is engaged in servicing certain needs of specific types of customers. For example, one product objective reads "to develop, manufacture, and market products meeting the heating and cooling needs of industrial and commercial establishments of all sizes." With this objective, note carefully, the company does not limit itself to specific products, rather it limits its market to given types of customers with particular needs. As the market and its needs change, the company adjusts its products accordingly.

## Need for Product Policies

Product policies are the general rules management sets up to guide itself in making product decisions. They should derive directly from, and be wholly consistent with, product objectives. If a product objective, for example, states that "this company desires to make and market products requiring only a minimum of service after their purchase by consumers," then a product policy (or policies) is needed to spell out how this objective will be attained. Generally, product policies take the form of a series either of short definitions or of questions arranged as a check list, and the most important objectives for most companies are sales volume, market share, and dollar profit.

## Planning New Products

While the details of new product planning vary with the company, generally they cover four major phases.

Phase One involves the allocation of new product planning responsibility. Since it is a nonroutine activity that can be easily overlooked, product planning responsibility must be delegated to a specific individual or group within the organization.

Phase Two involves creation of new product ideas. The planners evaluate the extent and importance of identified market needs (determined perhaps through marketing research and analysis of buyer behavior) and appraise the extent to which products fulfill them. They also evaluate the company's capabilities with respect to scientific knowledge and technological skills in terms of possible new products.

Phase Three focuses on more thoroughly investigating the competitive market situation and company resource with respect to each product idea developed in Phase One. Market research is critical during this phase since market potentials and competitive marketing methods can reveal, among other things, the size and type of marketing organization required. Analysis of company resources indicates the adequacy of plant capacity, product service facilities, marketing channels, engineering abilities, and other human resources. This phase ends with selection among alternative "product candidates," based on comparisons of each against specific product objectives, such as relative profitability, target market segment, and opportunity to attain product leadership.

Phase Four relates to actual development of the new product. A program is put together for management and execution of the development project. This includes, among other aspects, an overall plan for the product's eventual marketing.

## STRUCTURING THE PRODUCT LINE(S)

Controlling the composition of a company's product line(s) is a constant managerial concern. Structuring requires numerous decisions on adding new products, bringing out new versions of old products, and discontinuing individual items.

### Adding New Products

*Product Line Extension.*   When final buyers regard several products as a related group or line, management must decide whether to produce a "partial" or "complete" line. Consumers, for example, buy both kitchen and laundry appliances in the same retail outlets and are sometimes looking for several appliances at the same time. The manufacturer's decision to extend its offerings within a product line should result from evaluation of several factors. It must be financially able to add new items. It should analyze the likely effect of adding to the line on the profits of existing line members. If it finds that numerous buyers prefer to buy two or more products at the same time (as often happens with "matching appliances"), a more complete line may increase sales of present products. Similarly, as the line is extended, each item's marketing costs should be reduced, since little more promotion or selling effort is needed to sell the line than to sell an individual item.

Against these potential gains should be balanced the new item's probabilities of success. Does the company have the production, engineering, and general management "know-how" to develop and produce new products as good as its present products? Management also must evaluate the effect of the proposed additions on the reputations of present products; if buyers consider a new item inferior to those already in the line, the entire line's reputation may suffer.

*Diversification into Related Product Lines.*   Companies add related product lines for two main reasons: (1) to capitalize further on company "know-how" in serving particular market segments, and (2) to reduce the risk of obsolescence in the present product line: market segments do not disappear suddenly, but demand for a product line sometimes does.

How far a company should diversify into related product lines depends on various considerations. Will related product diversification reduce unit sales and distribution costs? Can the sales force sell the related line effectively? What promotional expenses are required? Who are the new competitors, what strategies do they employ, and what advantages do they have? Will a beneficial "halo" effect from the present line carry over to the related line? Can the items in the new line actually be developed, produced at reasonable cost, and differentiated in ways attractive to potential buyers? This type of analysis should permit management to estimate the profitability of adding a related product line.

*Diversification into Unrelated Product Lines.* This approach involves adding unrelated product lines sold to entirely different markets. Companies adopt it for reasons such as unexpected research breakthroughs or discoveries of profitable opportunities to develop products for new markets. Proposals for unrelated product diversification merit careful investigation, since both product and market are entirely new to the company. Generally, a company is well advised first to "fill out" its present line, then diversify into related lines sold to the same markets, and only then consider diversifying into new markets with new products.

*Product Replacement.* This defensive approach to new product addition aims at retaining the level of sales now coming from a particular market segment where an older product's sales are being endangered by competitors' new products serving the same uses. Examples of new products that replaced old ones are numerous; a few of them are: automobiles replaced carriages, diesel locomotives replaced steam locomotives, jet planes replaced piston-driven aircraft, the transistor replaced the vacuum tube, and the ball point pen replaced the fountain pen. For companies having products in the market maturity stage, new products should be "waiting in the wings," ready for market introduction at the proper times.

### Introducing New Versions of Old Products

*New Models.* Through introducing new models of old products, management seeks to stimulate sales. New models are not, strictly speaking, new products; they are variations of established products—new sizes, colors, designs, and the like. Management's hope in bringing out a new model generally is that it will come closer to "fitting" what present buyers really prefer.

Introducing new models is a regular feature of producer strategy for many products today, the regularity and frequency of model switching varying among industries and individual firms. Some switch models only when justified by significant product improvements. Others introduce new models on a regular, periodic basis even though changes are superficial. In competing with the American automobile industry, strongly committed to annual model changes, foreign auto imports have successfully competed under a strategy of changing the model *only* when technological improvements justify it.

*Planned Obsolescence.* Product improvement, whether real or contrived, provides a means for accelerating the rate of obsolescence. This is most important in mature industries whose markets have reached, or are approaching, saturation. In these industries, a manufacturer competes not only with other manufacturers, but with the products all have sold in the past. If a firm depends solely on physical obsolescence, gradual wear, and deterioration, its prospects for sales and profits are limited.

Products in consumers' possession can be made obsolete in two ways: by improving performance characteristics of new models and by altering consumers' concepts of the acceptability of models they already own. The auto industry's introduction of automatic transmissions exemplifies the first types of created obsolescence, and the regular change in auto body style is an example of the second. The term *planned obsolescence* describes both types.

Planned obsolescence of the second type is highly controversial. Some writers charge that it is economically wasteful, and many businessmen call it "wasteful" and "contrary to the country's best interests." Proponents defend it as a necessary support to a high-level economy and point out that the criticisms are based on the moral judgment that a desire for the latest thing is socially bad. Supporters feel that wanting "something new and different" is socially good. From the consumer's standpoint, creation of obsolescence through real product improvements generally is acceptable, but shifts in standards of acceptability (as in appearance) are more controversial. Yet, fashion, having been part of western culture for centuries, is not the creation of marketers.

***Trading Up and Trading Down.*** These two approaches involve bringing out changed versions of a product and altering the nature and direction of promotion. Generally, companies trading up or down do one or the other, but not both at the same time.

A company trades up when it adds a higher-priced, more prestigious product version with the main goal of increasing sales of a present lower-priced version. Thus, the emphasis is more on improving sales to an old market segment than on cultivating a new market segment. Ford Motor Company, for example, introduced the Thunderbird (a prestigious, relatively high-priced car) hoping to increase sales of the lower-priced Ford. Thunderbird was promoted separately, but the company made sure that prospective buyers of lower-priced cars knew that it was Ford-made. Companies trading up anticipate that a "halo" effect will carry over from the new prestige item to the older lower-priced and less prestigious item.

A company trades down when it adds a lower-priced product version in the hope that buyers who would not, or could not, buy a higher-priced version will now buy the new version because it carries some of the same prestige. In trading down, then, emphasis is on tapping a new market segment, one not tapped effectively earlier because the original version had too high a price. For example, Ford Motor Company, after successfully trading up with the Thunderbird, saw an opportunity to tap a market segment of "people who would like to have a Thunderbird but could not afford it." The traded-down version was the Mustang, a car resembling the Thunderbird but much lower-priced, that became an outstanding success.

### Product Line Simplification

Product proliferation is partially preventable through high selectivity in adding new products and models, but pressures always exist to offer greater variety. Marketing managers, in particular, frequently push for more complete lines and more models, as this helps them to satisfy widely varying market preferences. Production managers fight to keep product lines narrow and the number of models minimal, as this helps them hold manufacturing costs down and simplifies production scheduling.

Under increasingly competitive conditions, market pressures force manufacturers to offer greater and greater product variety; increasing consumer sophistication and increasing market segmentation also contribute to product proliferation. Well-designed procedures for screening new product ideas improve the chances that additions will be profitable but do not insure against product failures. Furthermore, today's successes become tomorrow's failures—products are born, grown, mature, and die, as the product life cycle concept indicates. Market and organizational pressures push in the direction of product proliferation; counterpressures are needed both to control new additions and to weed out "tired" products and models.

Product line simplification requires continual review of the line and the discontinuation of items not contributing directly (in their own right) or indirectly (e.g., as a repair part) to profits. However, simplification involves more than merely determining present profitability. Sometimes, a change in price, promotion, or marketing channels can make a currently unprofitable item profitable. At other times, dealers and customers expect, even demand, a "full-line" offering, preventing the weeding out of *all* unprofitable items. Some items, such as repair and replacement parts, may be unprofitable in their own right, yet have selling value and should be retained. Other unprofitable items must be kept in order to sell profitable items (e.g., when buyers regard a group of items as a "product system," as they do razors and blades).

Under some conditions, too, it is desirable to drop a profitable product. Management might discontinue an item, for instance, if the same resources would yield more profit if used in behalf of another item with a brighter future. Likewise, a profitable item might be dropped if it causes sales reps and/or dealers to divert their efforts from still more profitable items. In general, then, any item is a likely candidate for discontinuation if the company does not have the needed resources and/or talents to capitalize fully on its potential profitability. The grid in Table 11–1 shows the combination of product strategies and marketing strategies to improve profitability.

## PRODUCT QUALITY

Different kinds of marketers have varying degrees of latitude in determining product quality. Marketers of the products of farms, forests, fisheries, and mines, can exert little control over quality, defining it mainly

**TABLE 11-1** Grid of possible combinations of product-market strategies to improve profitability

| PRODUCT STRATEGY<br>MARKET STRATEGY | NO PRODUCT CHANGE | PRODUCT CHANGE | NEW PRODUCT |
|---|---|---|---|
| No market change | 1.<br>Design simplification<br><br>Greater integration—marketing, production, etc.—or "reverse integration" | 4.<br>Product line simplification and product discontinuance<br><br>New models<br><br>Planned obsolescence | 7.<br>Replacement of old product |
| Improved market | 2.<br>Remerchandising (e.g., branding change, change in guarantee, change in service policy, packaging change, etc.) | 5.<br>Product customization<br><br>Product systems | 8.<br>Product line extension<br><br>Diversification (related fields) |
| New market | 3.<br>New uses<br><br>New users | 6.<br>Market extension (e.g., trading up or trading down) | 9.<br>Product mix diversification (unrelated fields) |

*Source:* Cundiff, E.W., Still, R.R., Govoni, N.A.P., *Fundamentals of Modern Marketing,* (Englewood Cliffs, N.J.: Prentice-Hall, Inc., 1985), p. 145.

through grading. Even for some manufacturers, the limits of control over quality are narrow; a chemical company, for example, cannot change basic compounds; it can affect quality only to the extent its processing operations result in "absence of foreign elements." For most producers of manufactured goods, however, there is considerable latitude in determining product quality; most have a great deal of power to influence quality with respect to durability, uniformity, reliability, and other product features.

In its simplest terms, quality may be expressed as a function of price. Thus, if a product's price is high, its quality can also be high; and if its price is low, its quality will be necessarily lower. But, this is an oversimplification, since it is common, for example, for an item to compete successfully, at the same prices, against similar items of higher quality—provided that the lower-quality item is promoted more effectively. Nevertheless, promotion cannot compensate for really great quality differences. Effectiveness of the distributive network also influences the impact of quality differences. It is sometimes economically difficult to introduce a new brand of superior quality—even at equal prices—in competition with brands already enjoying strong demand and good relationships with middlemen.

To the extent that buyers equate price with quality, management should make its quality decisions in terms of the factors affecting price, particularly those of demand and supply. Both price and quality decisions should result from analyses of the nature of demand and competition at varying prices. Obsolescence is another factor limiting both quality and price. A rapid rate of product obsolescence tends to set an upper limit on quality, at least to the extent that quality affects durability. Many consumers will not pay more for a refrigerator designed to last for twenty years, if they believe the model will become obsolete in five or ten years.

## PRODUCT SERVICE

For many industrial products, service policies are indispensable; for some consumer products, they are important elements in marketing programs. For complex industrial products, such as computers, it is necessary to provide not only installation and repair services but, in most cases, training for customers' personnel. For many products, especially consumer items, the need for service is not so clear-cut. Nevertheless, if an item is a consumer durable or semidurable with a comparatively high price and a relatively low purchase frequency, it may be difficult to consummate sales unless the manufacturer or dealer, or both, provide service.

Manufacturers, however, sometimes overestimate the importance of offering certain services. Appliance makers, for example, at first were reluctant to sell through discount houses, mainly because these retailers did not provide repair and installation services. When these manufacturers learned to their surprise that many consumers were willing and able to handle both installation and servicing, their opposition to discount house distribution faded. The final decision over what customer services to offer should flow from an appraisal of customer needs and expectations.

Appropriate service policies and practices not only facilitate initial sales but also help in keeping products sold, stimulating repeat sales, and building customer good will. There is no place in a marketing program for policies that fail to accomplish these aims. Each customer service offered, or proposed, should be evaluated against two criteria: the extent to which it produces desired results and whether it contributes to net profit.

## PACKAGING

There are many reasons for packaging a product—to protect it, to differentiate and identify it, to make it more salable, or to improve handling convenience, to name only a few. Coal needs no protection against damage from the elements and handling, whereas photographic film needs protection from exposure to light; these are extreme cases, but the need for protective packaging of almost any product is usually just as clear.

If a product is packaged for brand differentiation and identification, it should remain packaged until purchased by the final buyer. Bulk packaging, removable before the final buyer buys, is for protection or handling convenience. Five-pound bags of sugar, for example, reach the supermarket inside a large paper bag—the small bags are designed for brand differentiation and identification, the large bag for protection and handling convenience.

When the brand name can be placed directly on the product, as with appliances, packaging for brand identification is not needed. But, if a product is hard to differentiate, as with nails, packaging may be the only way to differentiate it and secure, perhaps, some brand identification. For most consumer products, however, packaging is the main way to identify the brand at the point of purchase. The package, like a promotional display, relates the product to the producer's advertising and makes consumers aware of its availability in retail outlets. Beyond this, marketers expect the package to furnish consumers with needed product information and to provide the extra push at the point of purchase so often required to propel consumers into buying.

### Package Design

When packaging is primarily protective, design decisions are technical and involve comparative strengths, costs of materials, and shapes. When a package is primarily a promotional device, its elements must attract consumers' attention, hold their interest, and build their desire to buy. Package color, size, and shape are all important promotionally so decisions on these elements should reflect the target market segment's preferences. With more and more products being sold through self-service outlets, the promotional aspect of package design becomes increasingly important, since in these stores the package carries the promotional burden it formerly shared with sales clerks.

Package design must also consider convenience in product handling, by both middlemen and consumers. The shape should permit easy display on retail store fixtures. It should make it easy for the consumer to take the product home and to store it. The six-pack beer carton is an excellent example of a package that facilitates handling and stimulates consumption by increasing the unit of purchase.

### Package Size

The package-size decision evolves from consideration of several factors; the two most important are the consuming unit, and the rate of consumption. Cigarettes, candy bars, and toothbrushes are consumed by individuals and are packaged in units for individual rather than group consumption. Cake mixes and gelatin desserts are consumed by household or family units and are packaged for group consumption. Dry breakfast cereals are packaged both ways: in family boxes nd individual-serving packs.

Findings on the consumption unit and rate of consumption sometimes have to be modified when custom or habit strongly influences the package size. For example, the housewife is so accustomed to buying margarine in one-pound units that it would be very difficult to change to an unrelated unit, such as the pint or quart. She has learned to compare prices and to measure recipes on the basis of pounds and ounces of margarine and would resist buying in any other unit of measure.

Package size may also affect total consumption. When consumers have a plentiful supply of a product on hand, they may consume more than if they have to make a special buying trip to obtain it. The six-pack carton for soft drinks and multiple packaging of light bulbs have demonstrated the success of this approach.

### Package Cost

The protection needed to deliver the item to the user in good condition determines the package's minimum cost, but consumer preference and convenience often make it advisable to exceed this minimum. A metal container may be less expensive, but because of strong consumer preference, the marketer may use a glass container for certain products, such as jellies. Likewise, a reclosable package, although more expensive than a throwaway, allows the customer to store the product easily until it is entirely consumed without having to transfer it to another container. Each such addition to the minimum cost should be justifiable in terms of its beneficial effect upon demand.

When a package is aimed at achieving brand identification or other promotional goals, its cost is usually higher than if it is solely for product protection. Nevertheless, most marketers of consumer items expect their packages to help in promotion and see cost differences as worthwhile. At a bare minimum the package must carry the brand name, the marketer's name, a description of the contents, and other descriptive material (e.g., how to use the product). Once the cost of designing an attractive promotional label has been amortized, the cost per package may be no more than that of a purely protective-type container.

## BRANDING

The relative significance of branding as a means for enhancing a product's salability varies with the product and company. The truck farmer raising fresh peas competes for sales almost solely on a price basis, since buyers neither know nor care who grew the peas they buy. Yet, the food processor, canning or freezing the same peas, can build a strong consumer preference for its brand through differentiating and promoting it, convincing buyers of that brand's superiority.

Branding's function is to bridge the gap between the manufacturer's promotional program and consummation of sales to final buyers. Brand identification, then, is essential for the firm wanting to differentiate its product, giving the company some degree of control over the product's resale by middlemen, and at the same time enhancing promotional effectiveness. Through brand identification, a company prepares itself to compete on a nonprice basis.

Some products lend themselves less readily to brand differentiation than others. Many products of farms, fisheries, forests, and mines are difficult to differentiate because of their unprocessed form but, even here, brand identification coupled with imaginative packaging and promotion frequently achieves some product differentiation, thus insulating the marketer from the full force of price competition. Swift and Company, for instance, achieved this with its "Premium Butterball Turkeys." Product differentiation through brand identification and promotion is easier to obtain for consumer than for industrial products; highly standardized industrial items, such as sheet steel and nuts and bolts, can be identified by brand name but appear impossible to differentiate effectively.

The branding decision is especially important for products where the potential effectiveness of brand identification to secure product differentiation is unclear. A few years ago, for instance, "experts" contended that branding women's dresses was of minimal value because women bought according to criteria unrelated to brand—such as color, design, styling, and fit. Today the dress industry not only uses brand names but promotes them heavily. Manufacturers learned among other things that variations in women's sizes and shapes, not provided for by differences in standard dress sizes, provided opportunities for real product differentiation and profitable branding. Brand identification has the highest potential payoff where it is possible to differentiate the product effectively in terms of features consumers consider important. But it also has payoff potentials where present products have features shoppers look for—brand identification reduces the searching time shoppers have to spend in finding products with the desired features.

### Family Brands vs. Individual Brands

Most companies market several products so they must decide whether to sell each under a separate brand or to use a family brand. Many situations exist where substantial benefits can be realized through making one choice rather than the other. Decisions on family or individual branding require evaluation of three factors: nature of the product and product line, promotional policy, and desired market penetration.

*Nature of Product and Line.*  Similar products naturally related in consumers' minds, such as sheets and towels, benefit particularly from family branding. Favorable reaction to one item often leads buyers to buy others in the line. But this "halo" effect can also detract from a marketer's reputation if unfavorable experience with one item turn consumers against the entire line. Particular care must be taken that all items carrying the family brand conform to consumers' standards of acceptance.

Products lacking common marketing attributes are usually best marketed under individual names, since little benefit comes from jointly associating them. There may even be adverse sales reactions from family branding; for example, associating a food item with a soap product may handicap sales of the food since many consumers associate soap with an unpleasant taste.

All products do not lend themselves to sale under a family brand. The quality of family-brand products should be very nearly similar so that no single item in the line can lower the quality reputations of others. The products should also be fairly compatible: A woman may prefer a particular brand of soap, but she will probably not be at all interested in a new perfume carrying the same name because she is not convinced that experience in soap making will carry over to perfume making. However, some perfume manufacturers have been successful in selling soap under their labels, because of the use of similar scents coupled with skillful promotion. The products should also be sold to the same markets. Little is gained from applying a family brand to one item sold to industrial users and to a second sold to ultimate consumers.

*Promotional Policy.*  Using a family brand, rather than individual brands, usually makes possible a smaller total promotional budget. Under a family brand, much promotion can be directed toward the entire line, and even promotion emphasizing a single item tends to increase recognition and demand for the entire line. With individual brands, separate and often duplicating promotional efforts are required. Thus, a family-brand policy permits the most effective use of limited promotional funds for similar products. Yet, family-brand promotional programs restrict opportunities for emphasizing individual differences in items, and this may be important when introducing a new product.

*Desired Market Penetration.* Individual items in a product line face varying degrees of competition. A maker of kitchen and laundry appliances, for example, may meet only mild competition on dishwashers and electric ranges, but a competitor may make only washing machines and, through aggressive promotion, may have captured a large market share and be extremely difficult to displace. In such instances, where the same degree of market penetration is not possible for all items in the line, individual branding allows greater promotional flexibility. Items facing the strongest competition may be given larger shares of the promotional budget so that optimum market penetration can be achieved for each item in the line. This makes it easier to draw buyers' attention to changes and improvements in particular items. Individual branding also allows a producer to achieve greater market penetration by marketing similar but differentiated products appealing to different market segments.

### Multiple Brands for Identical Products

Producers of specialty goods often sell through a limited number of selected retail outlets to gain their dealers' cooperation in aggressively promoting the products. This has the effect of limiting the total sales potential because in any one market no single retailer or small group of retailers is normally in a position to attract all potential buyers. In such cases, market penetration may be increased by offering identical merchandise under a different brand to a second group of selected retailers.

Mergers frequently result in the use of multiple brands. The decision to retain the separate brands or to change to a single brand may depend on whether the different brands have developed dissimilar images that appeal to different market segments or on whether they have developed strength in different regional markets with well-known names that management is reluctant to abandon.

### Use of Private Brands

Private brands are those owned and controlled by middlemen rather than by manufacturers. Both manufacturers and middlemen face policy decisions on private branding. Manufacturers must decide whether to sell their products to middlemen for private branding. And middlemen must decide whether they can benefit from their own brands. The manufacturer's decision on the acceptance of private-brand orders should depend on the probable effect on the sales of its own brand, if it has one. A middleman's decision to promote private brands of its own should be based on its expectation of greater profits and/or greater control over the market.

## *CONCLUSION*

All businesses that "have something to sell" sell a product of some sort. In this chapter, we have focused on different kinds of products, analyzing mainly the ways in which buyers' attitudes, behavioral patterns, and purchasing procedures vary from one category of product to another. We also introduced the product life cycle concept, analyzed the need for—and process of—product innovation, and discussed problems involved in structuring the product line(s), determining product quality, formulating service policy, and making packaging and branding decisions.

# *12*

# MARKETING CHANNELS

In Chapters 7 through 10, we described the main types of middlemen who operate on the wholesale and retail levels of distribution and considered their main operating characteristics and policies. These middlemen constitute the building blocks that producers seek to link together into marketing channels as they attempt to bridge the gap between themselves and the consumer or industrial market. Marketing channels, in other words, provide the institutional linkage through which producers' products "flow" to the market. In the following discussion, we first consider some important problems confronting producers in choosing marketing channels; then we analyze some marketing channels in common use.

## PROBLEMS IN CHOOSING MARKETING CHANNELS

### Adjusting to Buyers' Needs and Expectations

One important problem confronting the producer in the selection of marketing channels is that of adjusting to buyers' needs and expectations at each distribution level. At the retail level, these buyers are the ultimate consumers; they are not even remotely interested in the producer's ideas about which outlets should sell its products. Ultimate consumers buy from those retailers who best serve their needs. An excellent case in point is that of the discount house. During the late 1940s and early 1950s, some manufacturers of nationally advertised products refused to permit discount houses to handle their lines. Nevertheless, discount houses managed to obtain these lines (through "bootleg" channels) and to obtain competitive lines from producers less particular about their retail outlets. Ultimate consumers in ever-increasing numbers demonstrated that they preferred to buy such items from discount houses rather than from conventional retailers. Manufacturers realizing the hopelessness of trying to keep their products out of discount houses—and the potential loss in sales volume if they succeeded—relented, many actively seeking retail representation through discount houses.

At other distribution levels, buyers' wants and preferences are also important. Once the producer determines which kinds of retailers are most acceptable to ultimate consumers, it must find the type of supplier from which retailers want and prefer to buy the product. Retailers may customarily buy directly from manufacturers, or they may buy from merchant wholesalers, or they may buy through agents of some sort. Whatever the normal buying pattern, a producer is well-advised to make its product available through the same sources. Similarly, the producer must analyze the needs and expectations of buyers at other distribution levels.

### Considering Marketing Needs of the Product

The product's nature, its unit value, its technical characteristics, its degree of differentiation from competitive products, whether it is perishable, whether it is a staple or a nonstaple—these and other product characteristics may limit the number of possible channel alternatives. Individually or in combination, they may restrict the alternatives to those in a given line of trade, to those containing a certain number of distribution levels, to those where middlemen are equipped to provide technical service and repair, or to those where middlemen have specialized storage facilities (for example, for frozen foods) or are specialists in some phase of marketing (for example, fashion merchandising). The crucial marketing needs of a given product, of course, may be quite unique. For example, the marketing needs for a line of power garden tools are quite different from those for a line of imported children's clothing. Often, formal marketing research is required to uncover the crucial marketing needs of particular products, especially radically new products.

### Determining Most Profitable Channel Alternatives

Through estimating the sales-volume potential and the costs of chan. usage for each channel alternative and through comparing these estimates, the producer attempts to identify the alternative that shows the greatest promise of contributing the most to maximum long-run profit. Certain market statistics, then, are required for making these comparisons. The most basic relate to the potential market. The producer must have short-term and long-run estimates of market potential, and from these, perhaps by applying some "target share-of-the-market percentage," it must derive short-term and long-run estimates of the firm's sales potentials. After considering these sales potentials, together with data on the "reach" of outlets at each distribution level, it tentatively determines whether a single channel or a number of channels are needed.

Marketing cost analysis is used to determine probable costs of performing required marketing activities under each channel arrangement. In each channel, there is implied some scheme for dividing up performance of marketing activities and apportioning some to the producer and others to different "channel members." The costs of performing each activity at each distribution level and the total costs of accomplishing the entire marketing task must be estimated for each channel.

### Obtaining Channel Usage

Obtaining channel usage requires that approaches be made to individual members of the prospective channel team. The producer's proposal must be "sold" to the managements of channel members, and, once this is done, there is usually also need to follow through and "sell" the team members' sales staffs. In other words, for each channel-member organization, someone must convince both the executives and those who do the actual selling of the worth of the product.

### Distribution Intensity

Not only must the manufacturer decide the kind of middlemen to be used on each distribution level, it must decide on *how many* middlemen there should be on each level. If it decides to sell directly to retailers, it must choose from among many different kinds of retailers; if it decides to use wholesalers, it must also choose from among the different kinds of wholesale institutions. Then, it determines how many retailers of the chosen types are needed to reach the consumers it wants to reach; and assuming that it decides to use wholesalers also, how many wholesalers of the chosen types are required to reach all the retailers it desires to use. If we think of the different kinds of middlemen as "institutional" building blocks, we can say that the manufacturer must decide not only on the kinds of building blocks to include in its marketing channel(s) but also on the number of each kind needed.

Decisions on the number of middlemen relate to distribution intensity. There are three general degrees of distribution intensity: mass, selective, and exclusive. These are arbitrary classifications for there are many intermediate gradations. Distribution intensity should be regarded as a broad band with mass distribution at one end and exclusive distribution at the other. Within this broad band, there is a very large number of points representing different degrees of selective distribution.

***Extremes of Distribution Intensity.*** The two extremes are mass and exclusive distribution. Mass distribution provides maximum sales exposure for a product, whereas exclusive distribution involves using a single middle-man—a retailer, for example—in each market area. Generally, a manufac-turer must use multiple channels, and frequently some rather long channels, to achieve mass-distribution intensity. By contrast, a manufacturer using exclusive distribution tends not only to use a single channel but also to sell directly to the chosen outlets.

*Selective Distribution.* Most manufacturers have neither 100 percent mass distribution nor 100 percent exclusive distribution, but, rather some form of selective distribution. Voluntarily or involuntarily, in pursuing a policy of selective distribution manufacturers restrict the number of outlets at each distribution level. Voluntary restriction occurs when a manufacturer decides in a given market area, for instance, not to use every conceivable outlet for its product but only a few "desired" outlets. Involuntary restric-tion occurs either when certain "desired" outlets refuse to handle a manu-facturer's product or when the available outlets in a given market area are fewer than the number that the manufacturer would like to have. Sometimes the number of middlemen is limited to those that can best serve the manu-facturer (that is, that can be the most profitable), but the more modern view is that the number of outlets should be limited to those that can best serve sufficiently large numbers of ultimate buyers (that is, not necessarily includ-ing *only* those outlets most profitable to the manufacturer but also other outlets, such as those situated in locations more convenient to ultimate buyers).

If skillfully implemented, selective distribution commonly results in greater profits for each channel member. The manufacturer gains because it sells to a smaller number of accounts (thus reducing selling expenses), and at the same time, should be able to sell more to each account. The middle-men gain because fewer of their competitors handle the manufacturer's product, permitting the middlemen to attract trade that might otherwise go elsewhere. Better merchandising practices also are likely to augment the profits of manufacturer and middlemen alike; there are fewer "out-of-stocks" because more adequate inventories are handled; more valuable re-tail display space tends to be used; at all levels there is more desire to cooperate in coordinating promotional efforts. Even the manufacturer's "small order" problem may disappear almost entirely.

*Deciding Distribution Intensity.* Particularly important in deciding on distribution intensity are a product's marketing characteristics. The more frequently end–buyers purchase a product, the stronger the argument for mass distribution or for an extensive form of selective distribution. The greater the gross margin is for the middlemen, the more persuasive the argument for something closer to exclusive distribution. The amount of product service expected by end–buyers may vary from none at all (a point in favor of mass distribution) to a large amount (an argument for exclusive distribution). If the useful life of a product is very long, distribution should usually be quite selective or even exclusive. Similarly, the more searching time end–buyers are willing to devote to finding a product outlet, the fewer outlets a manufacturer can afford to have.

The brand's market position also influences the decision on distribution intensity. If a brand has consumer preference, the manufacturer can afford to use some selective distribution. If buyers insist on a brand and refuse substitutes, highly selective distribution is feasible and exclusive distribution possible.

Many factors influence the decision on distribution intensity. A manufacturer must consider the strength of its desire to control price at each distribution level and its relation to the size of the "policing" problem. It must appraise the amount of market risk involved in each alternative—for example, exclusive distribution is like "putting all the marketing eggs in a limited number of baskets." It must know the attitudes of distributive outlets: Some actively seek and enthusiastically support "exclusives," others want no part whatever of "exclusives," and still others accept "exclusives" chiefly to deprive competitors of them. The manufacturer must also compare the alternatives in relation to its advertising program—both with respect to the probable amount of waste circulation (that is, appearance of its advertisements in geographic areas other than those where it contemplates having distributors) and with regard to the problems involved in coordinating middlemen's promotional efforts with its own. Management must decide whether it is more desirable to have competition inside retail outlets or outside them and the amount of protection that should be sought from in–store competition and in–market competition.

## MARKETING CHANNEL ALTERNATIVES
## IN COMMON USE

Marketing channels can vary widely, from the simple one a spark plug manufacturer uses to sell its entire output to one automobile manufacturer, to the long and complex channels employed in moving nonperishable farm products to market. Marketing channels are made up of different kinds of building blocks including producers, consumers or industrial users, wholesale institutions (both agent and merchant wholesalers), and retail institutions. Thus, the possible number of different channel alternatives is large. Figure 12–1 illustrates the more commonly used channel alternatives and brings out the point that the various channel building blocks bear a hierarchical relationship to each other. For example, if agent middlemen are present in a marketing channel, they generally are situated further back in the channel than wholesalers and/or retailers.

**Figure 12-1** Marketing channels commonly used by producers of consumer goods and industrial goods.

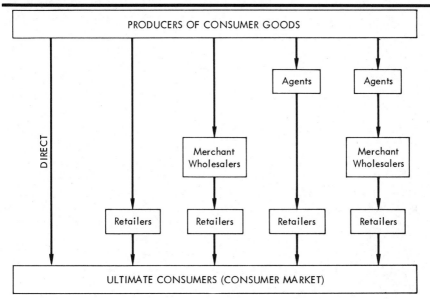

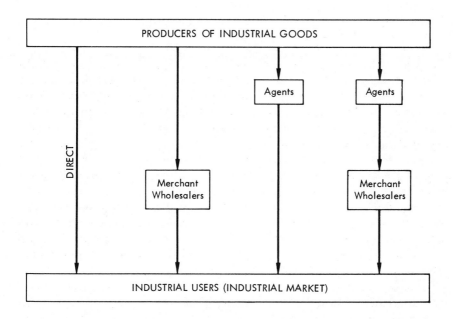

### Manufacturer to Consumer or User

There are two levels in the shortest marketing channels: the producer, and either the ultimate consumer or industrial user. The producer-to-industrial-user channel is the most common way to market industrial goods: (1) because many industrial products have markets composed of relatively few potential users; (2) the users of particular types of industrial products tend to be clustered in only a few market areas; (3) some industrial products require special servicing and installation which the manufacturer can best provide; (4) other industrial products are so technical that manufacturers deal directly with prospective users; and, in many cases, (5) industrial users insist on being permitted to buy directly and are able to buy in quantities large enough to make direct sales by producers economically feasible.

The producer-to-ultimate consumer channel is not nearly so important. But some farmers deal directly with consumers at roadside stands or from stalls in public markets. Some small businesses, such as bakeries and dairies, and larger businesses, such as tire manufacturers, sell directly to consumers, either through their own retail outlets or on a house-to-house basis. A *few* manufacturers, in such lines as shoes and shirts, sell directly to consumers through mail-order departments. However, not many manufacturers of consumer products rely wholly or even principally on the producer-to-ultimate channel. The reasons are fairly obvious: ultimate consumers are numerous, widely scattered, and accustomed to buying in very small quantities.

### Manufacturer through Agent Middlemen to Consumer or User

Some producers use agent middlemen as intermediates between themselves and the next level of distribution. (Agent middlemen, it should be remembered, generally operate at the wholesale level.) Agent middlemen are much used in marketing agricultural produce, partly because most farmers are too small to handle their own distribution efficiently and partly because the main growing areas often are separated geographically from major markets.

In marketing manufactured products, both industrial and consumer goods, agent middlemen are used usually, although not exclusively, by manufacturers who want to rid themselves of much of the marketing task. A manufacturer's entire output may be turned over to one or a small number of agent middlemen for marketing, in which case the manufacturer's marketing-channel problem is reduced to that of selecting and persuading certain agents to serve as its representatives. In other instances, the manufacturer may use agents to market its product in some areas—generally ones with limited market potentials—and either use its own sales force or sell directly to merchant middlemen elsewhere.

Agent middlemen negotiate the transfer of legal title to the producer's merchandise with institutions active on the next distribution level. In marketing consumer goods, they negotiate with either merchant wholesalers or retailers or both, or the agent makes arrangements for further negotiations by other agent middlemen situated farther along the marketing channel and nearer the ultimate consumer. For a product such as furniture, which is usually sold through a limited number of retail outlets, the agent ordinarily negotiates directly with retailers. For products sold through numerous retail outlets, such as most food and grocery items, the agent usually negotiates with merchant wholesalers, who, in turn, sell to retailers. However, in marketing food products, agents may also deal directly with such large-volume retailers as grocery chains and retail cooperatives. In marketing industrial goods, agents usually negotiate directly with industrial users; but in some lines, such as small hand tools, it is common for them to negotiate with merchant wholesalers, known as *industrial distributors* or *mill supply houses,* which, in turn, sell to industrial users.

### Manufacturer–Retailer–Ultimate Consumer

This is one of the most common marketing channels used for reaching the consumer market. Manufacturers using it generally have some compelling reason for avoiding wholesale middlemen: Their products may be perishable, either physically or fashion-wise—hence, speed in distribution is essential; the retailers involved may be predominantly large (such as chains, department stores, and mail-order houses) and, as a matter of policy, refuse to buy through wholesalers; the retailers handling the product may be located near each other, thus making it convenient for the manufacturer to sell them directly; the available wholesalers may be unable or unwilling to provide the type and amount of promotional support that the manufacturer feels its product requires; finally, the manufacturer may simply desire closer contact with ultimate consumers than that afforded through channels containing more distribution levels.

Manufacturers who distribute their products directly to retailers must finance the inventories that merchant wholesalers would otherwise carry. Furthermore, they need either a line wide enough to permit their sales reps to write fairly large orders or a narrower line of products generally ordered by retailers in large quantities. If the product line is not ordinarily purchased in large quantities by individual retailers, a manufacturer should have some other compelling reason for selling directly to retailers.

One important reason for distribution direct to retailers is the manufacturers' desire to make use of *franchising.* A franchise is a continuing relationship between a manufacturer (or an expert in the performance of some service) and a retailer in which the manufacturer supplies the retailer with manufacturing and marketing techniques, a brand image, and other knowhow. This method of operation which has existed for many years in such fields as petroleum marketing has increased enormously in importance.

The franchisor-franchisee relationship requires continuing close contact so that the franchisor can provide advice, supervision, and help when needed. The manufacturer to retailer to ultimate consumer marketing channel meets this requirement.

### Manufacturer–Merchant Wholesaler—Retailer—Ultimate Consumer

This consumer-goods channel is often referred to as the "traditional" or "orthodox" marketing channel. A manufacturer finds it suitable under some or all of these conditions: (1) it has a narrow product line; (2) it is unable to finance distribution direct to retailers or can put the necessary funds to more productive use elsewhere; (3) retail outlets are numerous and widely dispersed; (4) wholesalers are able and willing to provide strong promotional support or the product does not require such support; (5) the products are staples, not subject to physical or fashion deterioration; (6) the manufacturer's advertising to ultimate consumers exerts a strong pull in causing retailers to stock the product. Manufacturers who use this channel but desire closer contact with retailers often employ "missionary" sales reps who, while calling on retailers, ordinarily refer any orders they obtain to local wholesalers for filling and delivery.

### Manufacturer–Merchant Wholesaler—Industrial User

The manufacturer-merchant wholesaler-industrial user channel is used by many producers of such industrial items as small tools and other standard pieces of equipment. These are products of comparatively small unit value used by numerous and diverse industrial establishments. Merchant wholesalers serving the industrial market, though their operations in many ways resemble those of consumer-goods wholesalers, sell directly to industrial users. Such merchant middlemen are known to the trade by such titles as *industrial supply houses, mill supply houses, industrial hardware distributors, or equipment distributors.*

### Dual Distribution Systems

When the same product is to be sold to both industrial users and ultimate consumers, separate distribution systems are normally set up to reach each market. For example, the manufacturer of tires normally sells direct to automobile manufacturers and through retailers to the ultimate consumer. Some manufacturers, however, use more than one marketing channel to reach even essentially the same kinds of customers. The Select Committee on Small Business of the U.S. House of Representatives, in its investigation of competitive factors affecting small business described this sort of situation as "dual distribution." Dual distribution was defined by Richard H. Holton, former Assistant U.S. Secretary of Commerce, as situations in which "the manufacturer of a branded good sells that brand through two or more competing distribution channels" and where "the manufacturer sells two brands of basically the same product through two competing kinds of distribution networks."[1] An example of the first type of dual distribution is the widespread practice in petroleum marketing of selling gasoline and related products both through franchised independent outlets and through company-owned stations. An example of the second type of dual distribution is the practice followed by some appliance manufacturers of selling a nationally advertised brand through a network of wholesalers and retailers and selling an almost identical product under a private brand through a large chain or mail-order retail organization. Dual distribution may make it possible for a manufacturer to achieve deeper penetration of a market than it could obtain through a single marketing channel. However, there is a risk of alienation of channel members in either or both of the channels if they encounter strong competition from the other.

## *CONCLUSION*

In Part II, considerable emphasis was placed upon the dynamic nature of marketing institutions. This continuing process of change and evolution in institutions can be expected to continue, perhaps at an even more rapid rate, and only those institutions capable of making adjustments to the dynamic characteristics of markets are likely to survive over the long run.

The implications for the manufacturer are clear-cut. The continuing process of change and evolution in institutions means that there must be continuing adjustments made in marketing channels, because most channels contain middlemen. But other factors also contribute to the dynamic nature of the manufacturer's marketing-channel problems. Because a channel is a method of reaching a market, changes in markets require adjustments in marketing channels. Similarly, changes in products or in the consumers' or users' attitudes toward products may require changes in channels. And because competitors' activities may determine the aggressiveness of promotion necessary to sell a product successfully, so changes in competitive action may require changes in marketing channels. For all these reasons, the manufacturer must regularly reevaluate its policies on marketing channels.

---

[1] U.S. Congress, House Subcommittee No. 4, Select Committee on Small Business, "Hearings, The Impact Upon Small Business of Dual Distribution," *A Report of Subcommittee No. 4 on Distribution Problems to the Select Committee on Small Business,* 88th Congress, 2nd session, 1964, Hearing I, p. 4.

# 13

# PHYSICAL DISTRIBUTION

Physical distribution involves the actual movement and storage of goods after they are produced and before they are consumed. It is comprised of several interrelated activites, most importantly: inventory control, storage, transportation, materials handling, order size control, and order processing. Regarding physical distribution as a unified managerial responsibility places the major emphasis on the *total* costs of the integrated system, thus reducing the possibility of emphasizing one individual component at the expense of another. Since physical distribution costs bulk large in the overall cost of goods, adoption of the *total* cost approach has been rapid and widespread among well–managed companies.

## THE TOTAL DISTRIBUTION SYSTEM

Physical distribution is intimately related to other aspects of marketing. Consider what takes place as producers move through marketing channels, over time and through space, from production to consumption. Inventories are normally held by manufacturers, by middlemen at each distribution level, and by ultimate buyers at the end of the channel. In the distribution of consumer goods, for example, consumers add to their stocks by buying from retailers. This reduces retailers' inventories and eventually the retailers place replenishing orders with wholesalers, who, in turn, replenish their stock by placing orders with manufacturers. Thus, while products are flowing forward to final buyers, there is a reverse flow of orders causing alternating subtractions from and additions to inventories at each level. Each time a manufacturer ships an order, it initiates this chain reaction in the performance of transportation, inventory control, storage, and other physical distribution activities.

The details and manner of performing physical distribution activities at each level in the marketing channel may vary considerably. Often, the size of inventory varies between distribution levels, and among individual middlemen on the same level. When a channel includes certain types of agents, there may be no inventories at all on their levels. Similarly, middlemen differ markedly with respect to order quantities and frequency of order placement. Both the forward flow of products and the reverse flow of orders encounter interruptions of varying and often unpredictable durations. Either flow, and sometimes both, may fall to "just a trickle" or rise to "flood-stage proportions." A manufacturer may centralize warehousing and shipping activites at one or a few locations, or may decentralize them through branch warehouse operations or by using public warehouses. Middlemen, especially those operating multiple establishments, have similar options. Furthermore, in moving products from one distribution point to the next, different decisions may be made concerning transportation methods. These factors, present in all distribution systems, make managing physical distribution a challenging task.

From the manufacturer's standpoint, physical distribution management requires integrated planning of all transportation, storage, and supply requirements, plus the implementation of inventory policy. This requires decisions on the deployment and size of inventory at specific times and places, insuring that the right products are in the right quantities at the right places at the right times. The solution should strike an optimal balance between physical distribution costs and the expectations of end-buyers and users of the product.

Because manufacturers generally reach final buyers through intermediate distribution levels, they cannot completely "control" (that is, direct and regulate) physical distribution. They are bound to find distribution levels and points where they have little, if any, control over inventory size and disposition. A manufacturer does direct and regulate inventories at the factory and at its own warehouses; and here, at least, physical distribution decisions can be "optimal," but only in the sense that they are the best under the circumstances—considering such factors as costs, demand characteristics, and inventory eccentricities of distribution points farther down the channel.

A manufacturer normally must work toward optimum performance of the total distribution system by coordinating its inventory policies and practices with those of other channel members. How middlemen manage their inventories definitely affects the manufacturer's costs and profits. Their actions also determine the quality of service and product availability at the times and places desired by final buyers. If middlemen are overstocked, they may cut prices to make sales, thus jeopardizing future sales at normal prices, possibly damaging the manufacturer's reputation for product quality, and perhaps making themselves less enthusiastic about future relationships with the manufacturer. If middlemen follow unintelligent inventory practices, such as "hand-to-mouth" buying, the manufacturer is forced to enlarge inventories and, consequently, to increase costs. Furthermore, it and the middlemen suffer hidden costs from being out of stock and unable to fill orders when buyers want them. Unfortunately, out-of-stock costs are not recorded by conventional accounting systems, but profits and sales are both reduced when customers are sent away empty handed. Gains in physical distribution efficiency should be accompanied by improvements in net profits.

Estimates of physical distribution costs indicate that they account for as much as one–third of the manufacturer's selling price and from one–fifth to one–fourth of the price paid by the final buyer. A breakdown of these costs for large companies is shown in Table 13–1. Any area accounting for a great percentage of total costs should be a prime target for management's efforts to secure more efficient performance. Gains in physical distribution efficiency should be accompanied by improvements in net profits.

## DECISIONS ON SIZE OF INVENTORY

Inventories are, in effect, reservoirs of goods held in anticipation of making sales; that is, of filling demands from farther down along the marketing channel. Incoming quantities of the product ready for sale arrive, usually at irregular intervals, and are added to the inventory reservoir. The outgoing product flow is more continuous but still fluctuates considerably.

**TABLE 13–1** Physical distribution: Major elements of cost in 26 large companies

| COST ELEMENT | TOTAL DISTRIBUTION COST* (%) |
|---|---|
| Carrier charges | 44% |
| Warehousing and handling | 20 |
| Inventory carrying cost | 18 |
| Shipping room and administrative (includes order-processing costs) | 18 |
| Total | 100% |

*Averages for survey sample as a whole, based on available company data and/or author's estimates. Percentages assigned to various items vary as much as ±20 percent among the 26 individual companies.

*Source:* Cundiff, E.W., Still, R.R., Govoni, N.A.P., *Fundamentals of Modern Marketing,* (Englewood Cliffs, N.J.: Prentice-Hall, Inc., 1985), p. 178.

The volume in the inventory reservoir pulsates but not always with a regular rhythm; from day to day, changes occur in the rates quantities of input and output. Therefore, in deciding on inventory size, management must determine both maximum and minimum allowable inventory. In setting these upper and lower limits, both sales and cost considerations are involved.

### Sales Considerations

The main purpose in maintaining any inventory is to meet market demands; i.e., to make sales and to fill customers' orders. Since inventories are kept in *anticipation* of market demand, the upper and lower control limits should be attuned to forecasted sales. Thus, the more accurate the sales forecast, the greater the opportunity to maximize gains from economical inventory operations. The less accurate the forecast, the greater the need for substantial buffer stocks over and above "normal" inventory levels. With both a sales forecast and some notion of its probable accuracy, a decision-maker is prepared to set the control limits.

Two additional factors, however, must be taken into account. One relates to what management considers an acceptable level of customer service. Experience shows that, in a typical business, about 80 percent more inventory is needed to fill 95 percent of the customers' orders out of stock on hand than to fill just 80 percent. Each firm, then, must strike a balance between what it considers reasonable customer service and costs in line with managerial goals. It should also recognize that many customers may regard consistency of delivery at least as important as speed of delivery, particularly if they are buying for resale. Settling on some goal as to the proportion of all customers' orders which the stock on hand could satisfy without delay has a definite bearing on the upper inventory limit. The other factor is distribution-system responsiveness—the ability of a system to communicate needs back to the supplying plant and get needed inventory into the field. The amount of responsiveness determines how quickly the inventory can be adjusted to demand changes. Thus, distribution–system responsiveness directly influences the lower inventory limit.

### Cost Considerations

Three main groups of costs are associated with the inventory. *Holding costs* include warehousing and storage charges, cost of capital tied up in inventory, costs of adverse price movements, obsolescence, spoilage, pilferage, and taxes and insurance on inventory. *Cost of shortages* (that is, of having negative inventories) include special clerical, administrative, and handling expenses and, most importantly, losses of specific sales, of good will, and even of some customers. *Costs of replenishing* inventory differ in composition depending upon whether a business does its own manufacturing. Inventory–replenishing costs in a "make and sell" business are mainly manufacturing cost: labor and machine setup costs, costs of material used during setup testing, cost of production time lost during setups, clerical and administrative costs, and so on. Inventory–replenishing costs in the "buy and sell" type of business include: clerical and administrative work, transportation and unloading, placement in warehouses or stores, and performing necessary related activities.

Inventory decisions should be directed toward balancing the three types of costs. Whereas holding costs rise as inventory increases, the costs of both shortages and inventory replenishment decrease as inventory increases. Holding, shortage, and replenishment costs are all related, then, to inventory size; total costs are a function of the amount stored, and the problem is to determine how much to store in order to minimize total costs. Solving this problem involves balancing inventory–holding costs against either costs of shortage or costs of replenishment or both. One of the earliest and most significant contributions of operations research was the construction of models designed to minimize total inventory costs under different conditions.

## DECISIONS ON STORAGE
## AND INVENTORY LOCATION

Decisions on storage and inventory location are closely linked to decisions on inventory size. For instance, a decision to restrict inventory size drastically, so as to operate almost from hand to mouth, reduces total need for storage space. It is often necessary to increase some physical distribution costs to reduce others by a greater total amount. Marketers make three important storage decisions: geographic deployment of inventory, ownership of warehouse facilities, and number and location of warehouses.

### Geographic Deployment of Inventory

There are three possible decisions with regard to geographical deployment of inventory: (1) concentration at or near the plant or at some other central location, (2) dispersion at several distribution points located in or closer to the main markets, and (3) concentration of substantial inventories at a few distribution centers and redistribution to a larger number of distribution points dispersed throughout the market. The first two decisions are opposite extremes; the third is a compromise between them.

Comparison of inventory concentration and dispersion reveals opposite sets of strengths and weaknesses. The company that concentrates its inventory can minimize the number of customers' orders unfilled because of stock–outs; but in so doing it may increase total transportation costs and delay customer service. The firm that disperses its inventory needs a larger total inventory investment and, in effect, commits each subinventory to sale only in a particular market area; but it reduces total transportation charges and speeds up customer service. The concentration decision permits more rapid adjustment to changes in the make-up of incoming orders because unexpected demands originating from only a few markets usually can be met at once; the dispersion decision requires either that a large enough reserve stock be maintained at each branch to meet most emergencies or that there be some provision for moving stocks among branches. Thus, the dispersion decision requires the greater inventory investment because the sum of many small reserve stocks scattered over the whole market is greater than one large reserve stock held at a single location. Similarly, operating one large central warehouse should mean greater warehousing efficiency at lower costs per unit of product handled than can be achieved through decentralized operation of smaller storage facilities. But if the product line is made up mostly of bulky and low–unit–value items—the kind that usually must be shipped by truck or rail—total transportation costs may be lower when decentralized warehouses are used. This is because railroads and truckers normally charge less for full carloads or truckloads than for shipments in less-than-carload lots. Both decisions, then, have general strengths and weaknesses, and whether a marketer chooses one or the other—or adopts the third as a compromise—depends upon its evaluations of the relative importance of each factor. These evaluations, in turn, are influenced by the product line, marketing channels, pricing policies, and competitors' practices.

### Inventory Dispersion and Warehouse Ownership

Manufacturers deciding to disperse their inventories may choose between operating their own branch warehouses or using public warehouses. For any manufacturer, this choice depends upon the amount of sales volume originating in particular markets, its preference for fixed or variable warehousing costs, the desired degree of flexibility in making changes in the pattern of inventory deployment, relative warehousing efficiency, and the marketing channel used. There is relationship and interaction among these factors. If the volume of goods moved is substantial and shows little seasonal fluctuation, a good case can be made for branch warehouses owned and operated by the manufacturer. The costs of branch warehousing are mainly fixed and, with a large and steady "flowthrough" of goods, the costs per unit of product moved are likely to be low. Because public warehouses base their charges on the space and labor actually used, the scales generally tip in their favor only when a small volume is to be handled or when a large volume with great seasonal fluctuations is to be moved. The variable costs associated with the use of public warehouses also provide greater flexibility in making changes in the geographical deployment of inventory. Because most cities have many public warehouses, the manufacturer can easily close out stocks in some locations and place them in others.

The chief economic justification for the public warehouse is that it dovetails local storage needs of many manufacturers, which, in turn, makes possible efficient use of storage space, warehousing labor, and mechanized handling equipment. However, with a large and steady sales volume of its own, a manufacturer may realize comparable efficiencies in its own branch warehouses. Furthermore, if the product requires either specialized handling and technical service or special storage facilities, it may be forced to own and operate branch warehouses. Although some cities do have public warehouses that provide individualized handling and technical services (for example, those specializing in appliance warehousing) and warehouses that offer specialized storage facilities (for example, those with refrigerated storage space), they cannot be found in all cities. Thus, the manufacturer who uses them may still have to operate its own facilities in some markets.

Some manufacturers use public warehouses as substitutes for wholesalers, for local sales representatives, or for both. These manufacturers place "spot stocks" in public warehouses and furnish the operators with "accredited lists" of customers authorized to receive deliveries, including credit limits. The public warehouseman not only fills orders but often attends to billing and collections. Generally, public warehouses are not aggressive sales representatives so the manufacturer using them for that purpose may have to rely on exclusive retail outlets or heavy consumer advertising to "move the goods out of the warehouse." Still another reason for using public warehouses is that they issue warehouse receipts, which may be used as collateral for bank loans; however, this is only a source of short-term credit during the time the goods remain unsold.

### Number and Location of Warehouses

One problem confronting a manufacturer who practices inventory dispersion is that of deciding on the number and location of warehouses. The nature of this problem is influenced by several important variables including customers' buying patterns and delivery expectations, freight rate structures, service characteristics of alternative transportation media, warehouse operating costs, location of factories, production capacities and product mix of individual factories, and costs of building or renting suitable warehouses in different cities. It is possible to gather statistics and related information on each of these variables, but the number of possible combinations of the many sets of complex, and to some extent interrelated, variables is staggering. Thus, in the past, largely because of the mountain of work involved in calculating the probable results of each combination of variables, most decisions on number and location of warehouses were made intuitively. With the advent of the high-speed digital computer, such computations have become more routine.

Operations researchers have devised "simulation" techniques that permit mathematical representations of a company's distribution system, present and proposed, to be programmed on a computer. In a comparatively short time, a computer can provide the probable operating results under a number of different combinations of numbers and locations of warehouses.

Such simulations often furnish decision makers with much additional information needed for making decisions on related problems.

## DECISIONS ON MODES OF TRANSPORTATION

Decisions on modes of transportation are related both to decisions on size of inventory and those on storage location, both of which, of course, are themselves interrelated. No one of these decisions should be made without first considering the possible effects on the others. For example, decisions that seek only to optimize transportation costs may drastically increase inventory and storage costs. The important costs to keep in mind are the overall total costs of physical distribution, not the costs of any one aspect of a physical distribution system.

Decisions on modes of transportation should be made with the goal of optimizing the efficiency of the total physical distribution system. Relative costs, although important, provide only one basis for comparing the contribution of different modes of transportation to total system efficiency. There is a general trend toward providing shippers with more rapid transportation services (for example, increased truck speeds, and rail freight "piggyback" service). Transport time—the time required for moving goods from warehouses, for example, to customers—is a major determinant of efficiency in the distribution system. Reductions in transport time, though commonly accompanied by increased transportation costs, often result in significant savings in warehousing costs, packing costs, and inventory investments. For instance, switching from a distribution system composed of surface transportation and branch warehouses to one involving air transportation direct to the customer normally results in higher transportation costs but much lower storage costs. Net savings often result from such changes, largely due to reductions in transport time.

However, physical distribution costs can sometimes be lowered through the use of slower and lower-cost modes of transportation. For instance, Westinghouse Electric Corporation switched from air to surface transportation for deliveries of rush orders. By making improvements in all the distribution steps before shipment, Westinghouse saved so much time that it could use the slower surface transportation and benefit from the lower cost. Generally, transportation decisions should be based both on cost and transport time, and the relative significance of each depends on their combined relationship to the overall efficiency of the total physical distribution system.

## MATERIALS HANDLING DECISIONS

Materials handling is the area of physical distribution that has experienced the greatest change and improvement in efficiency in recent decades. The first major improvement was the elimination of "manhandling" of goods. Thirty years ago it was common practice to use manpower to transfer goods from storage to transportation and back to storage. Today most goods are not handled by human labor at all until they reach the retail or user level. Improved conveyer systems and fork lift equipment have made possible almost total mechanization. The second major improvement in materials handling was containerization—the development of methods by which a large number of units of a product are combined into a single compact unit for storage and transportation. Containerization has evolved from the simple pallet to complex and special-purpose containers. Containerization reduces both materials handling costs and time spent on handling shipments.

Materials handling decisions and costs are interrelated with other decisions and costs. Improved materials handling has not only reduced the cost of handling goods; it has also improved the relative effectiveness of transportation and storage. For example, containerization has so drastically reduced the "loading turnaround time" for ships that it has reduced their "comparative speed" disadvantage. At the same time, improved materials handling makes possible more effective utilization of storage space and, hence, a reduction of investment in facilities.

## ORDER SIZE DECISIONS

The size of the order also is closely interrelated with other facets of physical distribution. Therefore, order size decisions should take into account these other facets. For example, orders for amounts less than the contents of a normal pallet or container require that the goods be handled entirely by hand instead of by machine. Such manhandling appreciably raises costs. Less-than-pallet-size orders also increase the costs of storage and inventory control and add to their complexity. The size of an order may also affect the level of shipping costs, since bulk or carload shipping rates are generally a good deal lower than rates for shipping smaller quantities. It is important, therefore, for management to make decisions concerning minimum order sizes, units of increment in size, and preferred order sizes so that orders received will be at size levels consistent wiht the goal of optimizing total physical distribution costs.

## ORDER PROCESSING DECISIONS

The methods a marketing organization uses for processing customers' orders affects its service to them in two ways. First, reorder time is affected; second, the consistency of delivery time is affected. Variations in these two time variables exert influences upon the buyers' profits through changing the required investment in inventory, altering ordering costs, and changing the probability that items will be out-of-stock. Because of these considerations, buyers tend to shift their orders to suppliers providing superior order processing service. In a study of 700 retailers, it was found that store buyers could discriminate among even small differences in order service time and that their rating of this factor influenced their overall rating of a supplier.

Even small improvements in order processing service can provide a supplier with a competitive advantage; thus, it is worthwhile exploring possible avenues leading to greater efficiency in order processing.

### APPLICATIONS OF OPERATIONS RESEARCH TO PHYSICAL DISTRIBUTION PROBLEMS

Physical distribution decisions generally involve an attempt to optimize several variables. The conventional manual "pencil and paper" approach to such decisions is not only tedious but rarely successful, since restrictions of time and manpower require drastic simplifications of the problem. Consequently, executives have searched for new approaches, particularly those using computers.

Among these new approaches are those involving mathematical simulation, linear programming, heuristic programming, and integer programming. Mathematical simulation involves reducing the essential aspects of a company's distribution system to a mathematical representation and, with a computer's help, using this representation to test various schemes for improving distribution methods and/or lowering distribution costs. Management, then, after comparing the simulated results, selects the scheme that comes closest to meeting its objectives. The "transportation technique" of linear programming is used in solving "two-dimensional" problems, such as those involved in planning shipments from different origins to different destinations with minimum total shipping costs. The simplex method of linear programming is applied in solving multidimensional distribution problems. Heuristic programming is used for finding a "good" or "usable" answer quickly. Integer programming, a variant of linear programming, is used to determine the optimum solution from among a considerably larger number of alternatives than is possible with linear programming.

## *CONCLUSION*

Only very recently have many companies been aware of the many opportunities for cost savings that exist in the physical distribution area. But awareness of these opportunities has been sharpened since the logic of the "total cost" approach has received widespread publicity and been accorded equally widespread acceptance. In physical distribution, as in no other area of marketing, it is extremely important to strive for as rational an approach to decision-making as possible. Physical distribution decisions are major decisions, as difficult to make on rational bases as they are to reverse or change. They require considerable market information, both qualitative and quantitative and, in using this information, decision-makers are helped considerably if they clearly conceptualize the nature of the total physical distribution system, each of its aspects, and the relationships each aspect bears to others and to the total system.

# 14

# PROMOTION

Promotion is a key element in marketing strategy. Fitting the product and its features to market needs and preferences is important. Obtaining distribution is also important. Successful promotion is the third essential ingredient in marketing strategy; prospective buyers must learn about the product's distinctive want-satisfying characteristics and its availability. Establishing and maintaining communications with target market segments is the main task assigned to promotion.

There are many ways to achieve these market communications objectives. Both in terms of impact upon market demand and expenditures involved, the most important promotional methods are personal selling and advertising. Other communications methods, each appropriate and effective under particular circumstances, include: packaging, branding, direct-mail solicitation, point-of-purchase display, and premiums.

## THE PROMOTIONAL MIX

Close coordination of advertising, personal selling, and other promotional methods—both in their planning and implementation—is important. Considerable advertising effort may be wasted, for example, if personal selling effort does not obtain appropriate dealers for the product, if the package fails to draw buyers' attention to it, or if dealers do not display it effectively. Likewise, personal selling effort is wasted, for example, in explaining details (about the product and its uses) that are more economically communicated

**Figure 14–1** The promotional mix, promotional strategy, and overall marketing strategy

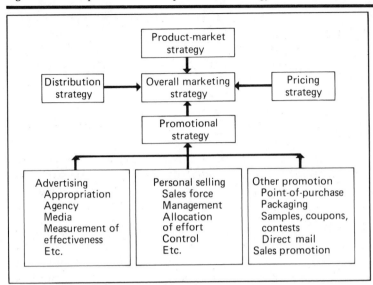

*Source:* Cundiff, E.W., Still R.R., Govoni, N.A.P., *Fundamentals of Modern Marketing*, (Englewood Cliffs, N.J.: Prentice-Hall, Inc., 1985), p. 306.

through advertising, the package, or point-of-purchase display. Figure 14–1 shows the relationship of the promotional mix, promotional strategy, and overall marketing strategy.

Determining the proper "mix" of advertising, personal selling, and other forms of promotion is one of marketing management's major problems. If management decides to rely mainly on personal selling, advertising and direct mail may be directed primarily toward making sales rep's calls more effective. For example, advertising may be used to make dealers more receptive to the sales presentation, or to convey part of the selling message, thus saving salespeople's time. In some situations, advertising may take care of the need for contact with smaller accounts, thus making it possible for salespeople to concentrate on larger and more profitable accounts. The opposite situation exists when management decides to rely mainly on advertising—advertising does the preselling, and display provides a reminder so order taking becomes the salesperson's chief function.

Before setting advertising, personal selling, or other promotional appropriations, management should determine the overall promotional appropriation, based on an optimum mix. Advertising, personal selling, and other promotional appropriations should then be apportioned according to their relative importance in the mix. Theory suggests that identical returns in terms of net profit should be produced by the *last* dollar invested in each type of promotion.

## ADVERTISING

The long-term objective of advertising, as of every other business activity, is to increase the firm's net profits. Perhaps the most important short-term objective is to provide support for personal selling and other forms of promotion, since advertising is rarely used separately from other forms of promotion. Under the marketing concept, it is important to remember that advertising also should serve as an effective and efficient source of information for present and prospective customers.

### Appraising the Advertising Opportunity

Advertising opportunities are most apparent: (1) when the product's demand is expansible, (2) when the product can be differentiated in buyers' eyes, and (3) when the nature of the product's demand is conducive to achievement of the marketer's objectives through advertising.

*Demand Expansibility.* If demand can be stimulated through advertising alone, it is said to be "expansible." An expansible demand exists if an increase in advertising results in greater sales of the product or brand with no change in price. An expansible demand is not a necessary condition for the profitable stimulation of selective demand (for a specific brand), inasmuch as selective demand advertising may succeed in winning away customers from competing brands. Nevertheless, existence of an expansible demand adds to the chances of success for selective, as well as primary, demand advertising. Moreover, advertising aimed at stimulating selective demand may win nonusers of the product type to the manufacturer's brand, may win some users of competing brands, and may even increase the brand's consumption among present users.

*Brand Differentiation.* A particularly critical factor in appraising advertising opportunity is the extent to which the brand differs from competing brands. Brand differences and similarities should be identified and appraisals made of their relative importance to specific market segments. Differences that large numbers of consumers consider important furnish the source of selective advertising appeals. If a brand is not very different from competing brands—and consumers know it—the most the manufacturer can hope to accomplish through advertising is brand acceptance. There must be brand differences of substantial importance to consumers if advertising is to succeed in developing brand preference or brand insistence.

*Nature of the Product's Demand.* The potential effectiveness of advertising depends importantly upon management's recognition of the evolutionary stage of the product's demand and management's skill in adjusting the thrust of the advertising appeal accordingly. Advertising appeals may be directed toward stimulating either or both of two broad categories of demand—primary or selective. Primary demand is demand for the *type* of product rather than a specific brand (e.g., demand for refrigerators rather than demand for Norge or Kelvinator). Selective demand is demand for a specific brand. Relative to the product life cycle, stimulation of primary demand precedes stimulation of selective demand. Consumers must want the generic product before they can want some brand of it.

### The Decision to Advertise

Should a firm advertise a particular product? The answer is "Yes, if *sufficient* opportunity exists for improving net profits through advertising." Determining presence of advertising opportunity is one thing, appraising its extent is quite another. Appraising the extent of an advertising opportunity is, in large part, a matter of taking into account: (1) the strength of basic underlying buyers' needs satisfied by the advertised item, (2) the effect of the advertised item's price, relative to unadvertised competitors, on consumers' purchases, (3) the item's distribution intensity, and (4) the costs involved in conducting an advertising program of the required type and magnitude.

***The Product and Basic Consumer Wants.*** Marketing experts have long recognized that if a product will not sell without advertising, it will not sell with advertising. For a product to sell at all, with or without advertising, it must appeal to and satisfy some wants of some consumers at least as well as competing items. Advertising, in other words, possesses no magic capable of causing people to buy things they do not want; however, it may help them to rationalize purchases of products they want but do not need in a strictly economic sense. Who "needs" custom-made shirts at double the price of factory-made shirts? Only a small percentage of men who require unusual sizes actually need custom-made shirts, but many men want them for prestigious reasons. Appeals to these other wants help consumers to rationalize uneconomic but satisfying wants.

In appraising a product with regard to advertising opportunity, the really important questions to ask are: "Do potential buyers have needs that this product or brand is capable of satisfying?" and "How important, or how strong, are these needs?" If there are strong basic needs for the product, the chances are that considerable advertising opportunity exists. If the product is capable of satisfying only comparatively weak and less basic needs, there is not nearly so much advertising opportunity. The extent of the advertising opportunity varies with the strength of the basic underlying needs that are satisfied by the product or brand.

***Price.*** Consumers should consider the product or brand worth the price that it is necessary to charge (including advertising costs). This does not necessarily mean that the advertised item should be priced identically with its unadvertised competitors or even its advertised competitors. Its price should represent reasonable value in the consumer's mind. If considered superior to competing brands, the price may be higher; if considered inferior, the price must be lower. Advertising will not persuade the consumer to pay what is considered an unreasonable price. Yet many consumers feel that an advertised brand is worth a higher price than an unadvertised brand because they are more confident that they are buying what they want. Manufacturers of nationally advertised brands are particularly careful to maintain consistent quality and service to retain customer loyalty.

Consumers usually are willing to pay a small premium because of their confidence in consistent benefits from an advertised brand. Beyond that, its price may exceed an unadvertised brand's price only by the amount at which consumers value its additional advantages. Consumers may determine this added value by personal observation and testing or by acceptance of the advertiser's claims when they are unable to observe and evaluate the differences for themselves. If the advertised brand has no important differences, hidden or otherwise, its price can be no higher than those of its unadvertised competitors.

*Distribution Intensity.* For advertising to attain maximum effectiveness, people influenced by it must be able to find stores that carry the brand. This is a matter of achieving the proper distribution intensity, considering the time consumers are willing to spend looking for the product. If consumers will spend only a little time looking for the product, its distribution should be widespread. If consumers spend considerable searching time on the product, its distribution can be more selective. Company policy on distribution intensity should be closely correlated with the coverage of the proposed advertising.

Even with proper distribution intensity, sales and goodwill may be lost if dealers do not carry sufficient stocks to meet increased demand resulting from the advertising. In order to prevent out-of-stocks from developing, the manufacturer should make certain that dealers know of the anticipated sales increase before the advertising appears. He or she should also see to it that dealers obtain reorders promptly.

*Amount of Advertising Expenditure Required.* The cost of an adequate advertising program not only affects the advertising break-even calculation but is often in its own right a major determinant of whether or not a company should advertise. Since advertising is but one part of the total promotional budget, the amount allocated for advertising should relate directly to advertising's role in the overall promotional plan. This amount, in turn, then must be allocated among the various media according to media rates and advertising messages planned.

The amount of the advertising expenditure will also be dependent on the advertising stage—pioneering, competitive, or retentive. Initial advertising for a product requires heavy expenditure to reach the threshold of awareness of prospective customers. Competitive advertising is determined largely by the level of advertising efforts by major competitors. It will vary from industry to industry, but it is normally much lower than initial advertising. Retentive advertising is at a still lower level. Its purpose is to retain current levels of consumption by reminding customers of the product.

With an estimate of the costs of an adequate advertising program on hand, the decision-maker needs next to determine whether the company can afford the expenditure. This depends partly on the advertising's ability to return sufficient additional gross-margin dollars to pay for itself. But it also depends on the funds the company has available. If there is not enough money to support an adequate program, it is generally best not to advertise at all and to concentrate instead on other promotional methods.

Whether the sales resulting from the advertising are immediate or deferred is also significant. If advertising can produce immediate sales, advertising costs may be met largely as they are incurred from the greater number of gross-margin dollars available. If the advertising investment pays off only over a considerable period, financing the advertising requires a much larger outlay. Companies short of working capital are often able to advertise under the first condition but not the second; this, in turn, causes them to use campaigns designed to produce immediate rather than deferred sales. Better–financed companies may choose advertising designed to produce either immediate or deferred sales or both, depending on the relative attractiveness of the different payoffs.

### Organization for Advertising

The top advertising executive ordinarily serves in a staff capacity, reporting either directly to the chief marketing executive or to a director of marketing communications or promotion. Management must decide either to have the company's own internal advertising department handle advertising production and placement or to utilize an advertising agency's services. How large the advertising staff is depends upon how much of the work is "farmed out" to an agency. Advertising policy formulation, because of its relationship to total marketing policy, generally is not delegated to an agency. However, whether the company should have its own pool of advertising talent or should tap the skills of an agency depends on who is capable of doing the best job. If advertising dollars are to produce the maximum possible impact on sales and profits, all elements in the program must be skillfully prepared and executed. Responsibility for advertising success, however, lies not with the agency, but rather with the firm's advertising manager. This placement of responsibility holds whether the firm's own advertising department discharges the entire task of advertising or whether all or parts of it are handled by an agency.

***The Advertising Agency.*** An advertising agency is a group of experts on various phases of advertising and related marketing problems. In its operations, it resembles other organizations that provide expert assistance on specialized business problems—the management consulting firm, the marketing research firm, and the firm specializing in design and administration of incentive campaigns for sales reps and dealers. But in the way it normally receives its compensation, the advertising agency is distinct from other consulting organizations.

*Compensation of Agencies.* The "commission system" is the traditional and still most widely used method of compensating advertising agencies. Agencies pay for space and time used on behalf of advertisers at the "card rate" less a certain discount, usually 15 percent, and bill clients at the card rate. Thus, agencies receive their basic compensation from advertising media rather than from advertisers, and this has been the source of considerable argument.

Advertisers, especially large ones, maintain that agencies may overspend for media simply because so much of their compensation comes from media commissions. Advertising agencies, as might be expected, have been the main defenders of the commission system, but more and more of them have been losing their liking for it. Part of the growing disenchantment traces to the consent decree entered into by the American Association of Advertising Agencies in 1956, resulting from an antitrust suit brought by the U.S. Department of Justice. This, in effect, made it possible for media to grant commissions to other than "recognized" agencies and in general made the commission system more difficult to enforce and more open to attack.

Even more of the agencies' disaffection for the commission system results from the increasing costs of providing a wide range of services to advertisers: services that include, among others, advertising pretesting, test marketing, conducting research on advertising effectiveness, and marketing counsel and aid in marketing research. At one time agencies performed these services "free," but there now is a growing tendency to bill advertisers for these "extras" on a "cost plus" or "fee" basis. Fees or charges now amount to roughly one-third of the gross incomes of advertising agencies. Some agencies have replaced the commission system entirely with a fee arrangement under which media commissions received are credited toward payment of the agreed fee.

*Advertiser-Agency Relationships.* Through long standing practice, certain relationships between advertisers and their agencies have become standardized. The five most important are: (1) The agency refrains from having two accounts whose products are in direct competition; (2) The advertiser refrains from using two agencies to handle the advertising for the same product; (3) The agency obtains the advertiser's advance approval before it commits him to expenditures; (4) The advertiser pays the agency for media and other invoices promptly and within the cash-discount period; and (5)

The agency passes on to the advertiser the exact dollar amounts of all cash discounts granted by media.

### Developing the Advertising Campaign

The first step in developing an advertising campaign is the clear definition of its objectives. Several other steps follow: determination of the advertising appropriation, selection of advertising media, creation of the actual advertisements and, finally, measuring advertising effectiveness.

*Determining the Advertising Appropriation.* Generally, the advertising appropriation should be "large enough to get the job done." If advertising objectives are profit-related, then the amount of the appropriation should be derived from advertising's predicted effectiveness in bringing in additional profits. If advertising objectives are not directly related to profit (e.g., if the objective is to improve salespeople's morale), then there generally is little basis for predicting either advertising's effectiveness or the amount required to reach the objective.

There is a difference, however, between the way advertisers *should determine* their appropriations and the way most of them actually *do.* The majority, mainly because of difficulties met in isolating the effect of advertising, rely on intuitive methods. However, the only conceptually correct approach is the incremental one, which involves setting the appropriation at the amount that maximizes advertising's net profit contribution. Lack of both understanding and the needed data account for the nonuse of this approach.

*Percent-of-Sales Approach.* In this method management applies some arbitrary percentage to past sales, forecasted sales, or some combination of the two and, supposedly, up comes the amount of the appropriation. The simplicity, in fact, is about the only thing good about this approach for it is difficult to defend on logical grounds. First, it assumes that advertising costs per unit of product remain constant regardless of the sales volume. More importantly, it implicitly assumes that advertising follows sales—advertising should result in sales and not the other way around. Further, the percentage figure, in most cases, can come only from past sales records and past advertising expenditures. There is no assurance that past percentage relationships will hold in the future.

*Objective-and-Task Approach.* There are three steps in this method: (1) Define objectives in terms of desired sales volumes, net profits, and the like; (2) Estimate the amount of advertising space and time needed to achieve these objectives; and (3) Express this amount of advertising in dollars to arrive at the amount of the appropriation. This method is logical in that it treats advertising as a *cause* of sales rather than an effect. If used to maximize net profit contribution of advertising, this method is equivalent to the incremental approach; however, unfortunately, most users appear to concentrate more on the effect of advertising on sales than on net profit. Without a profit-maximization emphasis, this method may produce an appropriation that increases costs rather than profits.

*Other Approaches.*  Three other common approaches to determining the advertising appropriation should be mentioned. The first is the *arbitrary method,* in which the appropriation is decided either "by pure guess" or "by allotting all the advertiser can afford." The second is called *matching competitors' expenditures;* the advertiser, in effect, permits competitors to set the appropriation. The third is the *tax per unit of product,* in which a fixed sum is put into the "advertising pot" for each unit of the product sold or expected to be sold. As should be clear, none of these approaches is defensible on logical grounds.

*Selection of Advertising Media.*  A number of factors influence the allocation of advertising appropriations to media. The nature of the market that the advertiser desires to reach and the type of product being promoted are the most fundamental. Also important are the distinctive characteristics of specific media; for example, newspapers are issued daily thus, some advertisers tend to use them and others to avoid them. Appropriation size is also important—small budgets usually mean that expenditures should be concentrated in a few media for best results, whereas large budgets ordinarily must be spread over many media to avoid a premature onset of diminishing returns. Ideally, media circulation (general exposure) should be heavily concentrated in the geographical areas where the advertiser has distribution.

Conceptually, the problem in media selection lies in determining optimum allocation of the advertising appropriation. The total should be so divided among the different media—newspapers, magazines, television, outdoor posters, and so forth—that the marginal returns from each type are all equal.

Cost may become a crucial selection factor, particularly when the choice is among media in the same classification—for example, between two magazines. In situations of this sort, each magazine typically has a different size of circulation and different advertising rates. The comparison technique is to convert circulation and rate figures to a common basis. Magazines, for instance, are normally compared according to the cost of reaching 1,000 readers with a given amount of advertising space. Newspapers are compared according to the cost of reaching one million readers with one agate line of advertising. Cost comparisons of other media follow similar patterns.

*Creation of the Advertisements.*  The actual preparation of the advertisements for a campaign involves creativity of a high order. It is difficult and probably impossible to evaluate such creativity on a quantitative basis.

The actual advertisements are produced by the advertising profession's creative people—the copywriters and artists—but the overall qualitative evaluation and approval of their outputs are the responsibilities of the advertiser's marketing and advertising executives.

*Measuring Advertising Effectiveness.* Most companies devote very little research effort toward improving advertising effectiveness. It is estimated that probably no more than one–fifth of one percent of total advertising expenditure is used to achieve an enduring understanding of how to spend the other 99.8 percent. Most measures of advertising effectiveness in current use are rather superficial. However, a few companies are carrying on promising experiments designed to hold other influences on sales constant and to measure the difference in results between experimental and control groups.

## MANAGEMENT OF PERSONAL SELLING

Personal selling is the most common, and often the most critical, element in the promotional mix. In fact, sales frequently are made without the support of any other promotional element. Even advertising, the next most common form of promotion, is not essential in many selling situations, particularly those in industrial marketing. However, only rarely is a sale made without a salesperson to clinch the deal. In some instances, salespersons are merely order-takers, but they are still necessary to "ring the cash register."

Personal selling is a highly distinctive form of promotion. Like other forms of promotion, it is basically a method of communication; but unlike others, it is two-way rather than one-way communication. Rather than individual behavior, it is social behavior; each of the persons in face-to-face contact, salesperson and prospect, influences the other. The sales rep's effectiveness is determined by numerous factors affecting both the customer and the seller. The outcome of each sales situation depends importantly upon the success both parties experience in communicating with each other and in reaching a common understanding of needs and goals.

### Determining the Personal Selling Strategy

There are both differences and similarities between the management of personal selling and the management of advertising. Unlike the options open in advertising, in using personal selling, a manufacturer assembles its own pool of selling talent, develops its skills, and directs its operations. It is, of course, possible for a manufacturer to shift personal selling activities to middlemen, but this is not nearly so common a practice as shifting advertising activities to an agency. There are problems, similar to those met in advertising, in determining the kind of selling force needed, its size, the method of compensating sales reps, the amount of the personal selling appropriation, and the allocation of personal selling effort among customers and prospects.

*The Personal Selling Appropriation.*   As with determination of the advertising appropriation, determination of the personal selling appropriation should come after the *total* promotional appropriation, which is based on an optimum promotional mix, has been set. Funds from the overall promotional appropriation should be allocated to personal selling according to its relative importance in the total mix.

Marketing plans drafted with a view toward achieving sales and profit goals ultimately must be translated into the types and amounts of marketing effort required. Sooner or later, management deals with the problem of converting these types and amounts of marketing effort into dollar cost estimates. Thus, an increase in the sales–volume goal may call for the hiring of a certain number of new salespeople, their training, providing them with expense allowances, securing and assigning additional supervisors, and so on. In allocating the personal selling appropriation, management must: (1) estimate the volume of performance for each required activity and (2) convert these performance volumes into dollar cost estimates.

The size of the sales force and the amount of the personal selling appropriations are related, but not necessarily directly so. The relationship varies not only with the company but with management's decisions. In apportioning the personal selling appropriation, management is continually faced with such questions as: Should we hire five additional salespeople at a total cost of $150,000 or should we invest the same amount in refresher training for the present sales force? Should we add sales supervisors or use the same number of dollars for conducting sales contests?

*The Job Description.*   In every company the job description outlining the duties and responsibilities of every selling job lies at the heart of sales force management. The nature of sales positions varies from company to company, for although sales reps in different companies have similar duties and responsibilities, the emphasis on specific tasks differs.

Effectiveness in managing the personal sales force depends considerably on the completeness and accuracy of the sales job descriptions. Through analysis of the duties and responsibilities making up the job, management derives the set of qualifications that sellers should possess. This furnishes guidance in searching out and in selecting for employment recruits with the desired qualifications. In addition, in some well-managed companies, the sales job description carries with it a statement of the performance standards management will use in appraising sales people's effectiveness.

*Rates of Sales Force Turnover.*   In determining the number of sales reps required for implementing a company's marketing strategy, management should consider the rate of sales force turnover. If a company has one hundred sellers, needs all one hundred for the coming year's operations, and has a 10 percent annual turnover, ten new reps must be recruited during the year. Not only is the rate of sales force turnover an important planning tool, it is also a widely used measure of efficiency in sales force management. This rate is defined as the number of salespeople separated, resigned, fired, etc., per 100 on the sales force. With increases in the rate of sales force turnover, costs of managing the sales force rise. Recent studies indicate that it costs as much as $12,000 to search out, select, hire, and supervise a salesperson until he or she begins to pay his or her own way.

Every sales force should have some turnover. When there is no turnover, the sales force may be growing stale, and inefficient salesmen may be staying on simply because the management has failed to replace them. Management must try to optimize turnover so as to eliminate "dead wood" and at the same time keep costs of turnover as low as possible.

*Size of Sales Force.* An individual salesperson performing the duties and responsibilities set forth in the job description represents one unit of sales manpower so that determining the proper number of salesmen is equivalent to determining the number of units of sales manpower needed to accomplish management's sales and profit goals. Logically these goals, both derived from the sales forecast, should establish the optimum size of the sales force. If the sales job description is accurate and complete, it should be possible to estimate the number of sales dollars that each sales rep should produce. Dividing this amount into forecasted sales and making an allowance for the rate of sales force turnover should indicate the number of salespeople needed. Difficulties in making these estimates vary both with the factor being estimated and the company.

The estimate for forecasted sales volume deserves some comment. In many situations, the magnitude of the sales forecast is itself influenced by the size of sales force that management plans to have. In fact, any realistic sales forecast must take into account the number of sales reps at management's disposal. When a company is young, especially when it is growing rapidly, its potential sales volume often depends primarily on the number and ability of its salesmen. In such a company, management actually may derive its sales forecast by multiplying the estimated sales productivity of an individual salesperson by the total number it has and can expect to keep, and the number it can recruit and train in the coming period. But as a company extends its distribution over a wider and wider geographic area, and as it approaches maturity, the situation reverses itself; then the size of the sales force is determined by making the sales forecast first, dividing this by the expected sales productivity of an individual sales rep and making adjustments for anticipated sales force turnover, needed time for training, and similar factors.

### Determining the Kind of Sales Force Needed

The kind of sales force that is appropriate for a particular manufacturer depends on many factors, but especially on the mix of marketing inputs or the overall marketing strategy. Salespeople in some situations must aggressively seek orders and in other situations need only take orders that come to them, but the degree of emphasis on order-taking and order-getting varies with different selling jobs. The driver salesperson for a soft drink bottling company is primarily an order-taker, since the product is strongly presold to consumers, and retailers reorder automatically for stock. The salesperson calling on householders to sell encyclopedias is much more of an order-getter, since the primary responsibility is to create demand.

Selling tasks can be grouped into four basic styles of selling that cut, to a large degree, across industry boundaries: trade selling, missionary selling, technical selling, and new-business selling. The trade seller develops long-term relations with a relatively stable group of customers; the selling is low key with little or no pressure, and it tends to be on the dull and routine side. The missionary seller is responsible for increasing the company's sales volume by helping direct customers with their selling efforts; the orders obtained result from the primary public relations and promotional efforts with the customers (retailers) of the customers (wholesalers). The technical seller deals primarily with the company's established accounts, and his or her aim is to increase the volume of purchase by providing technical advice and assistance. The new business salesperson's main responsibility is to find new customers—to convert prospects into customers.

### Managing the Sales Force

The chief sales executive's job is to insure that the sales force plays the roles assigned to it as a part of the overall marketing strategy. There are four main "sales force management" responsibilities: recruiting and selecting, training, compensating, and controlling.

*Recruiting and Selecting.* Recruiting involves determining who has the desired qualifications, identifying the sources of recruits, and choosing recruiting methods. Each previously used source should be analyzed according to the number of recruits obtained and their success or failure as company salesmen. Although company employees occasionally make good sales reps, external sources, such as colleges and other companies employing sales reps, are usually most productive. A selection system should be a set of successive "screens," at any one of which job candidates may be dropped from further consideration. The number and sophistication of screens depends upon the resources management is willing to invest in selection. Candidates surviving all screenings receive job offers.

*Training the Sales Force.* Most companies have sales training programs both for newly hired employees and refresher programs for "veteran" salespersons. For new sales reps the training program content normally includes: product data, sales techniques, evaluation of markets, and company information. Training methods for both new and veteran sales staff involve both group and individual instructional techniques. On-the-job training is the most common and generally the most important individual technique.

*Compensating Salespeople.* The duties and responsibilities inherent in each selling job determine the level of compensation necessary to attract and hold good men. Because sales reps enjoy high job mobility, they ordinarily must be paid approximately what competitors' salespersons are paid.

Every method for compensating sales reps represents some combination of four elements: (1) a fixed portion (salary), (2) a variable portion (commission, bonus, or a share in profits), (3) an element providing for either reimbursement of expenses or payments of an expense allowance, and (4) such "fringe benefits" as paid vacations, pensions, and insurance. Because "expense" provisions and "fringe benefits" are never used alone, they may be excluded from consideration so that three basic methods of payment emerge: (1) straight salary, (2) straight commission, and (3) a combination of salary and one or more variable features.

Each basic method represents a different balance of two underlying purposes of compensation: to provide management with the power to direct sales activities and to furnish salespeople with the incentive to work productively and efficiently. At the two extremes are the straight-salary and straight-commission methods.

*Supervising and Controlling Salespeople.* Effective supervision and control are essential to securing optimum performance from sales reps. This involves both the careful allocation of the seller's efforts and appraising his or her performance.

*Allocating Personal Selling Effort.* Once management commits itself to a certain size of sales force, it faces the task of allocating each salesperson's efforts to the best advantage. This involves assigning sales reps to territories and routing and scheduling their calls.

Assignment to a territory focuses the efforts on a given geographical area containing a grouping of customers and prospects. Each territory represents some potential volume of sales to the company. Whenever a sales rep is assigned to a territory, management has, in effect, matched some level of selling skill with the amount of sales opportunity that it believes to be present in that territory. Therefore, both the relative abilities of salespeople and the relative sales potentials of territories should be considered in assigning sales reps to territories. Too often, however, problems of appraising salespeople's efficiency and evaluating territorial sales potentials are treated independently. Because sales reps differ in efficiency, and because territories differ in sales potential, a *rational* assignment would put the best salesperson in the most fertile territory, the second-best in the second-most fertile territory, and so on. Only if the assignment is made in this way is it possible to maximize total sales in the entire market.

Once sales reps are assigned to territories, the next problem is to use their available selling time to the best advantage, limiting "waste" time and well–allocating productive selling time among individual accounts and prospects. "Waste" time includes: time spent in travel between calls, time spent waiting for interviews, and other time during regular selling hours not used for performing either selling or nonselling duties (that is, time "idled away").

Not every company uses formal planning and control of sales routes and call schedules. In some instances, management believes sellers to be the best judges of how they should spend their time. In other instances, formal routing and scheduling may be inappropriate. For example, it is difficult to predict the amount of selling time that each account will require for products designed to each customer's specifications or for door-to-door selling.

***Appraising Sales Performance.*** Success or failure in maximizing the contribution of the personal selling effort is the responsibility of management, not of the seller, and managerial excellence in making and implementing the key decisions determines the degree of success. The performance of salespersons, individually and collectively, directly affects the success of the personal selling effort, and management needs performance measures. Without performance measurements, management is handicapped in predicting the probable results of its decisions. Measurement is essential to deciding such questions as which salespeople to discharge, which to train further, and which to reward. Performance measures are needed, then, for both decision making and control. There must also be ways for distinguishing good performance from poor. Standards or norms against which to appraise the performance of the individual are needed.

One place to start in appraising overall performance is with the job description. Comparison of what the salesperson does against what the job description says he or she should be doing provides insight into the total performance. The trouble with the job description, however, is that many of the sales duties and responsibilities do not lend themselves to quantitative measurement. How, for example, can one measure how much good will a salesperson builds? Or what measures are there for quantifying his or her mental alertness in dealing with customers? Probably the best that can be done is to define, as clearly as possible, what performance is expected for each duty and responsibility. Some definitions may include quantitative performance standards (for example, the call frequencies for different classes of accounts), but most necessarily have to be phrased only as qualitative statements of what management expects.

Quotas are the most common yardsticks used to measure selling performance. A quota is a quantitatively expressed goal assigned to a specific marketing unit, such as to a seller or a territory. On the basis of his past performance, a sales rep might be expected to produce a predetermined volume of sales; or on the basis of measured market potential, a territory might be expected to yield a predetermined volume of sales. Quotas may be in terms of dollars or unit sales volume, gross margin, net profit, expenses, calls, number of new accounts, amount of dealer display space obtained, or other measurable quantities.

The dollar sales volume quota presents a major problem. Sales efforts do not always produce sales in the period for which the performance is being evaluated, and the results of a seller's current efforts may materialize only over many future periods. In addition, each sales rep is faced with different working conditions, many influencing the relative ease with which sales are made. Territory by territory, there are variations in competition, required travel time, and sales potential. Thus, it is rare to find a company that is justified in assigning identical sales-volume quotas to all salespeople. Because of competitive, physical, and sales fertility differences among territories, then, the sales volume quota for each seller should be set individually. Another important reason for individually set quotas is that salespeople also vary in selling efficiency because of differences in training, experience, and native abilities.

Distinguishing sales results produced by the sales force from those due to other causes is another major problem. Advertising, for instance, is often an influence in making many sales, but it is usually the seller who writes the actual order. At other times, the salesperson may write the order, but the supervisor or branch manager may actually have been the major influence in the customer's buying decision. In such cases, it is next to impossible to determine the sales rep's contribution precisely.

The sales forecast should be the main basis for setting sales volume quotas, since carefully prepared forecasts, when intelligently broken down, result in quotas that are reasonable and thus attainable. By breaking the forecast down into manageable parts—that is, into sales volume quotas for individual salesmen—management can specifically define the results it expects from each person's effort. However, it should be recognized that a sales volume quota can be no better than the sales forecast from which it is derived. If the forecast is little more than a wild guess, the quota derived from it will be no better. Improvements in sales forecasts and sales volume quotas go hand in hand.

## OTHER METHODS OF PROMOTION

*Point-of-Purchase Display.* The point-of-purchase display is the silent seller that calls the shopper's attention to the product, hopefully initiating buying action. Retailers rely heavily on in-store displays to provide customers with opportunities to examine and become familiar with the product, even in some instances to allow them to use or test it. Display ranges all the way from a dealer's showing of new automobiles, with promotional literature and pricing details, to a chewing gum display rack on top of a restaurant's cash register, or one for paperbacks in an airline terminal. Display is also an important promotional method in trade shows and expositions for industrial and institutional buyers. Display rarely bears the entire promotional burden; it nearly always is used in combination with personal selling or advertising, or both.

*Direct Mail.* While direct mail has much the same purpose as other printed advertising messages, it usually allows greater precision in selecting target receivers. For the same cost, a single newspaper advertisement might reach 10,000 readers, and direct mail only one hundred prospects. However, if the mailing list is compiled carefully, the one hundred direct mail messages may reach more real prospects than the newspaper advertisement. Direct mail provides an appropriate way to maintain contact with customers of industrial products between sales rep's calls. Also, like advertising, it can provide a product awareness and acceptance that increases purchase probabilities when buyers later are contacted by sales reps or see displays.

*Packaging.* Packaging, in addition to serving as a means of differentiating or protecting a product, also plays an important role in promotion. An attractively designed package both calls attention to the product in the retail store and provides a selling message. The package's promotional role is particularly important for products sold through self-service outlets. If three competing brands are placed side by side on a retail shelf, the consumers' attention more than likely will be drawn to the best designed package.

## *CONCLUSION*

There is no one best way to promote all products in all situations. The appropriate makeup for a particular promotional campaign depends upon numerous factors that vary in their influence at different times even for the same product. Probably the most critical factors are: product variations, purchase frequencies, market penetration, and market variations. In this chapter the two main components of promotion—advertising and personal selling—and the lesser elements in promotion have been analyzed. Basic to the management of these elements is the concept of the optimum promotional mix, from which should be derived the most appropriate proportions of advertising, personal selling, and other methods of promotion. Within the advertising area, not only must the extent of the advertising opportunity be appraised, but decisions must be reached regarding the advertising agency, the amount of the advertising appropriation, and the selection of media. Within the personal selling area, among the many problems met are those of determining whether salespeople should be mainly order getters or order takers, the number of salespeople, the amount of the personal-selling appropriation and its allocation, the assignment of sales reps to territories, the routing and scheduling of sales calls, and the appraisal of sales performance. Theory suggests not only that the marginal efficiencies of the promotional inputs should be equated, but that the same goal should be sought relative to the numerous subactivities that make up each major form of promotion.

# 15

# PRICING

Products may be matched with markets, but only when buyers and sellers agree on *prices* do ownership transfers occur. Without prices, there is no marketing. Either buyer or seller may propose a price, but it does not become one until accepted by the other.

Pricing generally is controllable. Marketers enjoy considerable freedom in making pricing decisions, defining pricing objectives, formulating pricing policies, and deciding pricing strategies. These activities, individually and jointly, have important effects on the relative ease with which "ownership transfers" are effected and, hence, upon sales volume and profits.

## FACTORS INFLUENCING PRICING DECISIONS

Numerous factors influence pricing decisions. These include both factors internal to the company and environmental factors.

### Product and Market Factors

***Stage in Product Life Cycle.*** The amount of discretion management has in making pricing decisions varies with the stage in the product life cycle. During market pioneering, the innovator enjoys wide discretion ranging from setting the initial price high to "skim" the market to setting it low to achieve market "penetration" quickly. Competitors enter during the market growth stage, but nonprice competition prevails and, at first, individual companies (because of differentiated products) have considerable freedom in pricing. During later phases of market growth and early market maturity, different competitors see opportunities to "widen the market," and price reductions become key factors in securing further market expansions. Sometime during market maturity, however, the market approaches saturation and price reductions no longer expand sales; emphasis shifts from selling to new users to making replacement sales to present users, through introducing new models or using other forms of product differentiation, and prices stabilize. Finally, during market decline, sporadic price reductions occur as different companies "clear out stocks" and discontinue the product.

*Product Differentiation.* If a marketer succeeds in differentiating its product, an opportunity may exist to cultivate buyers to whom product differences are more important than relative prices. Customers who consider product differentiation important do not wholly ignore price but they are not likely to buy competing brands solely because of small price differences. A prospective new car buyer with a strong preference for Chevrolet, for instance, will not buy a Ford or a Plymouth because of a price difference unless it is substantial. Price is not unimportant to such a buyer and he or she may shop around among several Chevrolet dealers to get the best terms, but in selecting the *brand,* product differences are more important than price.

*Customers' Buying Patterns.* Purchase frequency may affect offering prices. Items consumers buy frequently, for instance, are sold profitably by middlemen at low markups because of fast inventory turnover. When sales are high relative to inventory investment, a small profit per sale returns a large annual profit. High turnover products, such as most grocery items, are profitably retailed at 15 to 20 percent markups, whereas slow turnover products require higher retail markups—hardware, for instance, carries a 35 to 40 percent retail markup.

The usual quantity purchased also may affect offering prices. The larger the quantity bought at a time, the lower the marketing cost is per unit. Thus, for instance, it costs a retailer little more to sell six of an item than to sell one, so cost savings make possible profitable price reductions for quantity purchases. Purchases in larger quantities also tend to increase the buyer's total consumption because the item's increased availability often promotes greater use.

*Price Elasticity.* The relative sensitivity of sales volume to changes in price varies widely among different products. Demand for fresh strawberries is price elastic, since a small price change increases (or decreases) their sale considerably. Demand for coal is price inelastic, since a relatively small price change has little effect on the number of tons sold. These generalizations, of course, hold only within certain limits. A large increase in the price of coal, for instance, may cause buyers to switch to less expensive fuels.

When a product has a price inelastic demand, its marketer has little incentive to cut the price, since sales revenue per unit of product decreases more rapidly than unit sales increase. The marketer is much more tempted to raise it, as sales revenue per unit of product increases faster than unit sales decline. However, the availability and prices of substitute products limit the profitability of any sizable price increase.

When a product's demand is price elastic, pricing decisions generally are no less difficult. Unless a company has no strong competitors at all (a rare situation except during market pioneering), it cannot hope to take business permanently away from competitors through a price reduction, since they can and probably will quickly match or better it. Price reductions in such cases are profitable to individual companies only if they expand the industry's total sales so that the increase in the quantity the industry sells more than offsets the loss of sales revenue per unit. And, if close substitutes exist, declines in their prices may cancel out or reduce anticipated sales increases. Price increases are no more attractive unless competitors follow; even if they do go along, availability and prices of substitute products limit the profitability of any sizable price increase.

*Other Characteristics of the Product's Market.* Other characteristics of a product's market affect pricing. The size of the potential market makes a considerable difference: if a marketer can anticipate a large sales volume, it can realize substantial economies in physical distribution and promotion, thus reducing total marketing costs, and may use an accordingly lower price to improve the chances of attaining that sales volume. The relative density of the potential market (i.e., the degree of concentration of possible buyers) also affects marketing costs and, consequently, offering prices. Any factor that may change marketing costs affects pricing, since it shifts the level at which the price can be set and still be profitable.

### Marketing Channels and Distribution Policy

Pricing decisions take into account the size of the gross margins middlemen expect. Such expectations reflect individual middlemen's costs and their profit objectives as well as the scope and importance of the activities each is to perform for the manufacturer. In fact, each middleman's cost and the services performed are related; i.e., services involve costs. A wholesaler carrying an inventory and handling repairs, for instance, has higher costs and expects more gross margin than one who neither carries an inventory nor handles repairs. If the channel includes more than one level of middlemen, the gross margin requirements and services performed by each level need considering.

Similarly, if the marketer follows an exclusive or highly selective distribution policy, there are implications for pricing. Companies having such policies expect dealers to perform additional services. Dealers, in turn, expect larger margins. The manufacturer using mass distribution bears such costs directly; consequently, the dealers obtain lower gross margins on the product.

### Promotional Strategy

Promotional strategy affects pricing decisions. If a manufacturer, for example, uses massive advertising to "pull the product through the channel," it probably will allow middlemen somewhat less-than-normal gross margins. If the manufacturer expects them to assume some of the advertising burden, they expect greater-than-normal gross margins. If the manufacturer minimizes its use of advertising and other promotion, then it may offer middlemen lower prices (and higher gross margins) to get them to provide needed promotional support.

### Costs

The extent to which costs can or should enter into pricing decisions varies. Over the long run, sales revenues (i.e., prices × unit volumes) must be sufficient to recover all costs. But short-run prices do not necessarily have to cover costs; buyers neither know nor care whether sellers' prices cover costs.

*Nature of Cost Data.* Cost figures often are not as objective as they appear. Although costs are expressed in precise dollar amounts, their computation requires many subjective judgments. Production cost accounting involves numerous arbitrary allocations of overhead costs to arrive at unit cost. Distribution cost accounting often requires even more judgmental decisions.

Furthermore, cost data adequate for accounting purposes are often ill-suited for pricing decisions. Accountants work mostly with historical costs and are mainly concerned with controlling current operating costs. Pricing decisions are more closely related to future costs than to either present or past costs. Thus, pricing decision-makers are more concerned with "estimated" than "known" costs.

Estimating production costs accurately is particularly difficult for joint-cost products. A manufacturer making several products in the same plant, often on the same machinery, may find it impossible to allocate total costs among them except on a wholly arbitrary basis. The unreliability of the resulting cost data often leads to pricing individual products according to "what the traffic will bear," using cost data only as a general guide to insure that total sales revenue on all products is enough to cover total costs.

### Competition

While most modern marketers seek to compete on a nonprice basis to the utmost extent, they cannot entirely ignore competitors' prices. Nonprice competition may enable a marketer to gain partial "control" over a market segment through product differentiation or selective distribution for example. This may enable it to obtain higher prices than competitors, but when their prices change, it must keep its prices generally in line; otherwise, its "control" over the market segment slips away.

Furthermore, in making pricing decisions, a marketer must consider competitors' likely reactions. Will they follow a price rise? A price cut? How soon? A price change is the easiest switch in marketing strategy to copy, and copying can be almost instantaneous. That, perhaps, is why most marketers prefer nonprice competition—product, channel, and promotion changes are neither easy to copy nor can they be followed quickly. The first competitor making a profitable nonprice move gains more than a temporary advantage.

### Economic Climate

Because of the "stickiness" of administered prices, the company emphasizing nonprice competition tends to adjust slowly to changing economic conditions. Slowness in changing administered prices causes delays in price reductions at the beginning of a recession, causes inventories to build up to abnormally high levels, and necessitates even larger price cuts later on. Similarly, during periods of rapidly rising costs, which are often characteristic of business upturns, increases in administered prices lag behind the need, resulting in cost-price "squeezes." Therefore the company emphasizing nonprice competition should be alert to impending economic changes and make needed and timely price adjustments.

### Legislation and Governmental Pressures

Practically every country has legislation that influences pricing alternatives. In the United States, for instance, at the federal level the Clayton Act, as amended by the Robinson-Patman Act, prohibits several pricing practices that discriminate among like buyers: cumulative quantity discounts, noncumulative quantity discounts in excess of actual cost savings, "dummy" brokerage payments, and discriminatory promotional allowances. At the state level, some states have Unfair Practices Acts prohibiting sales at prices below costs (or *cost* plus some designated *markup*).

The possibility that governmental pressures will be brought to bear is a factor that decision-makers, particularly in basic industries where price increases might be regarded as inflationary, should consider. In industries whose members produce less "basic" and more differentiated products, the likelihood of governmental intervention is more remote but still possible. In fact, governmental intervention in pricing decisions is likely to become increasingly frequent and more influential in the future, especially during inflationary periods.

## PRICING OBJECTIVES

Pricing objectives derive directly from company objectives. They provide guidance to decision-makers in formulating price policies, planning pricing strategies, and setting actual prices. Probably most companies have profit as *a* main pricing objective.

It is not at all clear, however, that profit maximization is *the* main objective. Occasionally, a company "charges what the traffic will bear"— this may be short-run profit maximization but it is not the way to maximize long-run profit. Most experts suggest, in fact, that companies should deliberately refrain from maximizing short-run profits in order to maximize them in the long run. But it is impossible to prove that a short-run pricing strategy actually leads to maximum long-run profits.

Profit maximization, then, is more an ideal than a usable pricing objective. Recognizing the elusiveness of profit maximization, realistic decision-makers focus on other pricing objectives related, in one way or another, to securing, if not the maximum, at least a satisfactory long-run profit. Typical pricing objectives of large companies are: (1) to achieve a target return on investment, (2) to stabilize prices, (3) to hold or obtain a target market share, and (4) to meet or keep out competition.

## PRICE POLICIES

Price policies constitute the framework within which pricing decisions are made to achieve pricing objectives and the guide lines within which pricing strategy is formulated and implemented. Although price policies should be reviewed continually, they form an important part of the company's image and should be changed only infrequently. Each company needs a "bundle" of price policies appropriate not only to company and pricing objectives but to its overall marketing situation.

### Pricing Relative to Competition

Every company adheres to some policy, either explicity or implicitly, regarding the price of its products relative to those of competitors. If competition is mainly on a price basis, then each company generally prices its products the same as its competitors. If there is nonprice competition, each marketer chooses from among the three alternatives discussed below.

*Meeting Competition.* This is the alternative usually chosen. Marketers competing on a nonprice basis meet competitors' prices, hoping thereby to minimize the use of price as a competitive weapon. A "meeting competition" price policy does not mean meeting every competitor's prices, but only the prices of important competitors—"important" in the sense that what such competitors do in their pricing may lure customers away.

*Pricing Above the Competition.* This is less common but appropriate in certain circumstances. Sometimes higher-than-average prices convey an impression of above-average product quality or prestige. Many buyers relate a product's price to its quality, especially when it is difficult to judge quality before actually buying. In these instances, buyers may pay a little more for an item whose higher price implies higher quality.

Sometimes, too, a manufacturer "suggests" higher-than-average prices in the hope of improving middlemen's cooperation. If the manufacturer wants distributors and dealers to exert especially aggressive selling and promotional efforts, it may set relatively high "list" prices at which it suggests they resell the product to secure above-average markups. The higher markups are passed on to consumers in the form of higher prices, but the increased cooperation of the middlemen may more than offset the sales-depressing tendency of the higher prices and may even increase total sales. Generally, for a product to compete successfully at a price above the market, it must either be so strongly differentiated that buyers believe it superior to competitive brands or middlemen must enthusiastically and heavily promote it.

*Pricing Under the Competition.* Many firms price under the market. Some have lower costs because their products are of lower quality. Others substitute lower prices for the promotional efforts (which also cost money) used by their competitors. In all cases, however, firms following this policy must either have low costs or be willing to accept a lower profit per unit on a large sales volume.

### Pricing Relative to Costs

Every company has a policy regarding the relationships it should seek to maintain between its products' prices and the underlying costs. Long-run sales revenues must cover all long-run costs but short-run prices do not necessarily have to cover all short-run costs. Thus, some policy is needed to guide short-run pricing decisions toward attainment of long-run pricing objectives. There are two main alternatives.

*Cost Concepts.* The three cost concepts most relevant to pricing decisions are fixed costs, variable costs, and marginal costs. *Fixed costs,* often called "overhead costs," do not vary with the amount of sales; they include salaries, rent, heat, light, depreciation, property taxes, bond interest, and the like. By contrast, *variable costs* vary somewhat automatically with the amount of sales recorded; they include such costs as raw materials, labor paid on a piece rate or hourly basis, salespeople's commission, and packaging, packing, warehousing usage, and shipping costs. *Marginal costs* are the changes in cost when production is changed by one or some other given number of units.

*Full–Cost Pricing.* Under this policy, no sale is made at a price lower than that covering total costs including both variable costs and an allocated share of fixed costs. The reasoning is that if prices cover short-run costs, they will also cover long-run costs. Nevertheless, rigid adherence to this policy is not only difficult but often downright stupid: The price buyers are willing to pay may bear little or no relationship to the seller's costs, and there are complex and numerous problems involved in determining "real" costs. Furthermore, prices on items already in the inventory oftentimes must be cut below full cost in order to sell at all. Most businesses should try to keep prices above short-run costs in *most* situations, but they should also define the conditions under which departures are permitted. A full-cost pricing policy should be regarded only as a flexible guide to decision-making.

*Contribution Pricing.* A company with a contribution pricing policy uses full-cost pricing whenever possible but will price, under certain conditions at any level above the relevant incremental costs. Suppose a seller is offered a special contract to supply a large buyer who is not willing to pay the going price. The buyer may argue that the price differential is justified because of savings to the seller in selling time, credit costs, handling expenses, and the like. Still the demanded price concession may exceed the likely savings, so that total income from the proposed transaction is not enough to cover total costs. Emphasizing the short-run aspects, most economists would advise the marketer to accept the order, *if* the resulting revenues were large enough not only to cover all incremental costs but to make some contribution to fixed costs and/or profits. After all, current sales at established prices may already be large enough to cover the fixed costs, and the proposed sale at a special price will not raise fixed costs (assuming the incremental costs are all variable costs) so this sale need not bear an allocated share of fixed costs to yield net revenue. In other words, the argument is that so long as the proposed price more than covers the direct, or out-of-pocket, costs of the transaction, then the excess over direct costs represents profit.

Economists, however, often do not clarify all the conditions under which they make this recommendation. The important purpose of a contribution pricing policy, then, is to specify what offers at prices under full cost will be considered and under what conditions. Two important conditions should both be present for such offers to be accepted: (1) the company has the capacity *and* can put it to no more profitable use, *and* (2) the portion of the output sold below full cost is destined for a different market segment. Both conditions are important but the second is critical to the continuance of prices at full cost or above for the bulk of the output.

### Uniformity of Prices to Different Buyers

Every marketer should have a policy outlining the conditions under which it will charge different buyers identical prices and those under which it will allow price differentials. A contribution pricing policy, as explained above, details one set of conditions under which it might charge differential prices. But the question of uniformity of offering prices also arises in other circumstances.

*One-Price vs. Variable-Price Policy.* Marketers generally prefer to sell on a one-price basis, i.e., by offering all like buyers exactly the same price. In the United States, the one-price policy is used in selling most consumer products and most industrial products. Elsewhere, especially in the developing countries, sellers commonly use variable pricing even for consumer items.

Sellers regard the one-price policy as attractive for three reasons: (1) it provides a uniform return from each sale, making for fewer problems in forecasting sales and profits, (2) since prices are not negotiated with individual customers, selling costs are lower, and (3) there is less risk of alienating customers because of preferential prices given others.

Variable pricing, however, is common where individual transactions are large. It is hardly worth a consumer's or retailer's time to bargain over the price of a pound of coffee, and the loss of an individual sale is not important enough to cause reconsideration of the price. But, in buying an auto, many consumers exert considerable effort to obtain a lower price, and the sale is important enough for the dealer to "negotiate."

The bargaining power of individual buyers varies with the transaction size. In the industrial market, a large buyer generally represents a greater potential for future business than a small buyer so a seller may make concessions to gain or retain the large buyer's patronage. In addition, some buyers have greater bargaining power because of their ability to pay cash. For these reasons, negotiated pricing and variable price policies exist in many industrial markets and even in some consumer markets. Reluctant as many sellers of consumer durables are to admit that their prices are not fixed, often they "hold to" one price and negotiate on the value of "trade-ins."

### Price Differentials

Most marketers vary their prices under certain conditions even though they generally adhere to one-price policies. Price differentials may be based on size of purchase, type of customer, or buyer's geographical location. Normally, the marketer using these kinds of price differentials extends them to all buyers meeting the specified requirements.

*Quantity Discounts.* Offering price reductions on large purchases is common. Through quantity discounts sellers try to increase sales by passing on to buyers part of the savings resulting from large purchases. These savings can be considerable for it may take no more of a salesperson's time to sell a very large order than a small one. And the same holds for order–processing, order–filling, billing, and transportation costs, the last of which is cheaper per unit because of quantity rates offered by carriers.

United States firms using quantity discounts must keep two legal restrictions in mind (both included in the Clayton Act): (1) the price reduction can be no greater than the actual savings resulting from the larger quantity order, and (2) discounts must be made available on proportionately equal terms to all like purchasers. Within these restrictions, quantity discounts provide a way to reduce marketing costs and increase market penetration.

***Trade Discounts.*** A marketer often sells the same product to different classes of buyers. A paper manufacturer, for instance, sells typing paper to wholesalers, to retail chains, and to businesses buying for their own use. Some buyers in each class buy approximately equal quantities on each order, and one might expect the manufacturer to sell at the same price. But other conditions may cause different "trade discounts" from the list price to be offered to each class of buyer. Assume the manufacturer makes 75 percent of its sales through wholesalers; this marketing channel is essential to its success, and it hesitates to do anything that might antagonize or threaten the existence of its wholesalers and the retailers they serve. If it gives a corporate chain the same price it gives wholesalers, its outlets may underprice their independent retailer competitors served by the wholesalers. For this reason, some manufacturers extend lower prices to wholesalers than to even large retail chains regardless of the amounts purchased.

***Other Types of Discounts.*** Many marketers grant other types of discounts. Some offer cash discounts to stimulate prompt payments by buyers. Others allow special promotional discounts to middlemen providing local advertising or other promotional support, though generally such discounts are not offered continuously but periodically, as for short periods during the spring and fall. Still others use seasonal discounts to persuade buyers to place their orders in advance of the normal buying season.

### Geographical Price Differentials

The policy a marketer adopts with respect to "who should pay freight" has an important bearing upon its price quotations to buyers in different geographical locations. In general, the farther away the customer is from the factory, the higher the freight charge is for a given size of shipment. There are three major policy alternatives: (1) "f.o.b." or "free on board" pricing, (2) delivered pricing, and (3) "freight absorption."

***F.O.B. Pricing.*** The marketer using this policy quotes selling prices at the factory (or other point from which it makes sales), and buyers pay all the freight charges. Thus, buyers in different places have different "landed costs"—each pays the price at the selling point, plus the freight from there to its location, thus determining its total costs for the delivered shipment. Variations result not only in buyers' costs but in the wholesale and retail prices the product sells at in different parts of the country. This prevents the marketer from advertising the resale price nationally except in a general way, such as "Priced at $19.95—prices at your local dealer may vary slightly." The main attraction of f.o.b. pricing for the manufacturer is that it simplifies price quotations to those with whom it deals directly.

***Delivered Pricing.*** The marketer using this policy pays all freight charges but, of course, builds them into price quotations. In effect, it averages total freight charges for all customers and incorporates some amount, which may or may not be the "exact" average, into the price quoted. Prices quoted buyers are really f.o.b. destination prices—and the marketer's net return varies with the buyer's location. Delivered pricing is most appropriate when freight charges account for only a small part of the product's selling price or when a marketer attempts to suggest or maintain resale prices or to advertise them nationally. Standardized resale prices are most likely to be obtained when the marketer assures middlemen of uniform markups regardless of their locations.

*Freight Absorption.* Some marketers use a freight absorption policy to counter stiff price competition from sellers located closer to prospective buyers. Generally, this policy takes the form of quoting a price to the buyer that is the usual f.o.b. factory price plus an amount equal to that which the competitive marketer located nearest to the customer would charge. Thus, freight absorption pricing often is adopted to lessen the competitive disadvantages of f.o.b. pricing, especially where strong locally based competition is met in certain markets.

## PRICING STRATEGIES

Pricing strategies vary with the kind of competitive situation met by particular products. Choice of pricing strategy is most critical when the product is one of perishable distinctiveness. During market pioneering, management's choice is between skimming the market at a high price or penetrating it at a lower price. During market growth, management must take direct account of competitors' pricing behavior in formulating pricing strategy; thus, price-skimming generally becomes inappropriate and each competitor tends to set prices that will gain or retain some target market share. During market maturity, the product begins losing its distinctiveness and competition intensifies; the range of competitors' prices narrows and moves toward stability. During market decline, most companies "price competitively," but a few with sizable "hard core" markets obtain a slight premium, curtail promotional costs, and pursue "run-out" strategies. Thus, at each state of the product's life cycle, pricing strategies shift, as the competitive situation changes.

## PRICING PROCEDURE

Procedures for setting prices vary with competitive conditions. At one extreme—in the case of pure "commodities"—pricing is an uncontrollable, market prices being determined by the forces of supply and demand. At the other extreme, where monopolies exist, pricing is almost entirely a controllable, purely "administered" prices being set and held stable by management. In between the extremes—as under oligopolistic or monopolistic competition—in setting prices and in making price changes individual companies, by and large, anticipate and take into account competitors' likely reactions. However, in the vast bulk of American companies, prices are determined administratively rather than through market forces.

Specific price determination procedures differ. In some situations, such as competitive bidding, the buyer determines the seller's price. More often, the seller sets an "offering price," and potential buyers decide whether to accept or reject it. The most widely used price determination procedures are the manufacturer's cost-plus pricing and the middleman's markup pricing. However, variations of break-even analysis combined with demand estimation are seeing increasing use.

The ideal price determination procedure, of course, is to start with what the market will pay for different quantities and work back to the costs of producing and marketing those quantities, finally setting the price at the point of greatest spread between total sales revenue and total costs. Techniques for approximating the shape and nature of demand curves, however, are still crude. "Working back from the market" remains more an ideal than a practical method of price determination.

## *CONCLUSION*

In most marketing situations today, pricing is a controllable. This makes it possible for marketers to compete mainly on a nonprice, rather than a price, basis. While generally not the most critical factor in successful marketing, pricing is an important element in marketing. Pricing decisions require consideration of numerous factors including the company's objectives, other components of its marketing program, and environmental influences. Deriving directly from company objectives, pricing objectives generally relate to securing, if not the maximum, at least satisfactory long-run profits. Price policies comprising the framework within which pricing decisions are made should be consistent with, and contribute to the achievement of, pricing objectives. Pricing strategies represent adaptations of pricing policies and individualized tailoring of pricing decisions to fit particular competitive situations. Price determination procedures also vary with competitive conditions, but the most widely used are cost–plus pricing by manufacturers and markup pricing by middlemen.

# 16

# INTERNATIONAL MARKETING

## THE INTERNATIONAL MARKETING ENVIRONMENT

Basic marketing strategy inputs are essentially the same wherever marketing takes place. But the combination of these inputs into a final successful marketing strategy varies considerably from one market to another because of variations in environments. Differences in culture, geography, the economy, and the political–legal environment require different marketing treatments.

### The Cultural Environment

People who live in different societies or cultures are different from each other in many easily recognizable ways. You only have to listen to people who speak the same language—Americans, Canadians, Australians, and British—to recognize how different and easily identifiable each group is. The essence of any culture is imbedded in certain important factors that interact to determine cultural patterns—language, religion, cultural institutions, class structure, aesthetics, and social patterns.

*Language and Culture.* Language is the most important cultural input. Translation of ideas into another language must be done with great care to insure accurate transmission. The nuances of meaning for particular words vary from one language to another, and a literal translation often distorts the intended meaning. The international marketer needs awareness not only of surface differences in language but the more subtle influences it has on thinking and cultural identity.

*Religion and Culture.* Religion establishes moral codes and taboos for the behavior of its adherents, and it reflects their "core" values. Certain religions frown on certain types of business practices, and they affect the consumption or nonconsumption of certain goods.

*Cultural Institutions.* Each culture develops bases for daily relationships among individuals. The family's role varies in different cultures with respect to its influence on consumption. The educational system produces varying literacy and sophistication levels that influence consumption behavior. The influence of peers and peer groups ranges from highly important in affluent societies to of little or no importance in traditional societies.

*Class Structure and Social Mobility.* A high level of social mobility places a high value on possessions as a mark of status and provides opportunity to sell status–conferring goods. People at different class levels exhibit different buying preferences for similar products, and indicated marketing adjustments need making.

Although many cultural universals are common to all societies, the marketer must pay particular attention to the differences. Cultural differences require adaptations or adjustments of marketing strategy.

### The Political-Legal Environment

Business prospers when the political environment is stable. However, nearly always the potential exists for misinterpretations and misunderstandings between business and governments, and foreign business exacerbates the potential for mutual suspicion.

*Political Forces Affecting the International Market.* The astute marketer assesses the political factors that affect success in each foreign market. The political structure and philosophy determine the degree of governmental control over business and the roles of special interest groups. Level of nationalism is important; less developed countries often feel that the activities of large multinational firms threaten their very existence. Foreign marketers always face possible political risks of confiscation, expropriation, or nationalization.

*Strategies to Reduce Political Risk.* Changes in the political environment are the major sources of political risk. There is need for the international marketer to anticipate political instability as a precursor to change in the political environment. Not only is there need for identifying political vulnerability, but the international marketer must establish a positive political-business interface by identifying important benefits of its operations to the host country: resource transfers, balance-of-payments additions, employment or income contributions, and social or cultural benefits.

*The Legal Environment of International Business.* International marketers must understand often complex legalities in each national environment before determining marketing strategy. One problem is that no international commercial legal system exists. The foreign firm is often at a disadvantage in using another country's legal system because of unfamiliarity with the laws and the state of public opinion. Another problem for American business is that even though a company is operating outside the nominal territorial jurisdiction of United States courts, these courts still have jurisdiction if the business operations produce effects within the United States.

Marketers can take certain steps to minimize international legal problems. They are well-advised to use experts in local law. In writing contracts, they should insist upon using specific terms that are not bound to one culture. And every good international contract should provide for compulsory arbitration of disputes by neutral third parties.

### The Geographic Environment

The geographic environment often determines whether or not a particular country is a good potential market. It also affects the marketing strategy appropriate to those markets that seem promising. Several geographic elements besides climate and topography are of marketing importance: resources, population, and access.

*Resources.* Resources contribute to economic well-being. They take three main forms: raw material, energy, and agricultural land.

*Population.* People are a resource that deserves separate classification. Little doubt exists that it is a highly motivated, educated, and technologically trained population that makes the difference between Israel's economic productivity and that of neighboring Jordan.

*Access.* Countries that are easily accessible offer inviting marketing opportunities. Singapore, located on a major trade route between Europe and Asia, is a more important market center than New Zealand in the Southwestern Pacific. Access to the interior of a country is also important.

### The Economic Environment

Several economic factors affect a marketer's decision to enter a foreign market: income and its distribution, standard of living, currency supply, exchange rates, and economic barriers.

*Income and Its Distribution.* A country's gross national product consists of total production of goods and services and other values added. Total wealth has little marketing significance until it is related to people and income. Income per capita is more meaningful. A nation with higher per capita income is a better market for most goods than is one with lower per capita income. Even more useful is breakdown of population by income bracket. The marketer planning to export television sets may only be interested in the population with incomes over $10,000.

*Standard of Living.* Dollar income figures are somewhat meaningless in making foreign comparisons, since the equivalent number of dollars buys different quantities of goods in different countries. Real need exists for measures of standard of living. What portion of the people have only a subsistence income? What portion have substantial amounts of disposable income? Of discretionary income?

*Currency Supply and Demand.* The balance of payments is an aggregation of transactions in merchandise, travel and tourism, income and investments, military expenditures, and so forth. Some countries place controls on the exchange of their currencies to prevent deflation in value. The exchange rate and the supply and free convertibility of the currency in a country under consideration for market entry are of high importance.

*Economic Barriers.* Some countries restrict the free movement of goods into their markets. To protect local industry from potentially ruinous foreign competition, or to prevent outflow of scarce funds, countries impose quotas, duties, or tariffs. The international marketer's decision to enter a market is influenced by entry barriers and their strength. If, for example, tariffs make it impossible for an imported product to compete, the choice is either to abandon the market or to establish manufacturing facilities inside the country.

## SELECTION OF THE MARKETS

Hand in hand with the decision to market abroad is the choice of market or markets to enter first. Ideally, market selection is based upon a careful assessment of environmental influences, but objective assessment is not easy. Much data, particularly economic data, are inaccurate or incomplete. Collecting primary data may be too costly, and secondary data may consist of little more than the opinions of consular officials or reminiscences of tourists. Such assessments are never wholly objective. In comparing the relative promise of the French, German, and British markets, for example, an American marketer is strongly attracted to the British market because the common language makes the entire task seem easier. Ideally, though, the selection of a market is based on estimated market potential and growth, the likely market share, expected costs, and anticipated net return.

## MEANS OF ENTERING THE MARKET

A firm entering foreign markets chooses among several entry methods. These range from the simplest, indirect exporting, to the most complex, direct investment in the foreign market.

### Exporting

Exporting does not even require participation of the domestic manufacturer. An export agent in the home country may recognize a product's market potential in a particular foreign market and decide to manage its export—finding a middleman to sell it or even selling it directly in the foreign market.

In many instances, exporting is initiated and managed by the domestic producer who recognizes sales opportunities outside the home market, and markets and distributes in multiple locations. The exporting alternative is most useful when the product or products can be sold with minimal changes in several markets.

### Joint Ventures

Some international marketers decide to work with local partners in foreign markets. These dual relationships are called joint ventures and take several forms including licensing, joint ownership, and contract manufacturing.

There are three main reasons for using joint ventures. First, they provide a "locally owned" business identity and thus, resentment and harassment are less likely. Second, they are a low–cost method of market entry, since local partners generally put up some of the needed capital. Third, partial local ownership sometimes confers special status as to type and strictness of government regulation.

### Direct Investment

A company choosing to establish production facilities in a foreign country requires greater financial and other resource commitments than do other foreign market entry methods. Direct investments demand use of the firm's capital, personnel, and managerial talents. In return, the firm is in position to devise and execute the most appropriate marketing strategy for the foreign market. This entry method offers the maximum potential profits and control, and if tariffs and/or transportation costs are prohibitive, it may be the only feasible entry method in a particular market.

## THE INTERNATIONAL MARKETING PROGRAM

The international marketer and the domestic marketer deal with the same strategy inputs; inputs are used differently to adjust for differences in environments. Both make decisions on products, distribution, pricing, and promotion, but environmental differences make formulation of international strategy more complex.

### Product Decisions

For consumer goods, foreign market entry requires reevaluation of characteristics and policies applying to the product sold domestically. How and to what extent should the product be changed or adapted? How relevant are present product characteristics to the foreign market? What is the stage in the product life cycle? Are usage patterns different?

For industrial products, different decisions may or may not be required. Demand characteristics for industrial goods vary less than they do for consumer goods across national boundaries. What are the trends in industrial markets abroad? How does industrial purchasing behavior vary?

### Consumer Products

**1.** *Standardization versus adaptation.* The international marketer would prefer one worldwide product strategy, selling the identical product in all markets. But most products need adapting to the varying requirements of each market. For example, the bicycle manufacturer discovers that its product is viewed as adult transportation in the Netherlands, a child's toy in the United States, and a racing vehicle in France. To serve the three markets effectively, the manufacturer adapts the product to fit each market's expectations.

**2.** *Product attribute relevance.* Product attributes vary in importance among different markets. In affluent markets, convenience often is more important than price; for example, consumers willingly pay considerably more for a fully automatic sewing machine. In less developed countries, consumers can only afford the simplest, most basic machine.

Consumers in different countries have different attitudes about durability and styling. Preferences as to product size vary widely and usually relate to space availability. Products must be made compatible with local needs. Since most of the world uses the metric system, increasingly American manufacturers adapt their products to this scale. Electric power in different countries is generated in varying combinations of wattage and voltage, and exported products sold in foreign markets must conform to local conditions.

**3.** *The product life cycle.* A product can be at the maturity stage of its life cycle in one country and at the introductory stage in another. This sort of variation is useful to the marketer whose product nears decline in the home market—new markets abroad provide opportunities to participate in profitable growth stages elsewhere.

**4.** *Product usage patterns.* Similar products often have different usage patterns in different countries. In tropical climates sandals are regular footwear; in other climates they are summer sportswear.

**5.** *Government regulations.* Government regulations often dictate that products be adapted for sale in new markets. A classic example is that safety and emission standards for automobiles in the United States caused foreign importers to adapt their cars accordingly.

**6.** *Influence of country of origin.* Consumers often have stereotyped opinions about the products of individual nations or about certain types of products from specific countries. The foreign marketer must know these stereotypes; if they are unfavorable, they may prevent or reduce the effectiveness of market entry.

### Industrial Products

**1.** *Character of demand.* The needs of businesses are generally more similar thoughout the world than are the needs of individuals. Nevertheless, variations in factors such as economic development and politics and nationalism influence industrial buyers in different countries to act differently.

**2.** *Product features.* Perception of product quality varies between countries. Different performance levels are expected in different countries. Where the roads are good, speed may be as important as durability in trucks; when roads are bad, durability may be all important. Servicing is important because product users may not be in positions to maintain and repair their own equipment. The problems of providing adequate service and replacement parts increase in geometric proportions as the marketer moves farther away from the domestic market.

**3.** *Trends in industrial markets.* Immediately after World War II, most of the world's high-technology innovative firms were American. This dominance has since declined, and multinational firms have grown more important.

**4.** *Industrial purchasing behavior.* Industrial marketers unfamiliar with foreign markets sometimes mistakenly assume that business people act the same worldwide. However, in some countries not only is it difficult to make original contacts with industrial buyers, but once contacts are made it is crucial to build repurchase loyalty. How this is achieved, depending on the country, varies from providing superior service to outright bribery.

### Distribution Decisions

The international marketer often must devise an entirely new distribution policy when entering foreign markets. The kinds of middlemen in a particular country may be so different that marketing channel alternatives are different, and this may require the development of an entirely new distribution network. The factors affecting the selection of the best channel also can be unique to a country. Finally, the greater distances to be covered (internationally) increase the complexity of physical distribution decisions.

*Marketing Middlemen.* At the international level, some large merchant wholesalers have an enormous impact on trade. The manufacturer's representative is the most important agent middleman in international markets. The use of representatives gives a manufacturer access to local expertise and local sales personnel in a country without the managerial problems and expenses of setting up an organization.

Despite the enormous geographic, cultural, and economic differences among nations, suprisingly similar retail establishments have evolved. In underdeveloped countries, the typical retail establishment is a small, family-owned business specializing in a narrow line of products. In rural areas of developing countries retailing is much the same, but in the cities, department stores, chain stores, and other general merchandise retailers thrive.

Export and import middlemen have evolved to operate specifically in international markets. They find markets in other countries for products made in their home countries, or they seek products made elsewhere to sell at home. For the producer with little knowledge of foreign markets and foreign marketing, the export or import agent offers valuable contacts and expertise.

***International Marketing Channel Alternatives.*** Although the marketing institutions (retailers, wholesalers, and so forth) vary from country to country, the local options for basic channel structure are much the same. But in moving goods between nations where specialized import and export agents provide specialized services, channel alternatives are different.

***Physical Distribution in International Markets.*** Distribution represents between 10 and 25 percent of the total landed cost of international shipments. In addition, increasingly fewer international buyers accept prices quoted F.O.B. factory. Instead, they demand that the international marketer assume responsibility for delivering merchandise directly to their loading docks. Under these circumstances, the role of the distribution department in international marketing has grown in importance. Ocean transportation moves by far the largest volume of goods between international markets, but most international shipments require some combination of land and sea transportation, and air transport is growing in importance. The great distance and slowness of sea transportation often require the maintenance of large inventories in foreign markets. Exporters occasionally find inadequate storage facilities in some countries and must build or lease their own storage facilities.

### Pricing Decisions

In international marketing, four pricing inputs affect marketing strategy: (1) the market, (2) cost, (3) competition, and (4) the government. How these inputs affect the final price depends somewhat on management's perception of the role of price in its overall marketing strategy.

In each international market, price objectives should relate to the firm's overall market goals, to effects on the cost structure and profit goals, and to pricing in other markets. If penetration of a particular foreign market is critical to the firm's growth objectives, then that country's market and competitive factors must be considered in addition to costs.

Another important pricing decision is whether to have a standard price in all nations—an ethnocentric pricing policy—or to price independently in each market—a polycentric pricing policy. Polycentric pricing allows the marketer to maximize prices, but multinational customers resent being charged different prices for identical products in different countries.

### Promotion Decisions

A wide variety of promotion tools are available to the marketing planner. These tools are not equally available or effective in all cultures and societies, so the international marketer needs to adapt the promotional mix to each market served.

*Advertising in International Markets.*   Even in the United States, which has the world's largest volume of advertising, some consumers suspect that advertisers are manipulating them and view advertising as unproductive and, hence, a wasteful addition to the cost of goods. In overseas markets, such perceptions are even more strongly held and by broader and more influential population segments.

When a firm launches its first advertising campaign in a foreign market, the natural inclination is to choose themes and messages that have been successful in the domestic market. However, successful campaigns may not work well in new environments. Some of the most successful advertising messages rely on the turn or twist of a particular word or phrase that may not be directly translatable.

*International Media Decisions.*   The larger and more complex a society is, the wider the choice of advertising media. In the simplest societies the choice may be limited to radio and newspapers, and newspapers and other print media reach only literate people. Television is an excellent medium in the wealthier nations, but radio reaches a much larger audience in poorer countries. Posters and billboards are important media everywhere in metropolitan areas, and cinema advertising is an important medium in many foreign countries.

*Personal Selling in International Marketing.*   For many international marketers, personal selling is the most important promotional input. Sales personnel must be fluent in the local language and attuned to local purchasing customs, know company product lines and policies, and know how to sell effectively.

*Other Promotional Tools.*   Moving into foreign markets makes it necessary to reevaluate brand names. Names that are satisfactory in the domestic market may be inappropriate elsewhere. One ploy is to use different brand names in each country, permitting the selection of names that are appropriate to each language and culture.

## *CONCLUSION*

As marketers grow in size and approach saturation of their domestic markets, they look to international markets to provide additional growth opportunity. As more firms become interested in international markets, it is more difficult for the remaining competing firms to ignore these markets. International marketers build their strategies from the basic marketing inputs used by domestic marketers, but they operate in different national environments. These environmental differences are of supreme importance to the international marketers.

The level of commitment to international marketing ranges from minimal, indirect exporting of domestic products through export and import middlemen, to maximum, direct investment in production and marketing facilities in the foreign market, either alone or with foreign partners.

The international marketer adjusts marketing strategy inputs to foreign markets. Rarely can products be marketed in the same manner in new countries—they require adjustments to local differences.

# INDEX